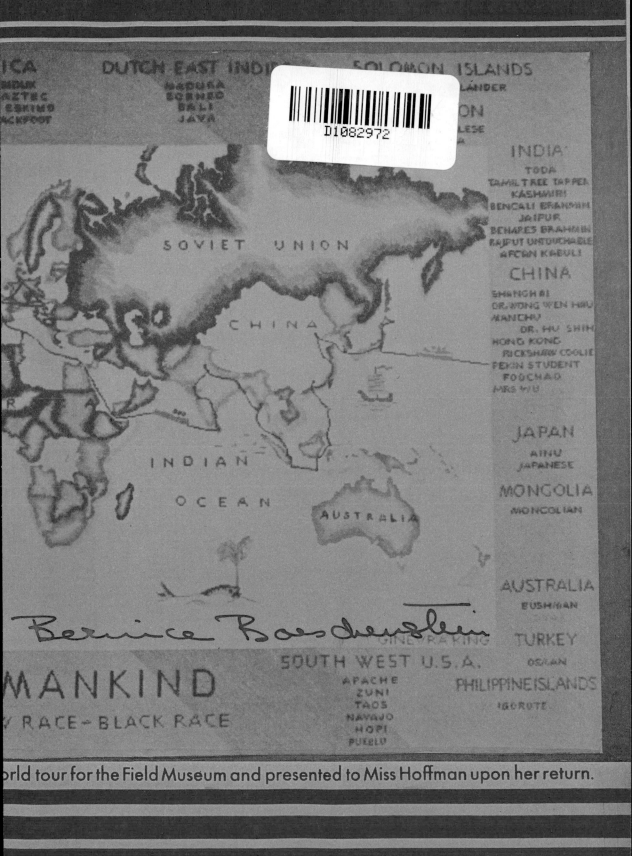

ICA
DUTCH EAST INDI
SOLOMON ISLANDS
LÄNDER
MADURA
AZTEC
BORNEO
ON
ESKIMO
BALI
LESE
ACKFOOT
JAVA

INDIA
TODA
TAMIL TREE TAPPER
KASHMIRI
BENGALI BRAHMAN
JAIPUR
BENARES BRAHMIN
RAJPUT UNTOUCHABLE
AFGHAN KABULI

SOVIET UNION

CHINA
SHANGHAI
DR. WONG WEN HAU
MANCHU
DR. HU SHIH
HONG KONG
RICKSHAW COOLIE
PEKIN STUDENT
FOOCHAO
MRS WU

CHINA

JAPAN
AINU
JAPANESE

INDIAN

MONGOLIA
MONGOLIAN

OCEAN
AUSTRALIA

AUSTRALIA
BUSHMAN

TURKEY
OSMAN

SOUTH WEST U.S.A.

MANKIND
RACE - BLACK RACE

APACHE
ZUNI
TAOS
NAVAJO
HOPI
PUEBLO

PHILIPPINE ISLANDS
IGOROTE

Bernice Boeschenstein

orld tour for the Field Museum and presented to Miss Hoffman upon her return.

HEADS AND TALES

HEADS AND TALES

By

MALVINA HOFFMAN

CHARLES SCRIBNER'S SONS · NEW YORK
MCMXXXVI

TO

IGNACE JAN PADEREWSKI

AND TO ALL THOSE FRIENDS WHO STOOD BY ME
THROUGH THE HURRICANE YEARS

ACKNOWLEDGMENT

During the time that I worked for the Field Museum, I enjoyed the whole-hearted and loyal co-operation of many minds, who advised and assisted me in every way. The unerring judgment of my husband, Samuel Grimson, and his splendid photographs and moving-picture records, have been of inestimable help. His understanding and encouragement armed me with strength to carry on the work which I never could have accomplished alone.

For the conscientious assistance of my fellow craftsmen and for the collaboration of the scientists and government officials in every country, my gratitude is sincere and unbounded.

The execution and installation of the Hall of Man was made possible through the bequest of Chauncey M. Keep, and through generous gifts from Mrs. Stanley Field and Mrs. Charles Schweppe, and, above all, by Marshall Field, whose devotion to the cause of the Museum has been an inspiration to its staff as well as to the President and Board of Trustees.

M. H.

CONTENTS

PAGE

ACKNOWLEDGMENT vii

I. THE HALL OF MAN 1

II. THE MAKING OF A SCULPTOR 17
 Youth in Forty-third Street 19
 Rodin, and Paris 33
 Breaking the Ice in New York 55
 Professional Adventures 68
 Mestrovic 79
 Behind the Scenes in Sculpture 86

III. THE STUDY OF RACES 115
 Hunger in the Balkans 117
 Africa 130
 Europe and the Elusive Alpine 159
 Maharajas in London 166
 Asia, Africa, and Oceania in Paris 172

IV. ROUND THE WORLD 179
 Packing with a Vengeance 181
 Hawaii—Sailing Westward to the East 183
 Japan and Hokkaido 189
 China 218
 The Philippines 250
 Bali 253
 Java 264
 Singapore and the Malay Jungles 272

ix

CONTENTS

	PAGE
Burma	290
India	298
Ceylon	327
The Return to Paris	331
V. THE END OF IT ALL	343
Finistère	345
If Atlantis, Why Not Mu?	352
My Trocadéro Exhibition	354
Our Aboriginal Americans	358
Taos	383
The Day After	392
Hic Incipit Vita Nova	395
"Know Thyself and Thou Shalt Know the Universe"	397
APPENDIX OF TRANSLATIONS	401
INDEX	407

ILLUSTRATIONS

PAGE

First gallery of the Hall of Man, Field Museum, Chicago   5

Nordic type in the Hall of Man   6

Blackfoot American Indian in the Hall of Man   7

Mr. Stanley Field and M. H. in her garden, Paris   8

The P. T. Barnum letter of August 14, 1850   25

Program of 1847   25

Portrait of Mrs. Hoffman   26

Portrait of Mr. Hoffman as he appeared in 1847   26

Chapel "St. Andrews by the Sea"   26

Old station stage-coach in front of Bachelder's Hotel   27

Hoffman family group at Little Boar's Head   27

M. H., at the age of two   28

M. H., aged twelve   28

Katharine Rhoades and M. H. on 43d St.   28

Three interior views of Rodin's studio at Meudon   37

Bust of Mr. Hoffman at the age of seventy-eight   38

Bust of Samuel Bonarios Grimson made in 1909   38

"Bacchanale" in the Luxembourg Gardens   39

M. H. in her 34th Street Studio   40

"The Column of Life"   40

Auguste and Rose Rodin on their wedding-day   49

Rodin and M. H. in August, 1914   50

Rodin's grave, surmounted by "The Thinker"   50

First group of "Russian Dancers"   59

Anna Pavlowa posing for her "Bacchanale" poster   59

ILLUSTRATIONS

PAGE

"La Gavotte"   60

Pavlowa and M. H. with telescope   60

Eight of the twenty-six panels, "The Dance of the Bacchanale"   61

"The Sacrifice." Detail of the Memorial   62

The Memorial as placed in the Cathedral of St. John the Divine   62

"Offrande"   63

Stone sections of the group for the Bush Building, London   64

M. H. finishing the head of "England"   64

The Unveiling at Bush House, London   65

Alabaster bust of Rita de Acosta Lydig   66

The plaster original   66

Portrait in colored wax of Anna Pavlowa   66

Marble bust of John Keats   66

Paderewski (three busts), the Friend, the Statesman and the Artist   71

"The Four Horsemen of the Apocalypse"   72

The Archangel of the Apocalypse   72

Ivan Mestrovic   83

Heroic figure in clay in Mestrovic's studio   84

Wood and iron armature for the horse   84

Eugène Rudier, maître fondeur   87

Sand process, section of plaster figure   88

Core inside of sand section mould   88

Core of "Brahman in Meditation"   88

Sand moulds, opened and closed   89

Pouring the molten bronze   89

Sand mould showing the wax channels   90

Upper section of the same figure   90

Bronzes being "chased" or finished after casting   91

Père and Jean Limet in their crowded studio   91

ILLUSTRATIONS

	PAGE
"Lost wax" process. Back of Navajo Medicine Man	92
Plaster figure of the Navajo Medicine Man	92
Navajo Medicine Man covered with coat of clay and plaster	93
Bronze figure as it emerges from the mould	93
Interior of the Valsuani foundry, Paris	94
Marble portrait of Mrs. E. H. Harriman	103
Jean de Marco at work in M. H.'s studio	103
Corner of M. H.'s studio showing fireplace	103
Equestrian statue of Louis XV	104
Cross section as seen from above	104
Air vents made of copper tubing	105
Brick towers through which metal entered the mould	105
Benin bronze, collection Louis Carré, Paris	106
Benin bronze, British Museum, London	106
Benin bronze, warriors, British Museum, London	106
Our Ford on the way to Kossovo on a flat-car	123
Landing at Karlobac	123
Mrs. Draper, of the American Red Cross, presenting flag	124
Bronze portrait of Colonel Milan Pribicevic	124
Sole surviving monk at Grachanitza, Kossovo	124
One of the mutilated Serbian victims of the war	124
Map of Africa showing the location of African tribes	131
Portrait of the Arab cook	135
Study of mixed type	135
Interior of Jewish synagogue on the island of Jerba	135
Senegalese tom-tom player	136
Black Belgian marble Senegalese head	136
Merchants of Old Tunis	137
Subterranean pottery dug-out, island of Jerba	137
City of Medinin, South Tunisia	138

ILLUSTRATIONS

	PAGE
Houm Souk, the capital of Jerba	138
"The Rabbi of Hara Srira," wood-carving	139
The Port of Salammbo	139
Jerba	140
Family group of South African Kalahari Bushmen	141
Native women filling ostrich eggs with water	141
Mother and child of the Kalahari Bushmen tribe	142
Pigmies of the Ituri Forest	151
A tribe of Ituri pigmy warriors	152
Monsieur Poirier and a pigmy chief	152
"Daboa," dancing girl of the Sara tribe	153
Shilluk warrior	154
Masai warrior with tribal spear	157
Mangbetu woman	158
Ubangi "duck-billed" woman	158
Zulu belle	158
Sudanese beauty	158
Portrait of Sir Arthur Keith	161
The elusive Alpine	161
"God's Gift to Women"	162
The Most Noble Marquis of Reading, Viceroy of India	167
H. H. the Maharaja of Patiala	168
H. H. the Yuvuraj of Patiala	168
Cock fight, island of Madura	175
Cambodian dancer of Ankhor	175
In the garden of the Villa Chauvelot, Paris	176
Reducing a sculptured head by pantograph	176
Madame Eames as Elsa in "Lohengrin"	176
Hawaiian surf-board rider	185
The five brothers Kohonomoku	186

ILLUSTRATIONS

	PAGE
Samoan warrior	186
Typical Hawaiian swimmer	186
Young woman of Tokyo	197
High priest of the Shogun temple	198
Japanese priests offering a prayer	198
Japanese athlete	198
Mother and baby, Japan	199
Cherry-blossom dancers at Kyoto, Japan	199
Dancing steps and accompanying musicians	199
Making wooden shoes, Japanese style	200
Wooden pillow with a silken pad	200
Our Japanese hosts in Tomakomai	201
Ainu mother carrying her baby	201
A beardless Ainu	201
Venerable Ainu of Hokkaido, greeting a neighbor	202
Ainus drinking from their sake bowls	202
A typical Ainu	203
The lone Ainu fisherman	204
A full-blooded male Ainu	204
Male Ainu before his thatched straw house	213
Ainu woman in native costume	213
Complex Japanese tattooing	213
A Japanese wood-carver	214
Kwannon, Bodhisattva of Compassion, Horyuji, Nara. A wood-carving	214
The Seated Goddess in the nunnery at Nara	214
The ever cheerful rickshaw coolie of China	223
Yong Ta Sen, rickshaw coolie	224
Mrs. Dan, a Manchu beauty	224
Woman of Central Mongolia	224
Mr. Li Yu Tien, a scholar of China	224

xv

ILLUSTRATIONS

	PAGE
Mongolian dancer	225
Peiping Union Medical College	226
Rickshaw coolie, with his Chinese pipe	226
Secretary to the Living Buddha of Outer Mongolia	226
Blind musician playing the sheng	227
One of the results of missionary work in China	227
Bronze portrait of Dr. Hu Shih	228
Abbot of a Mongolian monastery	228
The living Buddha of Outer Mongolia	229
Chinese woman in quilted winter costume	229
Christmas Day camel ride to the Temple of the Cloud	229
Dr. Lessing and the Secretary to the Dalai Lama of Tibet	230
Lama painting, known as *Mandala*	230
Arrival at the gateway of the Temple of the Cloud	239
Woman mud carrier of Hong Kong	240
Lama priest at worship	240
A Bali temple	257
Balinese wood carving	257
The star dancer of Den Pasar, Bali	257
Bali after the tropical rain	258
Ni Polog, a dancer of Bali	258
Golden bronze statuette of Balinese dancer	258
Ni Polog, a life-size portrait	258
The Towers of the Dead	259
The Harvest Festival	259
Papuan boy posing for his portrait	260
The portrait in pastel	260
Two leading ladies of the Balinese ballet	260
The Temple of Borobodour, Java	265
The Gamelon orchestra	265

ILLUSTRATIONS

PAGE

Two of the sculptured panels on the walls of the Temple of Prambanam 266

Dr. de Vink and M. H. beside the statue of Vishnu 267

The chief dancer of the Sultan's court at Jokjo, Java 268

Male dancer of the Sultan's court, Solo, Java 268

A boy brass-worker in Java 268

A Semang pigmy of the Malay jungle tribes 273

A family of the Jakun tribe in the Malay jungle 274

M. H. and two Sakai warriors 274

A group of Semang pigmies 275

M. H. preparing a clay head on the trunk rack 275

A Sakai chief 276

Model for M. H.'s Semang pigmy 276

A Solomon Islander in bronze 276

A male Sakai type 285

A female of the Sakai tribe 285

Our early morning visitors 285

Sakai warrior, bronze 286

Three Padaung ladies of upper Burma 291

One of the Padaung ladies in bronze 291

A young Burmese priest 291

Young Andaman Islander 291

The leading ladies of the court dancers in Rangoon 292

U. Aung Thin, in his native costume 292

Jeet Singh, our Sikh chauffeur 292

Andaman Islander in bronze 295

Pigmy Andaman Islander waiting to harpoon a turtle 295

The "wedding wail," Andaman Island 296

Jean de Marco at work, upon the steamer's deck 296

M. H. and S. G. with two gypsy dancers in Calcutta 299

Type of feminine beauty in Bengal 299

xvii

ILLUSTRATIONS

	PAGE
Doing penance	299
A Tibetan in bronze	300
Tibetan jewel merchant of Lhasa	300
Street beggar in Calcutta	301
Money lender of Afghanistan	301
Hindu woman of Rajputana	301
Merchant type of Kashmir	301
Sita Devi, Indian singer	302
Colonel Nawah Malik, Sir Umar Hyat Khan	302
Snake charmers at Agra, India	302
Pahalwan Nats	311
Dhul Singh of Rajputana	312
Acrobatic Pahalwan Nats	312
The Fighting Order of Priests, known as Bhats, Jaipur, India	312
M. H. drawing the portrait of Hamman Pershad Vaish	313
The woman of Jaipur	313
Royal courtesan dancers	314
M. H. on the royal elephant	314
A woman of Hieedley caste, of Jaipur	323
Khurshedji Nasarwanje Wadya of Bombay	323
Madam Sarojini Naidu	323
Janoo Singh, of the Bhat tribe, Jodhpur	323
The great temple at Madura	324
A typical palm grove, South India	325
Emaciated road mender of Madras	325
A Tamil climbing a palm tree	325
Tea-picker in the gardens of Ceylon	326
Untouchable Tamil woman	326
Group of devil dancers	326

ILLUSTRATIONS

PAGE

Symbolic group in bronze by M. H., representing the white, yellow and
  black races   335

Heads and hands by M. H.   336

Henri de Monfreid on his sailboat   336

Mascot Kiki, of Siam   336

If Atlantis, why not Mu? (map)   344

The fishing-boat *Malvina* in the port of St. Guénolé, Brittany   349

Guillaume Tanneau. Type of Breton sailor   349

Rocks and surf at St. Guénolé   349

Type of old Breton fisherman   350

La Fille de Roland. A lace maker of St. Guénolé   350

"Notre Dame de la Joie," drawing by M. H.   350

Monsieur Rudier and M. H. in the Paris foundry   355

M. H.'s exhibition in the Trocadéro Museum, Paris   355

Lieutenant Jean Julien Lemordant   356

Lieutenant Lemordant escorted by his Breton friends   356

Right hand of Lieut. Lemordant in bronze   356

The masked dance of the Apache Indians of America   365

Masked death ceremony of the Doggon tribe, bas-relief   365

The ancient Hopi Pueblo of Walpi   366

Hopi Indians, three generations   366

The Virginal head-dress, Hopi tribe   366

Santa Clara Pueblo chief   367

Puye Pueblo. Wall of the Kiva   367

Governor of Zuni Pueblo   367

Desideria, pottery-maker   367

Mural painting by Ma-Pe-We   368

Navajo woman   368

Navajo medicine-man   368

Symbolic Indian painting on deer skin   377

ILLUSTRATIONS

PAGE

Religious Indian sand-painting 377

Typical Navajo Hogan 378

The *Yurt* of Mongolia 378

Navajo rug-weaver 378

Navajo medicine man 378

An Apache brave 379

A Sioux Indian chief 379

An Apsaroke Indian 380

A Pueblo Indian woman 380

A pueblo of Taos, New Mexico 389

The courtyard 389

The outside stairway 389

Mabel Dodge Luhan 390

Albert Looking Elk 390

A young Taos Indian 390

The main house of Mabel's colony 390

*Photos of various bronzes and marbles by
Peter Juley and De Witt Ward, N. Y.*

I

THE HALL OF MAN

THE HALL OF MAN

In February, 1930, I went to Chicago in response to an unexpected telegram from the Field Museum.

"Have proposition to make, do you care to consider it? Racial types to be modelled while travelling round the world."

Sudden vistas of remote islands and mysterious horizons flooded over my imagination—escape from city life, discovery of new worlds, conflict with the elements. Infinite new windows of life seemed to open before me.

What lay beyond those windows is set down in this book, which describes my adventures and experiences of "head-hunting" in the near and far corners of the earth—and how the hundred racial types in the "Hall of Man" of the Field Museum in Chicago were selected and modelled on the road.

Perhaps the first question the reader would like to ask before embarking on the risk of reading this book would be: How did such an idea as the Hall of Man in bronze originate, and why in Chicago?

To know the answer, you would have to be interested enough in the subject of *Man* to explore the ethnographical museums and find out how this subject has been studied and exhibited up to the present time. The very name over the entrance to most of the halls—"Anthropology"—evokes in our minds dummies of sawdust or painted plaster with staring glass eyes and dusty false hair which has become partially unglued because—"there is never enough money for upkeep." You would also have to understand that the president and the trustees of Field Museum in Chicago are a very alert and courageous group of men. To keep abreast of the times, they decided, after investigating the reasons why the anthropology halls in all countries were generally empty and the snake and monkey houses always crowded, to step out of the tradition and take a long chance. They felt that "The Races of Man" should *look alive,* and be actual figures and heads that any one could recognize and feel to be authentic, without

3

being repulsive; so they decided to try sculpture as a means of revealing man to his brother.

To answer a second question: How did the Field Museum happen to select me for the interpretation of their project—perhaps you had better read this book and visit the Hall of Man in Chicago. This may give you a clue—although between you and me, I was never able to find the answer to the question myself.

Imagine yourself being asked to sign away your life and energy for an indefinite number of years, and to leap into the dark from a high precipice, as I did when, within eighteen hours after my arrival in Chicago, I decided to sign that memorable contract with the Field Museum. The job was a hundred heads—one head had I—but the chance was the best there was—"to do or die."

No one could give me the rules of the game—they had to be made as the game progressed. There could be no rigid limitations or calculations: we were taking a big chance, both of us, and there was only one basis of understanding between these gentlemen in Chicago and the artist from New York—it was that of complete mutual confidence.

Once launched I realized there was no turning back. If I started I would in all conscience and allegiance be compelled to carry the project to a finish—not counting its exhaustion or its costs.

I remember vividly how my knees shook as I stood facing the row of keen, observant faces of the men whom I had never seen before and who had come to Mr. Field's office to hear him read the outline of his original plan for the Hall of Man. The first idea was to engage four or five artists to collaborate on the scheme—sending them to various countries to model their subjects "on the spot." I cannot forget what courage it took on my part to say that I could not work under these conditions, but that I would like to present them with an entirely different scheme the following morning. They agreed to postpone their decision.

I went back to my little room at the Drake Hotel overlooking Lake Michigan, which under the gale had taken on the appearance of the North Atlantic in January. I faced the crucial moment that comes but once in a lifetime. Hour after hour I held my head in my hands

FIRST GALLERY OF THE HALL OF MAN, FIELD MUSEUM, CHICAGO

Showing life-size bronzes of African types on the right. Australian, Semang Pigmy, Solomon Islander, and Hawaiian on the left. The central symbolic group in the octagonal gallery represents the White, Yellow, and Black Races, with the globe of the world above. Beyond is the third gallery of Asiatic types. The total length of the Hall is 160 feet

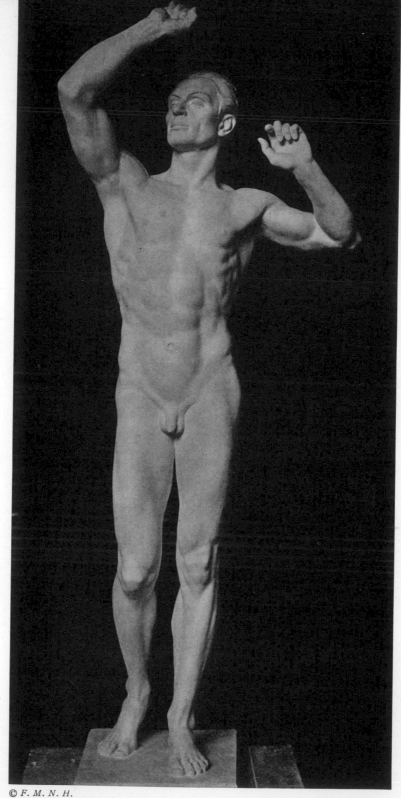

FULL–LENGTH FIGURE OF NORDIC TYPE IN THE HALL OF MAN

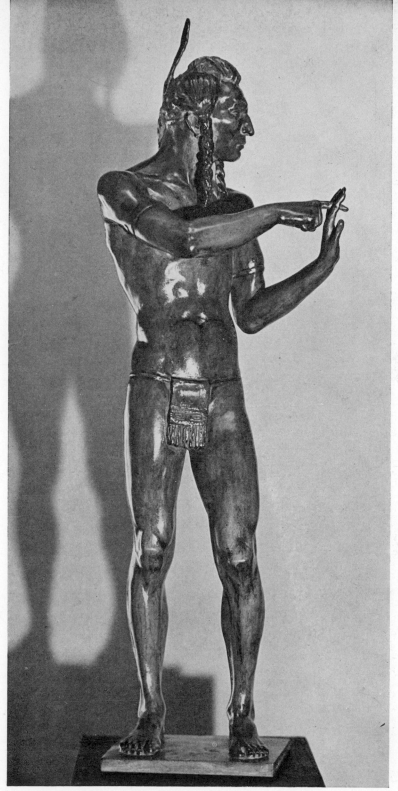

LIFE–SIZE BRONZE OF BLACKFOOT AMERICAN INDIAN
IN THE HALL OF MAN

The gesture of the hands means "I have seen my enemy and killed him"

VIEW OF OUR GARDEN IN PARIS, SHOWING MR. STANLEY FIELD, PRESIDENT OF FIELD MUSEUM, AND M. H. BY THE TUNISIAN TILED FOUNTAIN

and tried to think into the future, tried to face the inevitable problems and risks and find possible solutions. Many times I wanted to call my husband on the long-distance telephone and ask his advice—but I felt that to do this would be a lack of courage on my part. After all, it was my own risk and my own responsibility, and I knew that I could count upon his loyalty and complete co-operation. I feared that the years of intense effort and unknown complications that would be a part of this proposed long journey, with so much constant work, might be too much of a strain to expect either of us to withstand —and yet—something stronger than doubt and more inevitable than calculations took hold of me in the wee cold hours of dawn, and I started drafting the many pages of my proposed scheme. My Daemon had cast his spell over me and I was a mere instrument under his dominion.

By eight o'clock my plan was completed, and I engaged a typist to make it into a business-like looking paper—a good deal of red ink, and impressive numbered paragraphs.

At ten o'clock the three gentlemen met me at the museum in the same awe-inspiring office of huge dimensions, with a carpet so soft that I felt as if I were crossing the ninth green of a golf course. Everything seemed to my distorted vision to appear over-life-size and ominous in the extreme. I was acutely aware of belonging to the atom family.

I told them that the idea of getting a consistent, homogeneous ensemble by combining the works of many sculptors was impossible, to say nothing of the sanguinary struggle that would undoubtedly be waged during the years between the divergent opinions of the various artistic temperaments. I felt that the project must depend upon one artist alone, who would give himself or herself entirely and whole-heartedly to the enterprise and bear the responsibility for its failure or its success. I stated that, if I were chosen to do this work, I would be ready to assume all the risks and complete the task to the limit of my physical endurance. (I felt, after I had said this, as if I had entered the uncharted arena of no man's land.)

After my new proposal had been studied and accepted, I was instructed to return to New York and start work at once. Four months later it was decided that I should go to Paris and make all the necessary arrangements with museums and anthropologists to study the European and Asiatic types.

The Field Museum, in constant communication with all other ethnographical institutions, prepared the way, many months ahead, for our arrival in every place we visited. The spontaneous co-operation that responded to their requests to advise and aid the project was most encouraging to us all.

So intense was the effort and so engrossing the problem, that the first three years sped past us with an alarming rapidity. After this I felt an imperative necessity to visualize the compositions of the completed hall, before continuing any further activity. The figures were being cast into bronze and shipped to Chicago, and the problem of variety and arrangement was looming ahead of me. I cabled for time off to make a small scale model of the hall—so that each full-length figure and bust might find its eventual position in relation to the whole. Every pedestal and base had to be specially designed for each subject. Partitions, wall spaces, floor-covering, indirect lighting were now studied. Although there were about twenty racial types still left to be modelled, the general aspect of the hall was sufficiently complete to make it possible to open it to the public on June 6, 1933.

This was almost simultaneous with the opening in Chicago of the International World's Fair known as the "Century of Progress," and it was gratifying to the Field Museum to be able to record that over two million people visited the new Hall of Man during its first year of existence.

On entering the hall, the visitor sees a long gallery leading to a central octagonal room, beyond which is another long hall. The heroic-sized bronze group representing the three main divisions of the human race (White, Yellow, and Black) and surmounted by a globe, is the central point of interest in the octagonal room. Flanked on both sides of the galleries are thirty-four full-length figures standing against the flat wall spaces left between the alcove rooms of which there are four on each side of the long room.

In these alcoves are set the heads and busts representing the subdivisions of the main races which are shown in the full-length figures. All the lighting is reflected from the high ceiling and the walls are a pale golden beige color; the flooring is the color of natural wood. The pedestals and bases are of polished dark walnut, and the bronzes themselves vary from the darkest African negroes to the paler shades of tan and golden metal.

Before the end of this century many of the primitive races which are now represented in bronze in this hall and modelled from living subjects will have disappeared into the dim records of history.

The first contract did not include the possibility of *bronze* busts and statues (although I saw this quite definitely as an eventual and hoped-for goal), but called for painted plaster models with real hair and glass eyes. Here was a "dangerous crossing ahead"—but I sensed the fact that if I insisted at this point upon the sculptor's dream of bronze or marble, I would lose the chance of exploring the world, and that the museum would immediately turn to other artists who would gladly carry out the plan of painted plasters. The chance of combining art and science in permanent plastic form struck me as a step of vital importance, even if superhuman effort might be needed to accomplish it. Something told me that if I could prove this conviction by the first months of work, the idea of bronze as the ultimate medium would be automatically instilled into the minds of these men. My faith in things unseen was strong, and in a crisis there often comes the power for the need, and so it was that I signed up for painted plaster, real hair and glass eyes, knowing absolutely that within six months this part of the contract would be changed without a struggle. Such was the case.

The first subjects were the Blackfoot Indian chief and the Nordic male—both full-length figures, which I submitted for approval in the clay, having modelled the hair and eyes as I would quite naturally for any statue.

The result of this first try-out immediately removed any further idea of "real hair and glass eyes." The verdict was given quite painlessly and was unanimous. Half the battle was won.

During the first summer I made the full-length figures of two African types. These I had cast into bronze at my own risk, and patined to suggest the dusky skin and color of my models.

When Mr. Stanley Field saw these completed in Paris, he at once saw their added value in the metallic medium; the problem of glass cases and inevitable breakages and chipping of painted plasters vanished, and he immediately cabled to Chicago that his mind was made up to use every means possible to have all the figures and heads made in bronze, if financial assistance could be found to make this added expense a possibility. The cables between Paris and Chicago were kept busy until all was decided and a new contract was drawn up. My belief in the ultimate result was tremendously revived, and the secret goal was now entirely dependent upon the standard of my own work—with no further psychological barriers. Everything was to be in bronze, patined to suggest the varieties of skin colors, including the symbolic group fifteen feet high for the center of the hall—with the possibility of a few marble and stone heads still lurking in the background of my mind to add variety and interest to the ensemble. Four of these eventually came into being and are set in shadow boxes in the alcoves of the Hall of Man.

Each race left its mark upon my consciousness with a vivid impression. I have tried both by the gestures and poise of the various statues, as well as by the characterization in the facial modelling, to give a convincing and lifelike impression. I watched the natives in their daily life, fishing, hunting, praying, and preparing their food, or resting after a day's work. Then I chose the moment at which I felt each one represented something *characteristic of his race, and of no other.* To register accurately just these subtle gestures and poses, I had to efface my own personality completely and let the image flow through me directly from the model to the clay, without impediment of any subjective mood, or conscious art mannerism on my part.

For example, our own American Indian is caught in a gesture which in his indigenous hand-language is only understood by his own people to mean: "I have seen my enemy and killed him."

The Kashmiri Brahman is represented in a pose of extraordinary selfless meditation. Although it is quite natural for this man to sit as he does, it would be practically impossible for any of our American boys to assume this pose for any length of time, if at all.

'The Hawaiian surf-board rider is caught in a moment of extreme action—the sense of balance and speed being suggested by the position of his arms, and the intense expression of his face. If I had tried to pose him, I would have lost the essence of just what constituted his racial individuality.

The oriental calm of Asiatic types I have tried to represent in a varied collection of people, including high priests of Outer Mongolia, scholars, scientists, and ladies of high degree of China, Manchus, modern students, and rickshaw coolies—each one completely different from his neighbor in racial form, expression, and personal characterization.

Each subject was a new challenge. No human beings are ever alike, and in constructing their facial forms it was an ever-changing problem to determine just how their features were set, and how the line of their profiles could be drawn with such accuracy and definition that later on one of their own people might recognize at a glance from just what area I had drawn my material. My mind became sensitized like a photographic plate, and to keep the impressions vivid and apart demanded endless concentration at a high pitch.

Libraries are stocked with data on ethnography and anthropology. If those professors who by force of circumstances are obliged to draw their knowledge from these canyons of books and mounds of dusty skulls could be enabled to travel far and wide—what stimulating surprises they would have! How many reports would have to be moved from the "Fact" to the "Fiction" department!

We were told to limit ourselves to those races that were alive today, and so we had to exclude the Tasmanians, who have recently become extinct, the cause perhaps being that they were never known to have broken the seventh commandment. It was a great relief to me, for they were ugly enough to make celibacy an easy task, and sculpture an impossible one.

Even the scientific expert must be on his guard, for primitive races have a keen sense of humor, and delight in fooling the stranger. I recently heard the tale of a representative from Hollywood who wished to record a ceremonial chant of the American Indian on a sound disc. The Indian singers very politely consented to comply with his request, and he left the reservation feeling elated at his achievement. It was years later, when he met an Indian visiting California, that he asked for a translation of his unique record. To his dismay he was told that the words meant: "Does the White Man think that he can buy our secrets?" This was repeated in many variations, throughout the entire chant.

The more timid or apprehensive the model, the more important I found it to be entirely alone with him. These people, generally called savages, are far more intuitive and psychic than we are. It takes but a few seconds for them to discover if we are sincere or only bluffing. They sense this at once, and their actions are directed by this sensation. Words become quite unnecessary as a means of communication —a look of the eye, a smile, or a quick gesture can establish a relationship in which confidence and humor can flow easily from one individual to any other.

If a group of jungle folk or Indians gather about the white visitor, there is a tacit method of identifying the stranger at once. Is he to be taken within the circle of their confidence or not? If not, he might just as well fold up his tent and move along, for whatever he collects or observes will be falsified and his observations will be based on conscious misinformation.

The races of Man, studied as a whole, or in groups, such as nations, tribes or clans, would be a simpler problem than that of thoroughly understanding *one* man—the individual. For are we not all strangers? —to each other and to ourselves?

If we efface the surface differences of the various races, we come to their universal similarities—*"plus ça change, plus c'est la même chose."* We must learn the trick of removing masks and false fronts to study our unsuspecting victims—with the lid off. For a man to discover *himself* generally necessitates a calamity or some overpowering revelation of beauty.

Primitive races, so-called savages, civilized city-dwellers, and Siamese cats all share the same characteristics. The difference consists chiefly in the traditional manner by which they disguise their thoughts and evade the expression of their natural instincts.

Every race, creed, and color is caught in the same eternal struggle for existence—to eat, to sleep and to respond to the natural urge to procreate one's kind. The male seeks his mate, the eternal Eve seeks to find protection and leadership in her Adam. Throughout the ages primitive people have had instinctive pride in continuance of race.

Highly civilized humans often try to evade this responsibility of cultivating family trees. They appear as a challenge to their atrophied sense of courage and integrity. They seek to escape—escape situations, escape from each other, and above all the means to escape facing their own selves—to see themselves objectively.

Self-knowledge is the subtlest art of all. This is forced upon us sooner or later and the more we evade the issue the more layers will we have to penetrate before we reach the core.

What we experience is what we bring upon ourselves, but to acknowledge this is to walk through fire that consumes utterly. There is a code of ethics for each stratum of society—the wording changes, the titles of religion vary according to time, place, and founder, but when these ethics are studied, dissected, and revealed, the fathers of all creeds speak with the same meaning; even the headhunter defends his friend or his young at the risk of his own life. More than this cannot be asked of Christian or Pagan. The Great Universal Spirit comes close to those who seek him and when He does, mind triumphs over matter—in the temple, in the mosque, or in the Indian hogan, where men gather in concentrated prayer and conviction. If we watch the medicine man paint his age-old sacred symbols with the delicate streams of colored sand, and ask the sick man who is being healed by this how he feels after the ceremony, he will answer: "Better, stronger, more alive." Experience the force of will exerted by the Yogi in meditation; go to the River Ganges and see the ecstasy of faith in the eyes of the pilgrims who drink the same water that has laved the leper and the victims of the black plague; watch the mothers in Brittany who have given their sons to the sea and who, in their sorrow, find pride in their sacrifice to their Holy Mother. The Calvary stands stark and gray on the rocks of the sea, but brave men still give their lives and tears run down the cheeks of their sons who are still too young to go with them down to their Mother Sea.

Today the complexity of modern life has injected into the picture the question of eugenics, economics, and mechanics, to the destruction of many of the primitive forces which have given endurance, courage, and equilibrium to our aboriginal brothers. By reason of their loss, the present generation has a chronic case of nerves, while Mother Nature sits back in her easy-chair and smiles. She takes her toll if we evade her either by sins of excess or escape; man and animal alike, we are slaves to her omnipotence.

In telling the story of my study of races and of my work for the Hall of Man, I shall take the countries in chronological order as I studied them, rather than in any geographical sequence. The Balkan experiences that I describe go back to the year 1919 and the African journey took place in the winter of 1926–7. The journey round the world was undertaken in 1931, and for the following five years most of my conscious existence was dedicated to the Field Museum work.

This collection of 101 life-size bronze figures and heads is a sculptor's interpretation of Humanity, studied from three angles—Art, Science, and Psychology. It represents not only the actual study and work of the past five years, but the result of my observations and study over a period of many years previous to 1930.

II
THE MAKING OF A SCULPTOR

THE MAKING OF A SCULPTOR

Youth in Forty-third Street

Now that the *raison d'être* of the Hall of Man has been explained, it might be well to go back a few years and find out what the elements were that eventually combined to make this stroke of fate fall upon my unsuspecting head. (Probably it was a remark made by a friend at the right moment, or one of those accidents of circumstance which so often change the direction of our lives.)

Born and brought up as I was in the lurid atmosphere of Broadway and Forty-third Street, I was nevertheless one of a household which conserved the traditional and hidebound habits of Puritanical forefathers and conventional groups of numberless relatives.

The saving grace (for years, however, looked upon by the grandparents and the old New York families as a disgrace) was to my mind the fact that my mother broke away from the rigid expectations of her fond parents and their social standards and fell madly in love with her piano teacher, Richard Hoffman, an English infant prodigy who in 1847, at the age of fifteen, had come to America. Three years later he joined Jenny Lind on the first concert tour ever arranged in this country and under the management of P. T. Barnum, later of circus fame. Those were the days when the signboards hanging over the English inns read: "Musicians, play-actors and other vagabonds will not be entertained."

When a few years later he became a popular music teacher in New York, it happened that my mother became his pupil. After a few lessons in harmony and composition, my mother's heart began to spread its wings in the new ether of musical mysteries and her talent for the piano developed rapidly. Most probably her own evolution had reached the limit of social refinements and craved a new vitality of adventure and reality, and it was not long before Fidelia Lamson and Richard Hoffman decided to test their conviction and their courage. They ran away from social customs of the old order, and eloped. They were married in St. John's Chapel, Varick Street, New York, and soon after established their brave and defiant little menage in West Forty-third Street—at that time still a respectable-looking street with brownstone fronts and high stoops, but with a flourishing saloon on the corner of Sixth Avenue, whose swinging, knee-high doors remained a constant source of curiosity and hoped-for adventure throughout the years of my childhood.

The story of a city block like that in Forty-third Street is punctuated by many local events and personalities that leave their little dents or scratches on the waxen records of time.

One morning, about eight o'clock, I peeked out of my mother's bedroom window to see the snow-storm, and to my fascination saw the window in the house opposite to ours thrown open and the figure of a beautiful woman climb onto the ledge. A trained nurse ran after her from across the room and clutched desperately at the filmy transparent gown, out of which the lovely lady slipped. Her white body poised for one moment on the window-sill, glittering in the early sunlight—I was thrilled by a new beauty—then she jumped to the snow-covered ground some thirty feet below, just missing a venerable postman who was delivering the morning mail. It was my first study of the nude, and I felt a wave of excitement go through my body. This sudden revelation of naked young physical beauty in suicidal despair made a profound impression on me. With an instantaneous sense of chivalry the postman removed his coat, wrapped it about the fallen lady, who was uninjured, and sat on her chest calling for help and trying to prevent her from knocking her head against the wall in a final effort to end it all.

This incident added a glamor to the game of watching life from a window, and threw my eight-year-old mind into a state of bewilderment about the causes of such an act of desperation.

One of the most colorful personalities that lived in Forty-third Street at this time was Lillian Russell of music-hall fame, whose continuous stream of visitors gave me a panorama of entertainment that I could watch from our second-story window and yet be unnoticed.

Our back-yard, which could boast of a catalpa tree, a swing, and various dog-kennels and rabbit-houses, was the scene of endless games and adventures. The mysteries of planting seeds and watching them flower into life kept us busily occupied in the spring months. How the arid soil ever produced the necessary nutrition to keep these unfortunate plants alive even a few weeks seems even more of a miracle to me now than it did in those days of childlike faith in fairy-tales.

Instead of playing with the usual toys supposed to amuse little girls, I was forever experimenting with electric batteries and all sorts of mechanical gadgets. One of the rare treats to which I looked forward on Saturdays was the excursions to the power-house of the subway system. My father would accompany me and arrange with the foreman to let me watch the great dynamos in action, and the switchboard on which was recorded the number of trains leaving on their uptown trips. As the crowds increased at the noon hour, the number of trains was augmented, the levers were pulled to supply the necessary current, and the dials registered the flow and energy of the unseen power. This phenomenon seemed to me like a trip to Mars, and every moment I could find to experiment with batteries and cars on tracks was a thrilling adventure for me.

When I was in my early "teens" I can recall that on Saturdays I walked with my mother to the market on the corner of Eighth Avenue. I always took along my little fox-terrier. To pass the time out-of-doors while Mother was shopping, I would wander up and down the street, until one fine day, while curiously watching a group of familiar loiterers, it dawned on me that these pale-faced, hollow-chested men were not idle loafers at all but expert purveyors of forbidden drugs. I was excited by my discovery and by patching together the stray remarks overheard as I passed, I managed to weave a lurid and secret plot which could only be continued on the following Saturday morning. It became a well-known fact that this locality was the center of the "dope ring," and many were the raids upon the houses of that neighborhood.

All this came back to my mind years later, when, having shipped two plaster horses about three feet high from Paris to my New York studio in bond, I was waiting for the customs examiner to verify the work as originals and began to unbind the cotton waddings and bandages I had wound around their plaster legs to prevent breakage. "One moment there, lady," he said, "I'll do the unwrapping for you." I noticed how carefully he examined the bandages and my curiosity was aroused. "What do you expect to find in there?" I asked guilelessly. "Well, you never can tell, Miss, plaster casts and bandages can carry a big cargo of drugs sometimes, and if you will just cut a square window out of this horse's belly, we will see how he looks inside. The last horse I examined had 500 razor blades and $1000 worth of heroin in his tummy and he didn't show any outer signs of indigestion either." I confess to feeling rather flat and disappointed not to have hidden anything whatever either to amuse or surprise my imaginative examiner. The story of the Trojan horse must have given some barber a great thrill and led him to try it out in his own small way.

To bring up, feed, and educate five lusty youngsters on the spoils of piano-playing and teaching was a Herculean task, and many were the sacrifices made with magnanimous devotion by both my father and mother. The years of schooling and the crowded quarters of our little house must have been a daily and arduous problem of addition and subtraction, economics, and philosophy. In 1903, sickness and death threw a cloud of anxiety and tragedy over our family when my brother Richard, the eldest son, fell ill and died in Chicago at the age of twenty-nine.

When his body was brought home and the coffin left in our front parlor, I was told I could go in and say good-bye to my beloved brother. I touched his bronze-colored hair with my fingers, leaned over and kissed his forehead. The marble-like coldness of death sent a shiver through my body, and for a long time I could not move or control the terrible pounding of my heart. This first encounter with physical finality and spiritual immortality remained forever branded on my consciousness. I stayed alone with Death until the panic and fear in my heart were transformed into awe and reverence before the Silent Omnipotence.

The following years bound our little family closely together in a common grief in which we all felt inarticulate and helpless. My sister Elizabeth, whose radiant character was to be put on a rack of pain, developed a fatal malady from which no victim has been known to recover. At the age of thirty-two she had fulfilled her appointed time on this earth. Before she died she completely convinced me that the dead do not go away, but live on in our hearts to help the living. The loss of these two children laid a heavy load of grief upon the valiant spirits of my father and mother.

The first figure that I ever modelled was made in the little third-floor room of our Forty-third Street home. It was only about ten inches high, but it expressed to my sixteen-year-old mind all I knew of grief. The struggle I had trying to evolve an armature is unforgettable—a pencil stuck into a large wooden spool, and a metal shoe-horn lashed to this with twisted hairpins. On this grotesque skeleton I formed the desolate figure of a woman in the grip of despair.

It seemed to give me a certain sense of peace and satisfaction to feel that I had collected and concentrated my many conflicts and unshed tears into this concrete image. Perhaps the artist does regain a sort of equilibrium from the transference of his emotions into his art.

From the days of earliest childhood, I can recall my father's interest in everything the children did both at home and at school. He would question me each day on my return from a walk in Bryant Park—ask me what I had done, whom I had played with, and just what I had noticed on the streets. The fact that he expected to hear about all these things sharpened my powers of observation and memory, and I gradually learned how to collect enough impressions to force him to call a halt. Going over to the piano, he would lift me on to his knees and say: "Now, that's enough stories for today—listen to some music without words."

I was often found hiding under the piano so as to get *more* music than I could hear upstairs in the nursery.

Vivid memories come often to my mind of evenings by the sea at Little Boar's Head, New Hampshire—the eternal breaking of the waves along the moonlit beaches stretching away into the dark ocean —my father playing in the parlor of the Batchelder Hotel—the roads lined with buggies and four-wheelers, bringing neighbors from far and near to enjoy the informal recitals which he gave every Sunday evening for over thirty years.

Drenched in this atmosphere of salt sea-air, my recollections of annual summer holidays are filled with music—music mixed with moon-light, mysterious darkness, and the church bells of "St. Andrews by the Sea."

These Sunday evenings represented to my childhood something symbolic and inexpressible. The fact that I belonged so closely to this artist who was cherished by all these unknown people sitting about in silent groups, drinking in the beauty of his music, made me happy and excited. I was never conscious of the fact that there was a difference of over fifty years between our ages. It seemed perfectly natural that I should prefer to take my walks with Father rather than to play with children of my own age. He taught me how to harness and drive a horse when I had to stand on a chair to put the bridle over the horse's ears. Every morning I would go to the stable and hitch "Topsy" into a little red-wheeled runabout and proudly drive up to the front porch, and wait for Father to step in beside me and tell me where to drive. For every day we discovered new roads and wooded lanes, or trotted along the hard, wet, sandy beaches at low tide. Oh, the glorious days of golden sunlight—walks along the rocks and explorations at low tide into the crevices and caverns where creeping crabs and eels hid under the tangled, slippery masses of dank sea-weed.

It was not until my father's health forced him to give up many activities that I became aware of the fact that he was what was known as an old man. I could not bear to hear the word applied to him, and bitterly resented being told that on this account I should not ask him to participate in my youthful enthusiasms and excursions. I was frequently oppressed by a sense of ancient sadness and a desire to avoid laughter and games; and yet I was always expected to amuse others and be a sort of court jester.

It was years later in Paris that I began to cross-question my mother concerning my own arrival on this earth. Reluctantly she made the confession that for months before I made my appearance she had the firm conviction that I would be the cause of her death—that I had been a most unexpected and belated addition to the family, and that two months before I was born she had had herself photographed so that this picture could be given to my father by my sister Helen, who

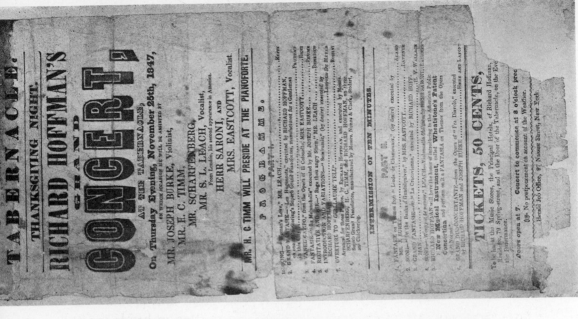

FACSIMILE OF A LETTER FROM P. T. BARNUM, DATED 1850, IN WHICH HE ENGAGED
MY FATHER TO PLAY WITH JENNY LIND IN AMERICA

FACSIMILE OF THE ORIGINAL PROGRAM (OF 1847) IN WHICH MY FATHER APPEARED
AS SOLOIST ON THE CONCERTINA

This same instrument was recently exhibited at the Museum of the City of New York

PHOTOGRAPH OF MY MOTHER TAKEN TWO
MONTHS BEFORE I WAS BORN

FROM AN ENGRAVING AFTER A DAGUERREO-
TYPE OF MY FATHER AS HE APPEARED IN
1847 AT HIS FIRST AMERICAN CONCERT

CHAPEL AT RYE BEACH, NEW HAMPSHIRE, "ST. ANDREWS BY THE SEA"

It was here that my father played the organ for many years. My Sister Elsie, my brother Charles, and I
sang in the choir. The stained-glass window in the chapel was placed there as a memorial to my father
by a group of friends

THE OLD STATION STAGE–COACH STANDING IN FRONT OF BACHELDER'S HOTEL

This four-horse conveyance was the regular means of transport for all arriving visitors and for occasional expeditions to Portsmouth and New-Castle, from where excursions were made to the Isles of Shoals, generally ending with a supper at "Ham's lobster-house" in Portsmouth

HOFFMAN FAMILY GROUP

Left to right, standing: Charles, Mother, Father, Helen, and Elsie. *Seated:* Malvina and Richard. Taken at Little Boar's Head

M. H., AGED TWO YEARS, HOLDING HER
PET WOOLLY LAMB

M. H., AGED TWELVE

KATHARINE RHOADES AND M. H. IN FRONT OF 116 WEST 43RD STREET

We were classmates at the Brearley School, and very proud of our new spring outfits. Miss
Rhoades is now a painter, and associate of the Freer Gallery of Art in Washington

was in her early teens at the time, and to whom my mother confided me and all my upbringing.

Apparently after I appeared on the scene, my mother's despondency and father's apprehension vanished, and they both succeeded in hiding any such thoughts from me during all my childhood. My mother then told me that she had frequently noticed a "sad, far-away" look in my eyes when I was a little girl, and that she had worried a good deal over the fact that I could not seem to derive any real pleasure from either toys or the companionship of children of my own age. The curious sense of responsibility that so often seemed to oppress me began to find its explanation, and as we threshed out many ideas that had been laid away in camphor for years, our understanding and love for one another deepened and grew into a perfect, complete relationship which nothing could ever shake or destroy.

During the years that my two sisters were being introduced to society, I was initiated into more of the complexities of life; the little household became far more active; a telephone was installed in our only bathroom—I never quite fathomed why, unless it was the only room in the house that had a key in the door and where one could be reasonably sure of being alone.

There were invitations to balls, parties, teas, endless scheming as to how the various callers and suitors could be received without meeting each other—for remember there was only *one* front parlor, and in this was my father's piano, where he gave lessons, rehearsed chamber music, and practised every available moment of the day.

About this time the great era of opera stars began to glitter in our musical firmament—Melba, Emma Eames, and Calvé, with the de Reszke brothers, Plançon, and Scotti. Signed photographs of these great artists began to grace every bureau and table in the house.

My father would take me to hear an opera occasionally, and after the famous arias had been sung he would drag me home, so that I would not become too tired or confused with too many impressions and emotions—for I was stirred to my depths by the music and above all by the pristine beauty of Emma Eames's appearance and voice.

After these excursions into the realms of musical fantasy, Father would play over and over the themes and arias of the performance, making me learn them and the words as well, so that they were indelibly impressed on my memory.

When the property on Sixth Avenue opposite Jack's famous chop-house became the Hippodrome, the local color of Forty-third Street was considerably keyed up. Private dwellings became rooming-houses for actors. Even Simpson's solemn and respectable grocery store, which was on the corner of Sixth Avenue, found the new pace too swift, and this landmark of another generation disappeared, with all its pungent aromas of coffee and tea and the crackling of stiff paper bags and the old-school manners of the venerable salesmen. Giants, dwarfs, freaks, white horses, giraffes, and elephants took their daily exercise up and down Forty-third Street; Henry Savage's theatrical agency blocked traffic between our house and Broadway with crowds of gay chorus "hopefuls." My parents felt they must move us into a calmer neighborhood. We were all very disappointed. So the little house, along with many others, was sold and torn down, and on its site rose the Elks' Club, and across the street the Town Hall came into being, replacing the former habitat of Lillian Russell and the unhappy lady who failed in her desperate plunge.

Throughout most of 1898 the Spanish American War filled the minds of every one with sudden new activities and responsibilities. My sister Helen plunged into the relief organization of the American Red Cross, to which she has devoted her best efforts and strength ever since, giving her leadership and inspiring service to the New York County chapter.

It was soon after the Spanish War that she married Doctor William Kinnicutt Draper. From then, and until his death in 1926, we all turned to him for his advice and devoted medical care.

Ruth and Paul Draper and I spent many days of our childhood together, playing games and tricks of every kind and learning pages of poetry, which we recited for our families. Ruth always took the first prize on any monologues or parlor entertainments, and developed her talents until she achieved international reputation and success.

We were living in Forty-third Street in 1908 when I first met Samuel Grimson. He had come to see my father with a letter of introduction from Mrs. William H. Draper, shortly after his arrival from

England. Soon after this Sam and my father played many chamber-music recitals together, and the young English violinist became an intimate friend in both the Draper and Hoffman households.

It was sixteen years later that Sam and I were married in the chapel of the Cathedral of Saint John the Divine, on June 6, 1924.

My father and Sam Grimson played the piano and violin together for two or three seasons, and I was permitted to turn the pages of music for my father, and by attending the rehearsals as well, I became familiar with most of the classical music, and grew to depend upon it as a vital life-force.

Gradually my father's health failed and I felt a sense of responsibility concerning my artistic future and the need of uninterrupted study. Attending day and night classes and trying both in oils and pastels to develop a technique which seemed always to recede just beyond my reach, sometimes a wave of encouragement would sweep over me and give me that divine confidence by which our youth is blessed and our studies intensified with passionate enthusiasm.

My desire to make some adequate portrait of my father eventually drove me into sculpture. I had studied painting enthusiastically for some time, when I felt the need of three-dimensional form. I made two portraits of my father, one in pastel and one in oils, and being dissatisfied with the results, I begged him to let me try to do his portrait once more in sculpture. He posed for me most of the time while playing the piano, and I could sense the strength of his will that I should do a good piece of work. I felt a strong collaboration of spirit, and at the end he was as convinced as I was that sculpture would be the medium I must choose for my art expression.

He examined the work very solemnly and laid his hand on my shoulder: "My child, I'm afraid you're going to be an artist. It's a long, hard road and you have to travel most of the time entirely alone. I am seventy-eight years old and can leave you very little of this world's earthly goods, but if I can leave you my ideals, perhaps they will be worth more to you than anything else. Above all, you must *be* an artist; after that you may create art."

As he said these words I remember feeling a shock of courage run through my veins. It was as if I had suddenly been given a sword of finely tempered steel, a defense against the inevitable battles that I would have to fight out alone in the future. Two weeks after this my father died.

This experience of a very young artist, exploring and discovering for the first time the inner character of a mature artist, who was her own father as well, was an overpowering one. I was thrown into the depths of loneliness and grief by his sudden death and the cessation of all his music, which had been the daily accompaniment of my life from dawn till eve.

The weight of this silence grew heavier with the years and to this day I have never felt so utterly possessed by any art as by music. My father had a fine classic style of pianistic playing, and a lovable nature which drew to him a crowd of friends and admirers during his fifty years of public appearances. My earliest studies of personalities were based on watching this procession of doctors, pupils, and friends which passed through our household. Sunday evenings were always consecrated to an informal gathering of artist friends. Father played for an hour and then the other musicians would sing or play the violin to my father's accompaniment, and generally I was made to sing a few songs by Brahms, Strauss, or Reynaldo Hahn before the evening was over.

It became an immediate necessity that I should direct my efforts to contributing to the family exchequer. The problem of each one of us was to earn a living and carry on the high purposes and ideals which our parents had so consistently practised. My maturing mind was filled with haunting memories of long vigils by sickbeds and frequent visitations of death. I felt mystified and under the spell of some tragic fatality. I studied drawing and painting while still at the Brearley School, and worked my way through years of incessant effort, trying to develop a technique that would respond, without too violent a struggle, to the sudden unreasonable demands made upon it. My mental machinery was uneven and sometimes flared up into a white heat without warning, sometimes prowled about in a jungle of confusion. I was driven on by an imperious need to express myself in form and color. For several years I worked under the direction of the painter, John W. Alexander.

Then my ideas suddenly crystallized. I bought a block of marble and diligently started in to carve my father's portrait. I was given space in a friend's studio in Macdougal Alley, and when the portrait was completed I sent it to the National Academy to be judged and exhibited. The fact that it was accepted and given a very good place was encouraging to me, and I decided to take up the study of sculpture, with more conviction than ever.

Rodin, and Paris

> "Vivre c'est rien, mais sacrifier sa vie pour un idéal est la seule chose qui donne sa véritable qualité à l'homme."—RODIN, in conversation.

Within a year, my mother decided to give up her life in America and devote herself to helping me in my artistic studies abroad. I had worked day and night trying to collect enough funds to pay for the steamer tickets, designing covers for sheet-music and patterns for wallpapers and linoleums, and making pastel portraits of babies and young children. We sailed away with a letter of credit for one thousand dollars left to my mother in legacy by a thoughtful friend. In the good old days of 1910 we were able to travel through Italy and Switzerland, to Paris and London, establish ourselves in various studio and alcove apartments, and live in the student quarters of the *rive gauche* for fifteen months, on this thousand dollars.

To any one who has had the good fortune of being an art student in Paris and who has been poor enough to know the joys of a Sunday lunch on the Boulevard Montparnasse, after a week of home cooking and dishwashing, when *dessert et café* were added to the menu as a real spree, it would be unnecessary to state that there were no obstacles ominous enough to dim the promise of even a distant horizon. Reading the menus from right to left during the lean years made everything edible seem precious and worth fighting for. Many were the laughs indulged in, when the inevitable *gateau de riz* would be suggested as a means of satisfying any stray hunger pangs that might still be lurking in the mind or body of a passionate young art student.

It was my determined intention to become a pupil of Rodin. While still in America I had studied his work from books and photographs, and from the varied and interesting collection of his clay studies, bronzes, and marbles owned by Mrs. John Simpson in New York.

When I had tried five times in vain to present a letter of introduction at Rodin's studio, Rue de l'Université, my hopes were almost frustrated and the situation had become pretty desperate for me. His concierge gave me little encouragement, but some last grain of hope drove me to extreme action on my fifth visit, and I said:

"Tell Monsieur Rodin that if he does not see me today I must return to America, but that I came to Paris to study with him, and that I must deliver a message to him from his friend Madame Simpson. I shall not leave, he must admit me today."

The surprised guardian seemed to sense my adamant determination, and in a few moments came back smiling.

"Well, at last I have permission to admit you," she said, and I followed her past the many studios until she knocked at Rodin's door.

I found myself in a room crowded with marbles and covered clay models on stands. There were four or five Frenchmen with black coats and red rosettes in their lapels, talking to Rodin, who looked me over with a hooded searching gaze that made me feel rooted to the spot and unable to move. He came forward slowly, and put out his hand. As I gave him the messages, in my unconjugated French, from his friend across the seas, his grip tightened and he asked me why I had not mentioned her name at my first visit. I began to feel my blood move again in my veins. "So you were determined not to leave without seeing me," he said. I nodded. "What have you under your arm in that envelope?" he asked. "Oh, just two photographs of the only sculpture I have ever done—I am just a beginner but I find I cannot escape it. Sculpture seems to have taken possession of me and my desire is to be your pupil if you will be willing to guide me and criticize my work."

"Let me see the photographs," he said. "Who are these two men?"

"Well, the marble is of my father," I replied. "He was a musician who, after a long life, was serenely meditative. The other is of a young violinist who is just making his début in America as a soloist."

Rodin looked at the photographs for some minutes, put them back into the envelope, and handed them to me. "Character seems to interest you. You have studied these men well. One is the mature artist with his life battles behind him, the other is the young dreamer with his battles ahead of him. Wait here a few moments. I am just describing this marble of mine to these gentlemen and then I am lunching with them." Rodin went back to the visitors and started to tell them that the figure represented a fallen angel that had broken his wings on a rock and that the idea had been conceived after reading a certain poem. He began reciting the lines in a deep monotone, but his memory failed him and he grew violent trying to recall the ending of the sonnet. He strode up and down before the great marble group.

By some extraordinary coincidence, I happened to know the poem, and when I saw that he could not recall the lines, I walked towards him. "Maître," I ventured, "I know that poem, shall I recite it?" He turned on me almost savagely—"What—*you* know it?—let me see if you do—recite it!" My blood was pounding, but I began the lines in a slow, quavering voice:

"*J'ai perdu ma force et ma vie,*
Et mes amis et ma gaîté;
J'ai perdu jusqu'à la fierté
Qui faisait croire à mon génie.

"*Quand j'ai connu la Vérité,*
J'ai cru que c'était une amie;
Quand je l'ai comprise et sentie,
J'en étais déjà dégoûté.

"*Et pourtant elle est éternelle,*
Et ceux qui se sont passés d'elle
Ici-bas ont tout ignoré.

"*Dieu parle, il faut qu'on lui réponde.*
Le seul bien qui me reste au monde
Est d'avoir quelquefois pleuré."

I stepped back once more to my place at the door, not daring to raise my eyes.

There was a murmur of surprise from the group of men. Rodin's voice suddenly rose in a tone of almost brutal abruptness—"*Allons, au déjeuner, mes amis—il est tard.*" He showed his friends out of the door, turned towards me—"Here," he said. "This is where my keys hang," and he lifted an old rag from a nail on the wall, on which hung two keys. "You may use them to open the other studios. Uncover all the work and examine the trays of plaster studies and I will see you when I return." He went out, closed the door and locked it from the outside. I had certainly not only been admitted at last to his studio, I was locked into it—for better or worse—and I wasted no time wondering what it all meant, but started in at once to pull the linen shrouds off the marbles. A new world seemed suddenly to engulf my imagination. When I had examined one room I went to the next and then to another and finally returned to where I had started and began making drawings of the small plaster hands of which there were thirty or forty in various positions lying in wooden trays. I worked so intently that I did not notice that the fire in the stove had gone out and that the studio had grown icy cold. I did realize quite definitely, however, that I was very hungry, for I had not had anything to eat since my cup of coffee at 7:30 A.M. and I suddenly noticed that it must be well into the afternoon as the winter light had begun to fade. I re-covered all the marbles, and as I went over to try the door, hoping to be able to open it from the inside, I heard a knock. Wondering what I should do, I made no response— for if it were some visitor what would he think if I said I could not open the door? The knocking became louder and then a key turned in the lock and the door opened. Rodin came in and looked about. He caught sight of me behind one of the marble blocks. "Well," he said. "What have you done all this time? Why is everything covered over? Did you not examine the work or did you not like it, that you have covered everything again?"

I explained hastily that the sight of so many of his groups was too much for me to cope with at one time, and that although I had examined them all, I had re-covered them carefully and had concentrated

Photos. M. H.   THREE INTERIOR VIEWS OF RODIN'S STUDIO AT MEUDON, OUTSIDE PARIS

Top: Plaster model for the "Gate of Hell." Below this, various portrait heads, and group of Ugolin and his sons in foreground. At right, study of one of the versions for the Victor Hugo monument. *Center:* Portrait of Clémenceau on table, Ugolin in foreground. *Below:* Draped groups in process of being made, and heroic bronze of "The Thinker." The glass cases around the walls contained innumerable studies of figures, hands, and heads in plaster. Hundreds of these were also stored in a large balcony at one end of the studio. This building has recently been rebuilt and entirely rearranged as a **museum.**

PORTRAIT OF MY FATHER AT THE AGE OF SEVENTY-EIGHT

PORTRAIT OF SAMUEL BONARIOS GRIMSON, MADE IN 1909

Photographs of these heads served as my introduction to Rodin

Elizabeth Watrous Medal, National Academy of Design.

BRONZE GROUP OF PAVLOWA AND MORDKIN IN THE "BACCHANALE," LUXEMBOURG
GARDENS, PARIS

Léonce Bénédite and M. H. on the day of the unveiling   39

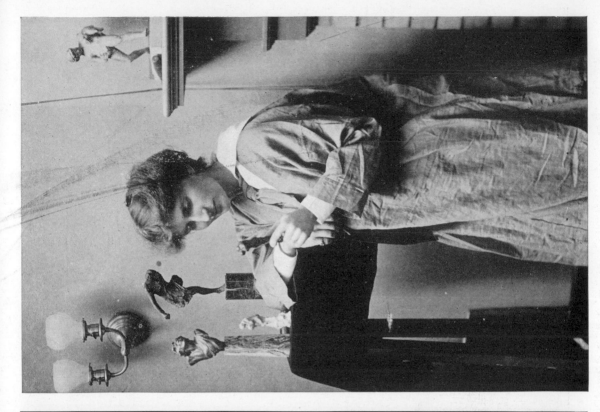

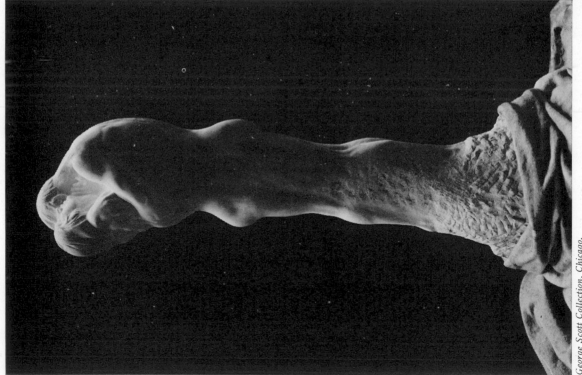

Right: M. H. in her 24th Street studio examining the small model which she had made in Rodin's studio, as described on page 43. To the left is "The

my attention on the little plaster hand which seemed to be more my size. I had made a few drawings of this and he examined my sketch book. After looking through it he said, "My child, do you think these are all drawings?"

"Why, yes," I answered naively, "I *did* think so, what are they?" for I could see he was not of my opinion.

"They are sketches," he said. "Michelangelo *never* made sketches, everything he drew was a study, a real drawing. See that you never make any more sketches. Beware of the weakness of your American artists," pointing his finger at me very threateningly.

"What is their weakness?" I asked.

"C'est leur sacrée facilité," he said, and then, going over to the stove, he realized how cold it had grown. The fire was out, and we were in semi-darkness. He came back and felt my hands; they were cold. He took off his heavy cloth cape and wrapped it about me and went to work remaking the fire. "Why did you let it go out?" he asked, and "Why do you look so pale and tired? By the way, did you have any lunch before coming to me at noon?"

"No, I had my coffee early but did not expect to be able to stay here so long today—it has been a great feast for a hungry artist, I shall never forget it."

He sat down beside me, drawing the little stools near the stove. "You forgot the fire, my child, because of the inner fire that burns you, but you cannot neglect hunger—nature is a stern mistress, and if you play tricks with her she will punish you every time. When I locked you in today, I never thought about food, I just wanted to make sure that you would be alone with my work, and that I would find you on my return." He rubbed my hands and held them near the glowing stove. "Now you must go home and take the little hand with you and make careful drawings for a week. Every day you must go to the Louvre and study and make copies of the old masters—Leonardo Da Vinci and Michelangelo and Raphael—not to copy their technique only but to understand it, and develop a technique of your own, and each week come back here and bring me what you have done—and be sure to eat plenty of beefsteak and potatoes"—at this point he encircled my absurdly small wrist with his strong sensitive fingers—"you are too thin and sculpture needs plenty of fuel for the fires of art burn fiercely. When you come back, I may be drawing from a model, if so you may draw with me. You know where the keys hang, from now on you may feel at home in my studio."

And so it was that my studies with Rodin began. They continued for over a year, until I returned to America in 1911. As I was leaving for America, Rodin urged me to study anatomy by dissection. "We have no facilities for such study in Paris but through your doctor friends you may be able to find a way in America to make your own dissections." I asked Doctor George S. Huntington at the College of Physicians and Surgeons in New York to admit me to the laboratories as a student. The sights and smells so shocked me that my determination was almost destroyed. One day as I stood wavering, Doctor Huntington suddenly appeared, scalpel in hand, and said smiling, "Well, well, Malvina, you look pretty green this morning—can it be that you regret having asked me to teach you how to dissect and learn the principles of anatomy?" His kindly blue eyes challenged me— "Remember you are the only woman up here and medical students are likely to jeer at you if you give any signs of funking."

My blood rushed up into my head again and I could feel the color come back into my cheeks. Doctor Huntington led me to the operating table; I put on my rubber gloves, and he said, "Now watch me closely, as I reveal to you the beautiful mechanism God built into our knees for you to see here the basic principles on which all bridges and levers are constructed."

The delicate accuracy of his technique (in spite of the fact that he had lost two or three of his fingers) was amazing. He turned his instruments over to me, and said he would return in two hours to see what progress I had made. "Be careful," he said as he left, "these scalpel blades are sharp; don't cut those tissue-paper sheaths that hold all our muscles in place. Remember everything you will discover is beautiful and wonderful, then you'll be all right." What a teacher! What sensibility and understanding he had for a cringing pupil—this man who spent his life searching for the hidden wonders of comparative anatomy and wading about in a gory laboratory from morning until evening!

42

After my first year, and by request of a group of artist friends, he was able to persuade Columbia University to open a special department of dissection and anatomy for artists. At first all the class attended enthusiastically, but gradually the numbers dwindled; the formaldehyde and grim surroundings were too repugnant for their eyes and nostrils.

A year later Mother and I went back to Paris and I continued my studies, dividing my time between night classes at the academy and working in my own studio. Each week I had a searching and constructive criticism from Rodin, sometimes drawing and sometimes watching him carve marble.

On Sunday morning I often went to the great studio of Rodin's home at Meudon, near Paris. He would show me the series of portrait heads in plaster, which he made while he was studying his sitters. Sometimes he would make six or seven different studies of the same person—varying slightly the pose of the head or the expression of the face. Frequently I knew him to start a portrait, and after a few sittings, to call in a plaster-caster and have a mould made as a record; then he would make a "squeeze," that is, the fresh clay would be pressed into the negative of the piece-mould and with this stage of the portrait safely registered, he would feel more free to make bold changes or experiments, without the fear of losing what had been achieved up to that point. The first plaster was a guide to which he could always refer if he felt himself in doubt during the subsequent sittings. He would hand me little plaster figures and ask me to cut off the arms and legs; then with white wax he would rearrange the groups, changing a gesture and adding action or some new suggestion of composition.

One incident which made a great impression upon me took place at the entrance to the Rue de Varenne studio. I was kept waiting a long time for Rodin to arrive. I took two small bits of clay and rolled them absent-mindedly into two pieces about five inches long. These I pressed together in my closed hand, and studying the result was amazed to find that the pressure of my fingers had clearly suggested the forms of two standing figures. I added the two heads and was tapping the base on the stone step to make it stand up, when

Rodin appeared. He asked me what I was doing and I showed him the little group. "Just an accident," I said, "made while I was waiting for you."

After carefully examining it from all sides, he said very seriously, "There is more in this than you understand at present. An accident, you say? Well, it is one of those accidents which one must catch and transform into science. You will keep this, and model this group one-half life-size and cut it in marble—but before you do it, you must study for five years. Will you promise to do this?"

"Yes," I answered, and wondered deeply how Rodin could see so clearly and decisively into the future. Eventually I carried out the idea and called it the "Column of Life."

Sometimes Sam would go to Meudon with me, taking his violin. Rodin would invite Rose Beuret to sit with him in the studio and listen to the music, after which she would bring us bowls of fruit, and milk and bread and butter. He told me, before presenting me to Rose, that she was "a violent nature, jealous, suspicious, but able to discriminate between falsehood and truth, like the primitives, and possessed of the power of eternal devotion. . . . You will be good friends, I know, but remember what I have said about her." His eyes glowed fiercely under his shaggy brows and then his face changed into a friendly smile.

It was years later, almost at the end of her life, that she became his wife—she who had been the "shadow of the sun" as she described herself to me, since her eighteenth year. Her love of music was almost pathetic; tears often ran down her thin cheeks while she was listening, so starved was she for any such emotional relaxation—her life had been completely devoted to the service of her beloved master, first as his model, then as his cook and housekeeper, and as the mother of his son. At the end of her long life he finally decided to marry her legally. After a few weeks of supreme pride and happiness, Rose Beuret Rodin died, and now the great bronze figure of "The Thinker" broods over the tomb in the Meudon garden where Rodin and Rose lie side by side under a common slab of granite.

While studying the first stages of my profession from the practical point of view in Paris, I became increasingly aware of the importance of understanding the *craft* as well as the *art* of sculpture.

Under the guidance of Emanuel Rosales, the Italian sculptor, I was introduced to the complexities of chasing and finishing my own bronzes. I watched for many hours how his deft fingers controlled the metal tools and how he was able to clean the surface of a freshly cast statuette, never harming in any way the modelling or texture of the forms.

During my first visit to a French foundry, I was quite overwhelmed by all the stages of handling through which every piece of sculpture has to pass. I listened to the remarks of the workmen and became friendly with the foreman of each department, and these men very patiently explained to me just what the workmen were doing and how to hold the tools myself and control them without damaging the metal. They would give me old pieces of twisted bronze to practice on, and I found it very exciting to be able to restore the surface to a smooth, even finish and have it approved by the founders.

The casual remarks of these master craftsmen concerning other sculptors were a revelation to me. It seemed that very few of the artists ever took the trouble to visit the foundry and in fact during the years that I have visited foundries so frequently, I have seldom encountered a sculptor who showed any active interest in how his sculpture was reproduced in bronze.

It was about this time that I began to realize what a serious handicap it was for a woman to attempt competition with the men in the field of sculpture. There was absolutely no traditional credit given to a woman in this field of activity, and I felt convinced of the necessity of learning my profession from the very beginning, so as to be able to control the workmanship of the great number of craftsmen with whom I was obliged to come in contact, both in France and in America.

I remember very well that Mestrovic, the Yugo-Slav sculptor, said to me when I first met him, that the first thing I must do as a woman was to learn the principles and technical side of my work better than most men, before I could start *even,* without the handicap of a preconceived idea that women were amateurs in art and generally took up sculpture as a diversion or a pastime. I wonder if the women in other professions, such as music and literature, have ever realized what a serious obstacle this femininity becomes in the field of sculpture—and with good reason, for the work itself demands that we stand on our feet from morning until night, lifting heavy weights, bending iron, sawing wood, and building armatures; we must know how to use carpenters' tools and plumbers' tools, and be able to calculate the strains and necessary supports to build up the clay figures. These last are often treacherous and collapse at just the moment when we are enthusiastically bringing them to completion.

In July, 1914, I was in Surrey recuperating from a serious illness when I received three telegrams from Rodin asking me to supervise the installation of his exhibition at the Duke of Westminster's (Dorchester House) in London. I worked two days with the movers directing the placing of the marbles and bronzes, reinforcing myself at frequent intervals with brandy and raw eggs. John Tweed, the English sculptor, who was a friend of Rodin's, came on the second day and gave me his friendly co-operation, for there were several very opinionated ladies who felt it their duty or privilege to object to the manner in which I was placing the marbles. Tweed had a broken arm in a splint at the time, but his contagious smile cheered us on greatly.

On the morning of the day of the official opening, when the Queen and her ladies of the court were to be present, Rodin suddenly appeared with Comtesse Greffuhle from Paris and asked if everything was in readiness. Luckily it was, and I asked him to look over the installation in the presence of the ladies who had been so convinced of my errors. He did so and said everything was quite as it should be. This was a most satisfactory reward for my efforts. When he left Dorchester House, Rodin ordered a hansom cab, asked me to accompany him, and told me to give the driver the address of the Leicester Gallery where a small group of my own bronzes was being exhibited at that time. I was indeed surprised that he had even remembered this fact. I was very happy to go into my modest little exhibit in the company of the great sculptor who could make such a *beau geste* of moral encouragement to his American pupil.

While we drove across London, I explained to him some of my difficulties with the titled ladies who had felt they knew more than I did about arranging the exhibition. "Malvina," he said, "an artist must learn the art of handling not only sculpture but human beings —there are all kinds in this world and you must learn to understand them all; you can enrich your own intelligence by studying their faults as well as their virtues—nothing is a waste of time if you use the experience wisely. *'Tout comprendre c'est tout pardonner,'* but don't waste yourself too often. It makes little difference most of the time what you say to people, they ask many questions but they seldom listen to your answers."

In the afternoon the Rodin exhibit was opened by the Queen— the court was in official mourning because of the recent assassination of the Austrian Archduke in Sarajevo. Mother and I managed to keep in the background during the reception. I remember we stayed in a little room with Gainsborough's "Blue Boy," watching the royal visitors from a curtained doorway.

A few weeks after our London experience, I was working at the Hotel Biron with Rodin, busily sorting and numbering the hundreds of drawings to be hung in his museum. He would pick up his pen-and-ink drawings, and turning them over slowly, would show me the old laundry-bills on which they were drawn. Quietly, as if talking to himself, he would muse, "Ah, those wonderful, terrible years when I had no paper to draw on, when Rose would collect these old bills and bring them home to me—it would seem as if they registered my best efforts, my agonies, my ecstasies. . . . Ah, youth, youth . . . the white flame burning . . . burning . . . day and night. . . ." For six weeks we arranged the bronzes and the marbles in their permanent positions on the ground floor of the building. One day a telegram from London was brought into the studio: "Consider risk too great to ship cases from Dorchester exhibit to Paris. Will hold until we receive your instructions." I translated this to Rodin, whose heavy brows frowned with anxious forebodings. "What can this mean?" he asked. "Go and consult the guardians and see what has happened."

War had been declared. Paris was aflame, soldiers were marching in the streets, excited groups were watching the bill-posters being put up on the walls surrounding Les Invalides.

I ran quickly back to Hotel Biron, stopping to call the plaster-caster from his work to be ready to go at once with Rodin to Meudon in a motor which had been loaned to him for the day. I picked up the black velvet beret and the long cape and went into the garden room where I found Rodin sitting with his head in his hands. When he heard the news, he seemed to be shaken to the depths of his soul. *"C'est la fin,"* he said, in a scarcely audible, husky voice. I helped him on with his cape, and as we passed his writing desk he stopped and picked up the first unbound edition of his book *Les Cathédrales de France.* "Give me a pen," he said. He leaned over the book and wrote in the fly-leaf with a shaking hand:

> *A mon élève Malvina, sculpteur sensible,*
> *son vieux maître Auguste Rodin*
> *Le jour que la guerre a été déclarée*
> *Paris—Août 1914*

He said as he gave me the book—

"Gardez ce livre en souvenir, vous m'avez dit une fois que les arbres dans l'allée de mon jardin lèvent leurs branches vers le ciel comme les mains en prières, aujourd'hui—tout le monde doit lever les mains, car c'est la fin de notre époque de civilisation."

A few days after this a telegram was sent to Rodin from a government office ordering the immediate removal of all his work into the cellar of the Hotel Biron, as the building was to be used for a day-nursery.

This blow was one which shattered the faith and happiness of Rodin's last years. It was, as he said, "the beginning of the end, the cracking-up of civilization"—*"qui n'est, après tout, qu'une couche de peinture qui s'en va quand la pluie tombe."* The days spent with him during the following months were charged with tension and tragedy. My mother was ill, and destiny decided that I should leave Rodin and Paris and sculpture and take Mother back to America and do my share in the Red Cross in New York.

In the autumn of 1914 Rodin went to England. One morning

AUGUSTE AND ROSE RODIN ON THEIR WEDDING–DAY IN THEIR VILLA AT MEUDON,
JANUARY, 1917

RODIN AND M. H. IN AUGUST, 1914, AT CHÂTELET EN BRIE, NEAR FONTAINEBLEAU
We had motored from Meudon

THE FAÇADE OF AN OLD CHÂTEAU ON RODIN'S ESTATE AT MEUDON
His grave, surmounted by "The Thinker," in foreground. Two plasters of the figure known as "The Shadow" were placed in the window frames

while visiting a friend in London, he heard the military band as the British Tommies were marching past the house where he was living, on their way to Victoria Station. He left the breakfast table and went to the window, waving his napkin at the pink-cheeked young Britishers. "Oh, my dear, dear boys!" he cried. "You are going over to fight with my French brothers, and to help them. What can I do to show my gratitude?" The tears coursed down his cheeks. He asked for a pencil, and wrote out a deed of gift to the British Government of every piece of his sculpture which had been exhibited at Dorchester House.

This collection is permanently shown at South Kensington Museum.

I never saw Rodin again, for he died in 1917, and it was not until after the Armistice when Mons. Léonce Bénédite, curator of the Luxembourg and of the Musée Rodin, sent for me to come and help him reinstate the collection after the war, that I was able to return to Europe. I devoted two months to helping in the task of arranging the vast collection, washing the marbles which had been covered with dust for many years, sorting hundreds of drawings, and unpacking the numberless boxes of antique carvings in ivory and dozens of Greek terra-cottas and bronzes, Egyptian reliefs and every kind of Etruscan glass bowls and fragile, iridescent vases. Many of these had lain in boxes so long, stored away in the chicken-houses and lofts on Rodin's property at Meudon, that when we attempted to lift the bowls, they crumbled into powder on the cotton wool, unable to withstand the sudden pressure of the outer air or of being touched.

This labor of love at the Hotel Biron was a liberal education for me, for I was entrusted with the mounting and arrangement of many cases of these objects and enjoyed the direction and advice of Mons. Bénédite and his brother George, then curator of Egyptology at the Louvre.

It was in those impressionable years that I was thrown into the realm of Boutet de Monvel (Aîné), Max Blondat, MacMonnies and Paul Bartlett, Pavlowa, Nijinsky and Diaghileff's Ballet, Gertrude Stein and Matisse, Brancusi, Rosales, and Mabel Dodge (now Mrs. Tony Luhan of Taos, New Mexico). Meeting so many creative minds was very exciting. There were writers, musicians, sculptors, painters—

an endless and colorful series of groups, opinions, and types. I was constantly amazed at the kindness shown me by the older artists. Some were always ready to advise and help me, while others gave me space to work in their studios. I began to sift them all into main classes—the "big people" and the "little people"—those who counted and stood out from the crowd fearlessly and welcomed any combat, those who were part of the crowd and would never have the courage to navigate alone; those who were listed on every card catalogue, and those who had no number or category into which they could fit; the tame type and the savage, the conventionalized plodder and the instinctive primitive.

During my student years in Paris my mother made every effort to enable me to work steadily and without too many domestic distractions or anxieties. She knew all my friends and quickly endeared herself to them by her sympathy and quiet charm. Having been born and brought up for the first years of her life in Paris, French was like her native language. When my artist friends were sick she would go to see them and take them hot-water bags and medicines. I well recall how many visits she made, carrying baskets of fruit, to my little dancing model, Loulou, who was forced to spend many months in a hospital.

My mother's breadth of literary and musical interests soon gathered many friends about us. In our modest little studio there was always a piano, and many were the Bohemian musical evenings that we enjoyed there.

These were the days of Jean Cocteau and d'Annunzio, of Maeterlinck, and Mary Garden's great performance in *Pelléas et Mélisande;* of Romaine Brooks, the painter, and of Georgie Duval and her coterie of musicians and poets on the Quai d'Orsay. Oh, the shimmering, fragrant spring evenings spent in her apartment with a new moon hovering over Sacré Coeur! The French windows thrown open to the balcony overlooking the Place de la Concorde; deep, soft divans and shaded lights; fumes of subtle incense floating about, and in the music-room a string quartette playing a delightful program of French music from the seventeenth and the eighteenth century composers. At the end of the evening some of the guests would sing and play modern music—which at that time was Debussy and Ravel—or a poet would recite his latest verses. The roof-garden served as an outside sitting-room, and the unique atmosphere created by our gifted hostess, Mme. Duval, made every one feel at home and informal.

From all these colorful experiences my senses derived great joy and satisfaction. These evenings seemed to complete the picture of my long days of hard work with a delicious and almost sensuous delight. The contrast of such beauty, intelligence, and luxury set off my stark little studio and the brutal, smoky atmosphere of the foundries.

There were very few events that I did not relate to my mother. Her understanding was so complete that I had no reason to dissimulate or hide anything from her. My experiences often amazed and alarmed her, but she heard them to the end and then she would sigh and say: "One lives and learns, but this new world of yours is all strange to me—you must have your own weapons for your own warfare; in my youth such things never seemed to happen . . . or at least they were never spoken of." This eternal "bridge of sighs" between the generations! What our grandparents thought and did was accepted as law by our parents up to a certain point, but they in their turn found new codes and new hungers threatening their young existence. There comes a tide for every one of us, and each in our own cycle of evolution grasps desperately for whatever solution may save us from destruction and decay. When Nature starves for new life and new blood, we puny mortals can but follow her dictatorship. Our parents may strive to force their will or their love upon us—it is of no avail. Youth, like a hunter, follows the fresh trail of the wilderness and no one may change his course.

Amidst the glamor and excitement of life there were frequent up-heavals of sudden tragedies and violent emotional experiences. I found that in my old diary of 1910–11–12 a quotation from Nietzsche was often repeated: *"Tu fus toujours ainsi, tu t'es toujours approchée familièrement de toutes les choses terribles."*

Something predestined seemed to draw me constantly into the depths of life, and there I so often found sanguinary traces. On an old drawing of the picket fence that used to wall off the upper terrace from the Butte de Montmartre, I made a row of hearts impaled upon the posts. Under this I wrote: "Between joy and pain is only an interval of blasted ecstasy."

In these years of white intensity my health began to give out under the strain. I became ill, and not daring to confess how I felt, I resorted to brandy and raw eggs at frequent intervals. It was under these conditions that I modelled my first portrait of William Astor Chanler and Robert Bacon, at that time the American ambassador to France.

My days were overcrowded with work. The mornings I spent as an apprentice to a sculptor; the afternoons I worked in my studio with models, or made portraits. The evenings were divided between night-classes in drawing and attending the concerts Touche in the *rive gauche* or studying at home. As my physical strength gave out, my enthusiasm and confidence sank into gloom and discouragement. Roads leading to my heart's desire seemed to grow interminably long, and at last the human machine gave out and I staged a complete collapse—mind and body. Ordered by the doctor to leave Paris and take an absolute rest, Mother and I went to the Forest of Loches where, after two weeks of immobility, we drove about in a two-wheeled cart which, with a huge white Percheron farm-horse, I hired from a neighboring peasant.

In those days boar-hunting was in full swing in the forest. One day we happened to come upon a hunting party just as the French horns were ringing their clarion calls through the forest. A white boar had been killed and the dogs and horsemen came rushing from all directions to the clearing where Mother and I, in our peasant equipage, had halted for a rest. With gallantry typical of the *grand seigneur,* the leading huntsman rode up to us and asked if we would like to join the party and return with them to his château of Montrésor and witness the ceremony of dividing the boar—inviting us to be guests at the hunt breakfast. We accepted with alacrity, and our own amusement at the way we must have appeared in our primitive cart, with the colossal white horse, helped to make the expedition informal and full of laughter. The Duc de Montrésor must have had a sense of humor to include us in the picture of his triumphant entry to the château courtyard, with the white boar carried on four spears ahead of us!

After a few weeks' holiday we returned to Paris. We visited the château country en route, driving our horse and cart from one town to the other and returning it very regretfully to its owner at the end of our journey.

I have always enjoyed violent contrasts—they seem to key up life in a most stimulating fashion—but when, after these exciting months, we sailed for New York and settled in a rather dark and grim apartment next to the Seventy-first Regiment Armory, both Mother and I would often sigh, remembering our gay evenings, and say: "This is not much like Paris and all its charms."

However, I managed to find a small studio on the fourth floor over a florist's shop across the street and there I embarked on my first professional adventures.

The first time I walked through Forty-third Street after my long absence abroad, I was to find its appearance transformed. I felt so utterly detached from reality when I saw the new buildings that I found it difficult to decide whether it was the *past* that really lived on in our minds or whether it was the *present* that had died.

When I looked at the place where our third-story window had been, and realized how my own destiny, past, present, and future, had been sealed and recorded in that room, and that no trace of any such place remained, I felt an uncanny sensation creep over me—something ghostly, an intangible "presentiment—that long shadow on the grass, indicative that suns go down, that darkness is about to pass."

Breaking the Ice in New York

I began to realize more and more that the making of a portrait included a good many things besides modelling.

To understand the submerged passion that burns in the human eye, to read the hieroglyphs of suffering etched in the lines of a human face, sometimes adding beauty and depth of expression, sometimes merely tracing their record of conflict and resistance; to watch the gesture of a hand or listen for the false notes and the true in a human voice—these were the mysteries that I found I must delve into and try to unravel when I made a portrait. There are no questions asked; there is simply a state of radio emanation set up between two human beings, which, if it is to reveal its secrets, must be sensed as a sort of sacred pact—an awareness to be transmuted into silent form. Over-powered by an unspeakable need to express some inner craving of the soul, the artist is driven along the difficult road towards the ever receding horizons, driven by imperious commands which come to him at unexpected moments, without warning, without mercy.

The only work that I brought with me from Paris was a group of Russian dancers. Pavlowa and Mordkin had posed for me, and although I had the original in plaster I saw no possibility of putting it into bronze. When I showed it to Mr. Bertelli of the Roman Bronze Works, he at once made me a sporting proposition. He said he would cast six copies in bronze and I could pay for them when they were sold. Such spontaneous encouragement gave me the necessary push to try my luck as a gambler.

I carried the first bronze to Mr. George Marcus of Marcus & Company, then at Fifth Avenue and Forty-fifth Street, and asked him if he thought he could show it in his window. (I was so frightened waiting for his answer that I fainted in his office and had to be revived.) He agreed, and within three months the six groups were sold and I felt as if my lucky star had found me.

That first winter I carved a marble portrait which took me many months. When it was completed, the base had to be levelled and made square. Laying it on its back and padding it to avoid any shock, I chiselled off and squared the corners. After a few minutes there was a crash—the head had been severed from the neck and fell to the floor. At such a moment sculpture can draw blood. I fled across the street, ran into my mother's room, and buried my head on her knees, sobbing as if my heart would burst. I shall always remember her tender understanding of that first accident and how she tried to console me.

When such casualties occur in marble there is nothing to do but start the work over again—it's like being caught "tweakin' the pears frae the neighbor's pear tree, *ye canna stick them back again!*"

After my début in Marcus's window, I made the "Gavotte" of Pavlowa in wax, and the "Bacchanale," and "La Péri" and "Les Orientals"; fountains, portraits, and statuettes kept me in a constant and insatiate frenzy of activity. My fighting spirit was up and nothing was too difficult to warn me off. When Mr. Adolph Ochs of *The New York Times* climbed the three flights of stairs and asked me to draw up plans for a Peace Monument, which was to include a statue forty feet high, a park, military barracks, and cascades of water running over garden terraces, I quite calmly accepted the challenge and in a few months submitted my plans and models and called it a "Modern Acropolis." Unfortunately, the war put an end to this project, as well as many others.

These were the early years of my friendship with Anna Pavlowa. I wanted to study all the poses of the dance known as "Autumn Bacchanale," to the music of Glazounoff, interpreted by her and her partner Mordkin. I had seen them give this performance in London in 1910. The impression they had made on me had been so overwhelming that I was determined to learn this dance from start to finish and reproduce it as a frieze in bas-relief. Pavlowa was as keen to help me realize this project as I was to carry it out. She arranged to have me take lessons from her assistant partner, Pavley. We worked in New York at the Century Theatre, and after thirty lessons she dressed me in her little red and white muslin costume, tied the bunches of grapes around my brow, and Pavley appeared in leopard-skin with his arms full of red roses.

My heart was pounding like a trip-hammer. We were to dance the Bacchanale on the actual stage, just before the performance began, and my audience was the empty house with Pavlowa standing beside the conductor's desk. When the pounding rhythm of the music started, everything in life evaporated except the liberation of a wild desire. We went through the dance in good style, and so enthusiastic was the applause (of the empty house!) of Pavlowa and some members of the troupe that we repeated our world *première* and *last* performance—at the finale of which I lay still on the floor, completely unconscious. I saw the lights go red and fade out into oblivion. The next thing I knew, Victor Dandré was bending over me, and spraying a bottle of Vichy down my throat and over my face. Pavlowa was rubbing my hands, and every one was rather alarmed, as I had put all my energy into this effort and it was not impossible that my heart could give out under such a strain. After that experience, I understood a good deal more about Russian dancing than is generally described. They go just that much further in every gesture and effort than other schools of dancing. The dancers try to go beyond themselves until it becomes almost a matter of life and death to them.

After this "heroic treatment," Pavlowa decided I was ready to start the interpretation of her Bacchanale, in bas-relief. At first I made a series of over a hundred drawings during the frequent performances of this dance. Perched on a soap-box behind one of the wings of the theatre, I watched each moment, trying to catch an instantaneous pattern or gesture. Then in the audience I caught other moments from different angles. After I had worked up these drawings in the studio with Pavlowa, I made studies of Mordkin, Novikoff, and Pavley. All of these men knew this dance and were more than willing to pose with their beloved "Anna." We often worked until one and two o'clock in the morning. Pavlowa and I had hoped to exhibit this frieze of twenty-six panels (showing fifty-two dancing figures) when she returned to America on her last tour, but fate willed otherwise, for in January of 1931 the greatest woman dancer of all time died of pneumonia in Holland, and joined the ever-living ranks of Immortal Artists.

The frieze was never shown publicly.

In 1919, when Mr. Robert Bacon saw my model for a war memorial, just before I sailed to exhibit it in Paris, he asked me to carve it in Caen stone in America. He was very ill at the time, and when I reached Paris, I received a cable from his widow telling me of his death and asking that I carry out his wishes to bring back the model to America after the exhibition at Knoedlers' in Paris. This heroic-sized crusader, lying at the knees of a woman, was carved from a ten-ton

MY FIRST GROUP, "RUSSIAN DANCERS," IN BRONZE
Showing Pavlowa and Mordkin in the "Bacchanale"

ANNA PAVLOWA POSING FOR HER "BACCHANALE" POSTER DESIGN IN THE
34TH STREET STUDIO
Marble group "Mort Exquise" and marble of my father's portrait in the background

"LA GAVOTTE," GOLD BRONZE STATUETTE OF PAVLOWA, BY M. H.
This was also made in colored wax. (Metropolitan Museum, N. Y. Stockholm Museum, Sweden)

PAVLOWA AND M. H. LOOKING THROUGH OUR TELESCOPE AT HARTSDALE, NEW YORK
Pavlowa had tied a fur scarf about her head in true Russian style

EIGHT OF THE TWENTY-SIX PANELS IN WHICH THE DANCE OF THE "BACCHANALE" BY PAVLOWA AND HER PARTNERS WAS INTERPRETED BY M. H. IN BAS-RELIEF

Photo. A. B. Hervey.

DETAIL OF THE MEMORIAL, "THE SACRIFICE"

THE CAEN STONE GROUP AS IT WAS PLACED IN THE CHAPEL OF THE CATHEDRAL
OF ST. JOHN THE DIVINE, BEFORE THE THREE STONE STEPS OF THE BASE WERE
FINALLY ADDED

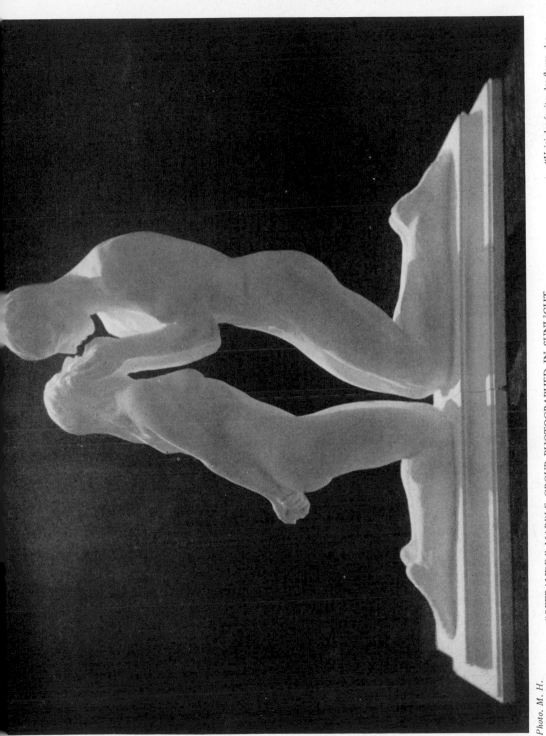

Photo. M. H. "OFFRANDE," MARBLE GROUP PHOTOGRAPHED IN SUNLIGHT

George D. Widener Memorial Medal, 1920, Penna. Acad. of Fine Arts. Helen Foster Barnett Prize, 1921, Natl. Acad. of Design

"Voici des fruits, des fleurs, des
feuilles et des branches
Et puis, voici mon cœur, qui
ne bat que pour vous . . ."

63

ASSEMBLING THE STONE SECTIONS OF THE GROUP FOR THE BUSH BUILDING, LONDON, OUTSIDE THE STONE CARVER'S STUDIO IN CLOSTER, NEW JERSEY

M. H. FINISHING THE HEAD OF "ENGLAND" IN SITU

THE MOMENT OF UNVEILING THE GROUP DEDICATED TO "THE FRIENDSHIP OF ENGLISH–
SPEAKING PEOPLES," BUSH HOUSE, LONDON

(Harvey Wiley Corbett, architect. Irving T. Bush, donor of the group)

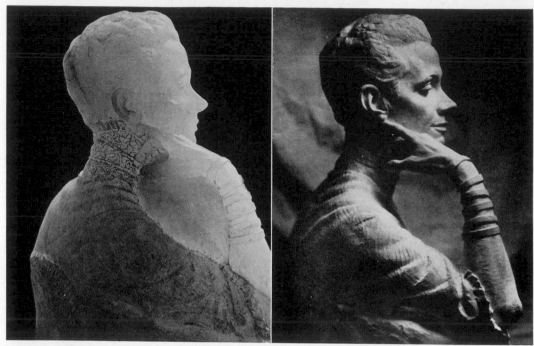

ALABASTER PORTRAIT OF RITA DE ACOSTA LYDIG   THE PLASTER ORIGINAL

PORTRAIT IN COLORED WAX OF ANNA PAVLOWA   MARBLE PORTRAIT OF JOHN KEATS

(Metropolitan Museum of Art, New York; Corcoran Art   (University of Pittsburgh)
Gallery, Washington, D. C.; Carnegie Art Institute,
66   Pittsburgh. Pa.)

block of Caen stone in the front room of my Thirty-fifth Street studio, which I had rented and transformed from a stable into a two-story studio building.

It took fifteen months to model and cut the memorial. The chains of the warrior's armor had to be carved without a hammer, as this would have chipped off the delicate links. This group was placed temporarily in a beautiful chapel in the Cathedral of St. John the Divine and later was moved to Cambridge, Massachusetts, as it had been presented to Harvard, and was placed in the war memorial chapel. My original title for it was "La Douleur est la Mère de la Beauté" (Sorrow is the Mother of Beauty), but later it became known as "The Sacrifice."

This work was done during the last year of my mother's life. She was able to come to the studio to see it completed. The tall candles were lighted at the head of the group. She said no word to me as we stood there together alone, but her fragile little hands were folded in prayer. She seemed to feel a sense of peace, and after I blew out the candles she said " 'Leave there thy gift upon the altar and go thy way.' " We went into the back studio, and Ernest Schelling was there waiting to play for her. He was always most kind and generous about her desire to hear him play, and I know that those hours of informal music were the happiest experiences of her last years.

On Easter Day of that same year Pavlowa came to see us—she had always loved my mother dearly. When she found Mother dying, her pale thin face was bathed in tears. She knelt quietly beside my mother's bed and laid her head on the little delicate hand that lay so still—so still. I left them alone together, and when I went back she beckoned to me to kneel beside her; she said a prayer, and my mother's smile was the only answer.

> ". . . The world, at best,
> Is but a dream by way of growing old,
> And then the closing of mortality."

Pavlowa's thoughtfulness and devotion to me during the dark and terrible weeks that followed my mother's death were a bond which endeared her to me more closely than ever. She who had been my muse and inspiration, always keen to help me by posing for hours after the late performances, and watching over me when I travelled with her as if I had been her little sister—this great artist, the incomparable dancer, found time and opportunity to express her human sympathy in boundless, immeasurable ways.

Professional Adventures

Every time I returned to Paris I spent many hours scrutinizing the marbles in the Greek and Roman collections at the Louvre, and the great series of portraits by Houdon of the French eighteenth century. His vivid portrayal of character greatly impressed me, for I was constantly faced with this challenge of how to give distinction to my various sitters and reflect their individuality.

One of the most absorbing problems I ever tried to solve was the portrait of Rita de Acosta Lydig in alabaster. She had always attracted me as an exotic and fascinating personality, the perfect hostess who knew the art of making each guest feel himself the special attraction of the evening. No dull moment was ever permitted in her brilliant salons, at which were gathered together the various leaders of the intelligentsia, musicians, poets, and artists of her time. During the last year of her life she suffered from a most painful and fatal illness; her courage and endurance were almost superhuman. While she was still in the hospital, I told her that I would like to carve her head in alabaster. She said that if I would make her portrait in this transparent material, with her high collar of Spanish lace, African gold bracelets, and glittering black hair, the thought of it would help her to recover. She would, she said, make one more effort to hold her head high until the end. And so it was decided, and we began to work as soon as she was strong enough to come to my studio. When the portrait was completed it was shown with a large group of my work at the Grand Central Gallery. Rita Lydig came to the opening reception, and enjoyed showing her portrait to her friends. Alas, it was not long after this that she had a serious collapse, from which she never rallied.

During the next few years in New York I became very much interested in the problem of how sculpture was being taught in America, both in the art schools and in private classes, and I visited a great many of these in the hope of finding one in which the pupils were taught the practical handcraft of their art as well as the composition and interpretation of form. I was impressed by the great number of requests I received to engage graduates of art schools as assistants or studio-helpers. When I tried out these boys, to test their ability to enlarge sketches by the compass or build solid and well-planned armatures for the heavy work, I was amazed at their lack of training, as well as their lack of interest in the practical side of sculpture. Hardly any of them knew the first principles of how to cut and carve in wood, stone, or marble. They could not sharpen the tools necessary for this work, and seemed to feel it beneath them to make a plaster cast or to be expected to saw wood with any degree of expert skill.

My European training had given me such respect for just these details that I felt it a very serious lack in the program of the majority of our art schools that all this side of sculpture was so completely neglected. These young men were able to make academic charcoal drawings and build up figures from the nude, generally between two or three feet in height, with a certain sense of accuracy and ability. They did not seem to feel that they were lacking in any particular branch and had no hesitancy in asking a good salary for their services. It was with difficulty that I could persuade any of them to clean the tools that they used, or to leave the studio in any state of order at the close of the day.

I found that nearly all the art students I questioned about their studies had no idea of perspective and very little knowledge of the skeleton or the muscle structure in human anatomy. When they modelled heads, they instinctively felt that the white race, as they had seen it, would form an average basis upon which to model any head that might come into their path. There are courses in anatomy and perspective available to our students, but I think in most cases these subjects are not considered by students to be of any vital importance and so are often neglected.

It was in Geneva, during the early sessions of the League of Nations, that I studied Paderewski as the Statesman. He seemed to be listening in a majestic, sphinx-like silence to the arguments and disagreements of all the other nationalities. I was able to make notes and drawings of him without being noticed, and from these I began the portrait for which he posed later on in New York.

While I was visiting my friends the Ernest Schellings at Céligny, Mr. Paderewski came to dine occasionally, and I would continue my observations during the long sessions of bridge lasting well into the early hours of the next day. This game I could never manage to learn beyond the point of committing more unpardonable errors than were ever recorded in the book of warnings and rules—so I was permitted to be a silent and harmless observer. His face had an impenetrable expression of intense concentration. When he foresaw the inevitable defeat of his opponents, a subtle smile would pucker up the corners of his eyes, and every one knew that the next and deciding tricks were his.

The following season I attended his Chopin recital in Carnegie Hall. From my seat in the second-row-center, I watched the ever-changing emotional expressions play over his face. During the playing of a mazurka, the clear-cut impression of an entirely different personality made me decide to make another portrait of Paderewski as the Artist. I hurried to my studio and worked all night after the recital. When, on the following morning, Mr. Paderewski came to my studio, this second interpretation of his musical mood was finished in clay. He felt, after studying it, that it would not be possible to carry it further by posing again, as the mood was so definitely evoked by the music, and could not be repeated to order in the studio.

For the Statesman, however, he was able to recall the Geneva experiences and isolate himself. After a short interval his face assumed the expression I needed, and he posed like an inscrutable sphinx.

During the years of my work for the Field Museum, I was greatly

71

PADEREWSKI, THE FRIEND

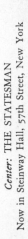

PADEREWSKI, THE ARTIST

American Academy at Rome. (Presented by Mrs. Wm. Church Osborne)

Center: THE STATESMAN

Now in Steinway Hall, 57th Street, New York

"THE FOUR HORSEMEN OF THE APOCALYPSE"
Plaster model for a stone monument to be twenty-six feet in height

THE ARCHANGEL OF THE APOCALYPSE

This figure in gold bronze surmounts a stone shaft at the four sides of which are
equestrian groups in black bronze of the Four Horsemen. These two models have
never been executed in their final medium

encouraged by the visits of Mr. Paderewski to my studio in Paris, and by his constant interest in the project which sent me to so many of the far corners of the earth where he had played and observed with his keen eye the character and formation of many races. It was astonishing to see how accurately he could pick out the Samoans, Indians, and others among the motley crowd of types that filled the studio.

When the Hall of Man was opened, the long strain of overwork began to take its toll, and for many months I was obliged to give up all activities in sculpture, and learn some of those lessons which are branded upon us by illness and enforced solitude. It was during these months that my friends suggested to me that I should write some record of my work and experiences. The Indian chapters I read to Mr. Paderewski in the summer of 1934, and although I was not at all convinced that I could accomplish anything even resembling a book, I was persuaded by him to continue writing. Six months later, in Paris, he asked me to read him the completed manuscript, which at that time did not, however, include any of the autobiographical matter. The magical influence of his friendship at these dangerous curves of my existence could never be realized by him—but when a little ship in a storm gets signals from an ocean liner that it will stand by, all sense of fear vanishes and new courage and faith are born.

Once in a blue moon a single personality can stand out above all his compatriots with such power and nobility that he alone can represent all of his country's best qualities far better than any scientific selection of types, or even crowds of his contemporary fellow countrymen.

Poland has been twice blessed in this living exponent of her highest ideals. Her other immortal artist, Chopin, has been re-incarnated in the art of Paderewski. Those of us who have heard Paderewski interpret Poland's tragedies and triumphs, who have known the mysterious haunting memory of his words and his music, may well be grateful to have been his contemporaries. What he has stood for as an example to mankind, and what he has revealed in the magic of his music, and by the courage of his convictions, is so rare and inspiring that his influence will be remembered in every corner of the world where he has left the seal of his genius.

"The half of music, I have heard men say, is to have grieved." The poet who said this knew one of the secrets that go toward the understanding of all art. Paderewski has lived through many tragedies and has tasted the dark red wine of human suffering. He has transmuted the sorrow and beauty of life into his immortal music.

In 1924 I had been given the commission to make two stone figures fifteen feet high over the entrance of Bush House, Kings Way, London, to be dedicated "To the Friendship of English Speaking Peoples."

This problem was one which presented many angles of interest, such as the correct scale and style of the figures to fit in with the architecture, and the perspective effects from the street and other buildings. The group was to be in American limestone, carved in America but transported in sections to London, there raised six stories in the air by a hand windlass set on a steel scaffolding, and set in place on the narrow plinth supported by two gigantic columns about seventy feet high. The stone sections varied from three to nine tons each, and the entire group weighed fifty-two tons. The shipping and setting of these stones caused me many white nights of anxiety. When at last I reached London and watched the sections being lifted into place, there was one hair-raising incident—among others—that was typically British. The two workmen were slowly winding up the section of one of the great figures, and just as it reached the edge of the plinth and the corner was resting on it, there was a shrill whistle from the foreman and everything stopped. The men dropped the ratchet into the gear of the winding drum, got up, and went inside. The stone remained suspended on its cable, with one corner on the edge. I was on the street below, and frozen to the spot with nervous apprehension. When I could collect my wits, I took the elevator to the sixth floor and ran out to the scaffolding to ask what had happened. All the men had disappeared down the ladders; only the foreman remained and was lighting his pipe.

"Why, what's the matter, Miss, ye look all pale and agitated?"

"Why did you blow that whistle and stop the men pulling up my stone?" I stammered.

"Why bless ye, it's tea time, Miss—at four o'clock we takes our tea and nothing stops us. Now don't be worried, your lad'll be standing quiet on his own feet before night and it would be a cold day before he takes another step."

Every day for five weeks after that I spent on four boards slung along the edge of this plinth or sitting astride the stone shoulders of my big figures, finishing the carving of their faces and darkening the shadows on draperies, shields, and inscriptions. For we found that the sun never struck the stone group which faced due north, and details had to be cut deeper and made more legible, owing to the lack of sharp sunlight which does a great deal of such accentuating on out-of-door sculpture. My constant fear was that I might drop a chisel on the head of some one walking below us; the fear of my two vigilant and faithful stone-carvers, Robert Baillie and Charlie Semino, was that I would step off the boards myself, and fall down eighty feet to the sidewalk.

On the Fourth of July, 1925, when Lord Balfour pulled the ropes of the curtain of flags which unveiled this group, there was one person in the crowded street who breathed a sigh of relief—and had to be nursed back into a normal condition of nerves and health, during weeks of complete exhaustion. Sam and I went to Windsor for a holiday.

One of the most cherished gifts I ever received was given me at the King's Library at Windsor during this visit. The librarian presented me with a set of reproductions that had been printed from the original drawings of Leonardo da Vinci. These wonderful anatomical studies are kept in fireproof steel cases, with hundreds of other precious originals by the Old Masters, and it was a most inspiring privilege for us to be allowed to examine all these treasures, spread out on a big table in a private room, and study them at our leisure.

After Windsor we visited Paris and there I made the portrait of my great friend, Edward Schuré, the Alsatian philosopher and author, while he read aloud to me the poems he had dedicated to his beloved *inspiratrice,* Margherita Albana Mignaty.

During one of Sam's innumerable wanderings about the streets and byways of old Paris, he came upon an object of rather gruesome interest. It was one of those shrunken heads of the Ecuador Jivaro Indians, hidden away in an old junk-shop of Montmartre. Knowing its value and rarity, he sat down and chatted over a glass of porto about his quest for "singing birds" and musical boxes of the eighteenth century. On his way out he bought the head *pour effrayer quelqu'un à notre pension.*

This tribe has a secret process by which they reduce the size of a human head to about one-half life size, leaving the hair its usual length, still attached, and the features of the face quite intact and proportionately smaller, without distortion. They submit their decapitated enemies to this process and carefully sew up their lips and close their eyes, so that they will not reveal what secrets are performed upon their mummified heads!

When he arrived in our *chambre meublée,* I watched him unwrapping the parcel, which I knew was liable to contain anything from an ivory snuff-box to the latest example of "English plum cake" for tea. To my astonishment, the eery head of some unfortunate mortal came to light. The long, silky, black hair was woven into strands of colored tape; shells and feathers were attached to the head, and the lips were lashed together with long strands of colored string. He very calmly set it on its wooden post and placed it on the small mantelpiece! Then he rang the bell for the maid to bring us tea. When she had set the tray on the table, he said, *"Émilie, regardez sur la cheminée, vous verrez un nouveau pensionnaire pour Mlle. Guilhou . . . ! Ne vous effrayez pas, il ne mange pas tant de cake que nous."*

A few days later this head was acquired by a museum in London, where it joined its many mates in the ethnographical collection of out-of-door sports of Cain's children living in Ecuador and Peru.

When Sarah Bernhardt visited Peru she was presented with a necklace apparently made of pearls, but when the gift was explained to her it was disclosed that the pearls were actually human eyes petrified by the secret process known to a certain tribe of Indians. We can imagine the expert diplomacy which must have been called into play on the part of the Divine Sarah when she was forced to accept such an eery gift with grace and appreciation.

Returning to America once more, I completed the portrait of John

Keats in marble, and of Agnes Yarnall, of Philadelphia, in stone.

About this time the verses of the Revelation of Saint John, with their dramatic imagery, cast a new spell over me. Now, in 1926, the impressions of my trip through Yugo-Slavia in 1919 (which I shall describe in my first chapter on the study of races) seemed to be taking form at last. The ensuing months were spent searching for some way by which I could express the Four Horsemen.

". . . Behold a white horse: and he that sat on him had a bow; and a crown was given unto him: and he went forth conquering, and to conquer. . . .

"And there went out another horse that was red: and power was given to him that sat thereon to take peace from the earth, and that they should kill one another: and there was given unto him a great sword. . . .

"And I beheld, and, lo, a black horse: and he that sat on him had a pair of balances in his hand. . . .

"And I looked, and behold a pale horse: and his name that sat on him was Death, and Hell followed with him. And power was given unto them over the fourth part of the earth, to kill with sword, and with hunger, and with death, and with the beasts of the earth. . . .

"I saw under the altar the souls of them that were slain for the word of God, and for the testimony which they held. . . .

"And I saw another angel ascending from the east, having the seal of the living God: and he cried with a loud voice to the four angels, to whom it was given to hurt the earth and the sea,

"Saying, Hurt not the earth, neither the sea, nor the trees, till we have sealed the servants of our God in their foreheads. . . .

"What are these which are arrayed in white robes? and whence came they? . . .

"These are they which came out of great tribulation, and have washed their robes, and made them white in the blood of the Lamb. . . .

"They shall hunger no more, neither thirst any more; neither shall the sun light on them, nor any heat.

"For the Lamb which is in the midst of the throne shall feed them, and shall lead them unto living fountains of waters: and God shall wipe away all tears from their eyes."

These verses haunted me night and day and decided me on a plan of stopping all my work and going to Africa and Italy and Yugo-Slavia to devote my time to the study of architecture and monumental sculpture, and to free myself from the cramping habits of city life and social engagements. An artist is often driven by inexplicable need to change his environment and to tap new fountains of elemental strength. Overcome by the ancient weariness of frustration, the artist is consumed by an untamable desire to be reborn, to wipe out failures, and to start on a new road, with faith in beauty yet to be born.

In Africa, even more profoundly than during my post-war visit to Yugo-Slavia (both journeys are described in later chapters), I was startled by the necessity of an artist's studying the different races in order to be able really to appreciate the enormous variety, both in form and characterization, that goes to making up the features and expression of a single human countenance. The violent contrasts between the white race, the central-African negro, and the flat-faced, high cheekboned appearance of the Asiatics were each one in their own sphere a new challenge to any power of observation.

It was in 1927, after the African journey, that I went to Rome alone. I spent the winter studying there, living in a little room in a pension for three months and exploring the museums and drawing the architectural monuments of that immortal city. Through the courtesy of the director of the American Academy at Rome, I was invited to use the facilities of the Academy's art library. As a number of the resident students at that time were friends of mine, we had many happy evenings together and talked over the problems that were facing the artists of America and Europe in this distracted atmosphere of the post-war period, when art had become almost a drug on the market in comparison to the other more vital necessities of life.

Mestrovic

After Rome I decided to go to Zagreb in Yugo-Slavia and study
under the direction of my friend Ivan Mestrovic, whom I had met in
New York on his first trip to America in 1926, when he accompanied
his great collection of work. This consisted of over one hundred
marbles and bronzes, most of them of heroic size, which were exhibited at the Brooklyn Museum, and then were sent on a tour of
many other museums throughout our country.

I spoke to him of the difficulty of learning the principles of sculpture, and it was in answer to this question that he took me one day
to his academy to see how he had trained his pupils to become craftsmen first and artists afterwards. He felt most strongly that the sculptor
must understand his medium as a very important part of each problem; that if the subject was treated in one way, it would demand being
carried out in bronze, whereas if treated in a heavier and more plastic
fashion, it could stand being interpreted in stone or marble, and be
enhanced by the use of just these materials. He agreed with me that
the sculptor must be familiar with and love the materials and tools
of his profession. Tools are, after all, only the prolongation of our ten
fingers and should be controlled as accurately as the hands themselves.

I remember one incident in his studio, when by misfortune I had
broken one of my wooden tools. He heard it crack and came over at
once to see what had happened. "What a pity!" he said. "This is a
beautiful tool and we must mend it at once." He stopped his own
work, and carefully filed it off, reshaped it, polished it, oiled it and
returned it to me in perfect condition, only slightly shorter. This was
an indelible lesson to me.

We went together to the academy, where he showed me the work
that was being done in all materials and in every form of sculpture
from wooden bas-reliefs to heroic stone figures. After we had examined the work in the classroom, where hundreds of students were
studying painting and sculpture in all its branches, Mestrovic seemed
very depressed, and as we walked across the ice-covered courtyard on
our way to his home, he murmured:

"Oh, the long procession of art students—hundreds, thousands of talented, ambitious pupils all over the world. . . . *Why* are there so few real artists?"

I answered by asking a question: "How many out of your big class are given diplomas each year on graduation?"

"Oh, quite a number receive the grade of capable craftsmen. These can carve in wood or stone for other sculptors, but if I can find *two* worthy of being called artists I am encouraged. They generally work hard and under difficulties; they cut down their own trees and drag the logs to the school. They collect old bits of stone from buildings that have been torn down; they learn to temper and make their own tools, and often there is no coal to heat the studios, so they have to work violently to keep warm."

"What do you feel is the greatest lack in their make-up—what prevents many others of talent from measuring up to this standard?" I asked.

"C'est la qualité d'âme qui manque, Malvina. Vous le savez aussi bien en Amérique qu'en Yugo-Slavie. Ils travaillent avec leurs mains et pas avec leurs âmes."

I remembered again my father's saying to me after I had finished my portrait of him: "One must *be* an artist first of all, and *then* one can create art."

When I had explained my desire to study architectural drawing and perspective, Mestrovic arranged for me to study with an Austrian professor who gave courses in these studies at the Zagreb University. The fact that I had to learn my lessons in German added considerable difficulty, although I could understand and speak the language in my own fashion. I found the work intensely interesting and instructive from many points of view.

One day, after visiting the foundry, Mestrovic and I walked through the picturesque streets of Starri Grad—the old city that overlooks the new Zagreb. We turned into the street of the sculptor's home and studio.

A great wooden door creaked on its hinges as Mestrovic turned the key and pushed it open. We crossed a paved courtyard and entered the studio.

He had instructed one of his pupils who was studying wood-carving to transfer his design of the "Annunciation" to a panel of thick boards about six feet high and four feet in width, and to start chiselling out the entire background about two inches in depth.

Mestrovic threw off his coat and hat, lighted a cigarette, slipped on his corduroy blouse and picked up his wide chisel and wooden mallet. He began driving the wood in a shower of flakes and ribbons all over the studio. The figure of the angel seemed to come to life by the magic of his swift, sure strokes. The position of the Madonna, however, did not suit him; he stepped back and called to me: "Kneel down here, Malvinushka, and show me what you would do if a voice suddenly whispered to you that you were to be the Mother of Christ!"

Astonished and startled, I merely said: "I couldn't be more surprised than I am at this moment by such a command."

"Oh, before you forget it, be quick about it, give me the position of a head thrown back and of hands praying."

I knelt on the floor and he pushed back my head against the wall— "Hold it," he said, and went on pounding the chisel with all his force, until he had cut the new, sharp outline he was searching for.

"There, that's all—you can go now. Something had gone wrong in the neck of my drawing. Now I can go ahead without any trouble."

After a while he calmed down and darkness threw its veil over the strange, silent world of figures and bas-reliefs.

He held his wrist, and confessed that his injured arm still gave him much pain. He had slipped on the gangplank of the steamer on his arrival in America and had broken his right forearm. A few years previously he had fallen through some hole in the roof of his studio during its construction and had broken his other wrist; so this recent accident was, as he described it, "Just one more way of making sculpture difficult."

I could sympathize sincerely with him about his arm, for I had myself been tormented by an accident to my right wrist, which had torn the interior tendon bracelet and forced me to wear a plaster cast for many weeks and a steel-bound gauntlet for over a year. A sculptor, under such circumstances, envies the construction of modern motors, which enables the owner to replace broken parts and proceed merrily on the way.

When Mestrovic was in New York on his second visit, he very patiently acquiesced to my request that he should pose for a portrait in his studio blouse and rope sandals. As we were both busy working all day, he planned to dine with us and pose in the evening. Before beginning the clay portrait, he advised me to make three or four life-size charcoal drawings of his head, and after this we started in on what was really hard labor lasting into the small hours of the morning. When I had about half completed the head and shoulders, I felt that the composition would be greatly enhanced if I could persuade him to give me the extra time needed to make a full-length figure—but I dared not ask him.

The following day, Zuloaga, the Spanish painter, came to see the portrait, for he was a great friend and admirer of Mestrovic. When I confessed my fear of asking Mestrovic to pose longer for the full-length study, Zuloaga, in his enthusiastic manner, asked for a ladder, and, picking up a large paint brush which happened to be lying on a stand next to a pot of red paint, climbed up the steps, and wrote in large letters on the wall of my studio *"OSEZ!"* Dare! When he clambered down he shook the brush at me and commanded me to start the framework at once, so that when Mestrovic arrived for the evening's séance, all would be in readiness. He then left me, and I was faced with a difficult problem. The bust, which was well over life-size, was far too heavy for me to lift and was, besides, nailed onto the three-legged stand to make it more secure. I knew just the pose I wanted to model, so in sheer bravado I rigged up the framework, using the three legs of the high stand as my supports for the legs and the trunk of a tree against which the figure stands.

It was stiff work bending over to block out the mass of heavy clay, but by evening when "Mestro" came unsuspectingly into the studio, he was pleasantly surprised, and encouraged me to complete the whole figure. The idea that the stand had served its double purpose down to the actual floor of the studio caused him much concern, for he guessed how my back would ache before I had finished his sandals!

IVAN MESTROVIC
Over-life-size figure in bronze. (Brooklyn Museum of Art)

HEROIC FIGURE IN CLAY

During process of construction in Mestrovic's studio in Zagreb—one of his two American Indians on horseback (Michigan Avenue, Chicago, Ill.). Head of Moses in the background

WOOD AND IRON ARMATURE FOR THE HORSE OF THIS SAME GROUP

I could just stand up under the horse's belly. This framework is thoroughly shellacked and then covered
84   with the clay. The proportions are enlarged from the original smaller-size plaster model

I pointed with my tool over my shoulder to the dripping red letters on the wall, and said: "Your friend, Zuloaga, was here today and left this visiting card."

"Mestro" and I had a good laugh. When, a few years later, Sam and I were in Spain studying the Basque and Spanish types and visited the enchanting home and studio of Zuloaga on the seacoast south of San Sebastian, one word on a scrap of paper served to announce us to our host—*OSEZ!* He came out and welcomed us with open arms. To know a Spaniard in America is one thing, but to see him on his own beloved soil, drenched in hot golden sunlight on the edge of the sea, is to get the full color and exuberance of his character.

When Mestrovic received the commission from Chicago to make the two heroic American Indians on horseback for the two great pedestals that face the bridge on Michigan Avenue, he decided to use this commission as a demonstration to his classes in Zagreb. The best pupils were allowed to build the huge wood and iron armatures which were to support the clay. These twenty-foot equestrians were enlarged from the four-foot plaster models. When the full-size models were finished and cast into plaster, they were moved over to the little one-story foundry building on the grounds of the Art Academy. Here it was found necessary to dig down a whole story in depth into the ground, to enable the full-size models to be sunk into the ovens and bricked under the level of the foundry floor—the solidity of the ground itself serving as retaining walls of the oven. These statues were cast in the "lost-wax" process, which I am going to explain further on.

Mestrovic purchased the finest quality of English copper and tin, and had it shipped to Zagreb. He then engaged the most expert bronze founders in Florence to come to Zagreb and instruct his pupils, and the young Yugo-Slav founders, just how to prepare for every stage of this complicated procedure. The intense cold weather added a very serious situation to contend with, but in spite of what would have seemed to most people insurmountable difficulties, the work was accomplished, and after much persuasion Mestrovic actually submitted to the plan of making a series of moving-pictures during the preparation and casting of these two historic statues.

Behind the Scenes in Sculpture

I have found an inordinate interest on the part of the general public in the exact processes that constitute the actual making of a statue in marble, or the casting of a bronze. Through many long hours I have endeavored to reduce the complexities of this subject to a capsule form. The questioner has no conception of what a vast field of information he must absorb before he can in any way begin to comprehend all the ways and means to the final accomplishment of a work of art.

People in general seem to enjoy sculptural art more easily than painting, because of its more tangible and three-dimensional reality. Color, however, usually excites the eye and mind more. Now that the public has been slowly but surely weaned from the gentle school of Barbizon to the violent dynamics of modern abstractions, it may seem academic and old-fashioned to make any particular effort to describe the practical means needed before any piece of bronze, whether by Rodin, Brancusi, or Maillol, may come into being—regardless of its maker, style, or meaning.

In case there are still those, however, who feel the urge to clarify their minds on this subject, I shall plunge without further warning off the deep end, leaving the uncurious to skip this chapter if they feel inclined.

If we follow the work from the original model in clay, which the sculptor himself has to handle, through the next stage of plaster-casting, where the sculptor steps aside and confides his original clay to some capable plaster-caster, we may watch this man flick the plaster over the clay by dipping his hands into the bowl of thick creamy liquid, having tinted the first layer with a dash of bluing to distinguished it from the next outer layer, which is absolutely white, letting it all dry in a thick, strong shell which is divided into sections. One way of making these sections is to lay a linen thread on the surface of the clay, pressing it lightly along the lines of the desired seams and letting the two long ends hang out freely before the plaster is poured. By pulling this thread before the plaster hardens a neat cut

86

EUGÈNE RUDIER, *MAÎTRE FONDEUR,* STANDING BESIDE RODIN'S "THE THINKER," WHICH
WAS CAST INTO BRONZE AT THE RUDIER FOUNDRY, PARIS

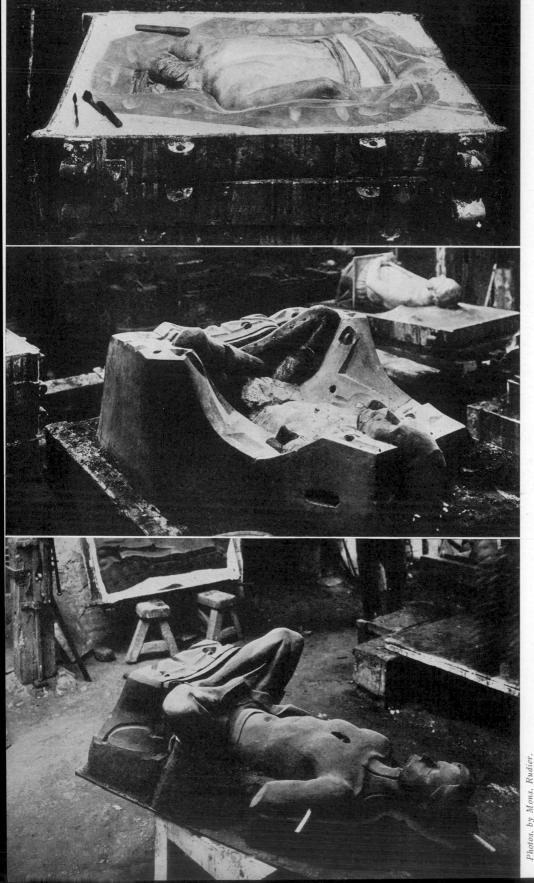

CORE OF "BRAHMAN IN MEDITATION"

Showing channels cut in neck where metal is to be reinforced by heavy veins of bronze on inside of cast

CORE INSIDE OF SAND SECTION MOULD

SAND PROCESS

Section of plaster figure of Kabuli type shown packed into the sand mould before being cast into bronze. The sand is held firmly within iron frames which are subsequently bolted together

SAND MOULDS OPENED AND CLOSED

The hook by which the sections are lifted is seen at the right. This fits into rings shown on the edge of the closed sand mould

POURING THE MOLTEN BRONZE FROM THE CRUCIBLE INTO THE MOULD

The two men control the pouring of a thin even stream of white hot metal

SAND MOULD ON THE LOWER SECTION OF THE SHILLUK AFRICAN WARRIOR

The wax channels are shown darker. The metal flows in from the end and is fed to all parts
of the figure evenly

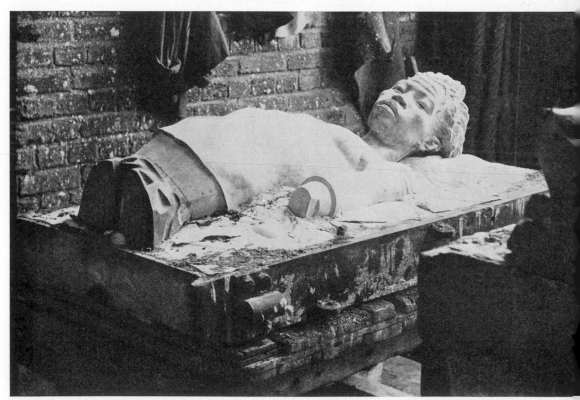

UPPER SECTION OF THE SAME FIGURE SHOWING PLASTER ORIGINAL PARTLY EMBEDDED
IN ITS SAND MOULD

The section of arm shows where joint is bolted and welded together when completed

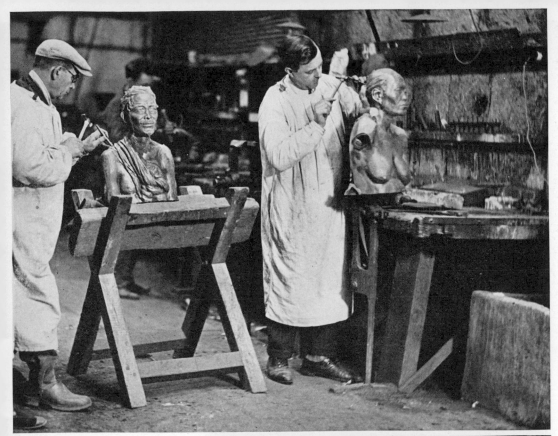

Photo. M. H.

THE JAKUN JUNGLE TYPE AND FEMALE MUD CARRIER OF HONGKONG

Shown here as they are being "chased" and finished after having been cast into bronze

PÈRE AND JEAN LIMET IN THEIR CROWDED STUDIO ON THE BOULEVARD ARAGO

The Nordic Male is on the table, the Basque, Senegalese Drummer and Wahima Sultan in foreground. Père Limet is patining the female Eskimo

Photo. M. H.

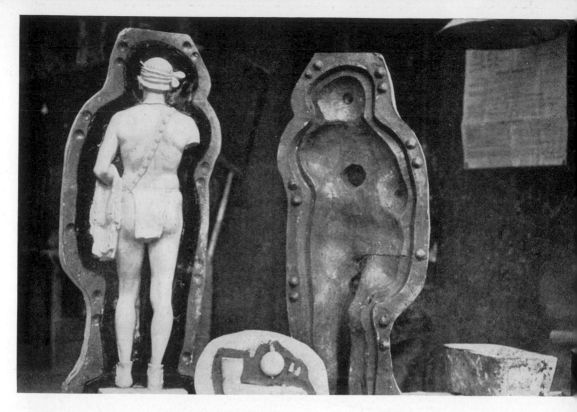

LOST–WAX PROCESS

Back view of the figure of Navajo Medicine Man in plaster. Outside of this is the layer of gelatine covered by the shell of plaster. The holes in outer edge fit over the "keys" in the right-hand negative plaster section so the two parts of the mould fit exactly and cannot shift. The arm and gourd are shown in their gelatine and plaster moulds

THE PLASTER FIGURE OF NAVAJO MEDICINE MAN ON THE LEFT—REPRODUCTION OF SAME IN RED WAX ON RIGHT

Photos. M. H.

SAME FIGURE COVERED WITH THE FIRST COAT OF FINE GRAIN CLAY AND PLASTER APPLIED WITH A SOFT BRUSH

This is covered with a coarser, thick coating of the same

SHOWING BRONZE FIGURE AS IT EMERGES FROM THE MOULD WHICH HAS BEEN BRO– KEN OFF AFTER THE METAL CAST HAS COOLED

The tubes are the metal channels by which the cast is fed during the pouring. These and the air vents projecting on shoulders and head must all be removed by expert chasers

Photos. M. H.

Photo. M. H.

VALSUANI FOUNDRY, PARIS

The head founder is stirring the boiling metal in the oven. Asbestos gauntlets protect the hands and fore-arms. The assistant (*left*) prepares the buried moulds to receive the molten metal. This primitive instal-lation has been the birth-place of many famous bronzes by sculptors of many countries. Founded by Mons. Claude Valsuani in 1898, it is now carried on by his son Marcel and by Mons. Spohr, the head founder. Against the wall leans the carrying bar for transporting the crucible from the fire to the buried moulds; their vent-holes are marked by twists of paper which pop out when the molten metal is poured into the central opening. The cylindrical collar prevents the metal from running over the top of the moulds

is made for the division. If pulled too soon, the thread would slide out and the plaster would ooze together over the seam; if pulled too late, the thread would be set in the plaster and could not be pulled out. This sounds simple, but try it and see!

Another method is to make a partition wall of thin brass strips which we push carefully into the surface of the clay before the plaster is poured and which project out about one inch from the clay surface. To know just where to make these partitions takes years of practical experience, for no two originals are ever alike.

Plaster-casting is a matter of great skill, for to remove the shell-covering it is necessary to dig out and destroy the original clay model, and if the plaster mould is not perfect, the sculptor has lost the only record of his work. When the shells are securely reinforced outside with irons, bent to follow the exterior contour, and attached by the help of wads of burlap soaked in plaster, they are thoroughly cleaned and soaped and set together again and bound with ropes. Now a supply of liquid plaster is prepared and mixed just to the necessary point of thickness. The fresh liquid is poured into the empty hollow mould, and this is turned and rolled about so that all crevices and hollows are sure to be filled. The inner surface is covered to the thickness of an inch or more, depending on the subject, and left to dry and harden. Incidentally, a great deal of the plaster is swished out over the beginner, until he looks more like a clown than a would-be caster and the floor of the studio is a mass of white débris.

Then the outer shell is chipped off very carefully with a chisel, great attention being given to *not* driving the chisel too deep, so as to scratch or damage the surface of the interior plaster cast. It is at this point that the bluish tint of the first layer is watched for. This acts as a warning—for only a thin layer remains now between the original cast's surface and the steel chisel hit by the caster's wooden mallet. The beginner is generally so eager to see his final result that the surface is covered with nicks and scratches from his nervous and uncontrolled chisel. When the mould is all removed, the artist should have an exact replica in plaster of his original clay. The sculptor who has learned how to cast well in plaster, and has been obliged to do his own work on the road, or in places where casters are not available, has respect for this craftsmanship, which plays such a vital part in the early stages of every piece of sculpture. During the first few trials of casting a simple model, it is amazing to find how many things one is called upon to remember at exactly the right moment, and how easy it is to make a perfectly hopeless fizzle of anything that appears to be so simple when we watch an expert workman doing a quick clean job for us.

When a sculptor has finished his original model in clay, and has had it cast into plaster, he may decide to have this carried out in marble. To do this, he selects a man who has had years of training and experience as a marble-carver, and who can select for him a piece of material without flaws or veins which would mar the effect of the finished work. Sometimes the block of marble appears quite perfect on the surface, but I have had the bad luck to strike a dark vein or striation on the inner part of the block, and have sometimes carried a piece of work almost to the finish before running into this kind of trouble.

Few sculptors of modern times do much of their own marble carving. It is a slow and tedious profession, demanding expert skill and endless patience and accuracy. Very often the work is prepared by the *metteur au point* or "marble-pointer" who takes off the surplus materials to within an eighth or one sixteenth of an inch of the finished surface; at this point the sculptor takes up the problem of finishing the details and giving to the surface his individual texture and vibration of light and shade. This "pointing of marble" is done with the assistance of a delicately adjusted three-point compass known as a pointing machine, which is hung on the original plaster. By means of a steel needle about seven inches long, the heights of the surface are all registered by hand and the needle is set. The compass is then transferred to the stone, and hung on three identical points to correspond with those on the plaster model. The excess stone is cut away until the needle can be pushed in to the same depth as on the original. It is not unusual to take three or four thousand points, to prepare a portrait for the final surface. If the machine shifts, or the needle is not accurately set, the entire effect will be ruined by errors in the pointing.

Many people have stated that Rodin never carved his own marble. He did engage several outside carvers and assistant sculptors. One of them was Despiau, who has since won international fame as a master sculptor. I have watched Rodin carving his own marbles at his studio in the rue de l'Université, and have marvelled at the way he could suggest soft feathers of a great broken wing, carving them directly in the block, without referring to the small plaster model. The pressure of an arm against another arm or the weight of a foot on the ground were certain problems which Rodin solved by himself, explaining to me just how the desired result was obtained in marble. He avoided any sharp edges, and used the light reflections almost as a painter would, to envelop his forms. He had a horror of deep holes or sharp outlines. He had a perfectly definite technique which is easily recognized, and he told me he had spent many hours identifying the strokes of certain tools, and just what effects they were capable of giving, in the collection of Michelangelo's sculptures in Florence.

To teach me what surfaces and planes could do to a piece of marble, Rodin would take me to the Louvre late in the day, just before closing time, and, standing in silent admiration before the great Egyptian statues or the "Venus de Milo," would pull a candle out of his pocket, light it, and hold it up so that its light fell on the smooth, strong planes of the statues.

"This is the test," he would say to me. "Watch the sharp edge of light as I move it over the flowing contours of these great *chef d'œuvres* of Egypt . . . you will see how continuous and unbroken are the surfaces . . . how the forms flow into one another without a break . . . no unnecessary dark cavities to break the massiveness, no scratchy lines too deeply cut into the precious *matière*. They knew—those old Egyptians! They never cut away too much; they knew where to leave the details enveloped, and only suggested by the perfect outline of the stone left uncut. One feels sure of their intention and of their knowledge of anatomy, without being troubled by it."

Rodin's absolute modesty and self-effacement in the presence of these eternal masterpieces was one more proof of his true greatness. His endless searching, day and night, was to know how to translate Nature into a simple continuous line, and the thousands of drawings which I had the privilege of sorting and cataloguing with Monsieur Bénédite, the first curator of the Musée Rodin, in 1919, will always be a visible and instructive testimony of his indefatigable study.

The art of bronze statuary developed only after hollow casting was discovered, and the first objects were usually votive offerings and ornaments used in the Hellenic and Roman period. When I visited the Naples Museum in 1910, I found it a revelation to my hungry young mind. It has perhaps the finest collection of early bronzes in the whole world. I recalled the skeptical remarks of certain friends and sculptors who had considered America plenty good enough to teach artists all they need to know. Then I discovered the fine examples of the art of the Middle Minoan age; I felt when examining the sword blades so beautifully decorated, so exquisite in their designs, that it must have been a real pleasure to be transpierced by such a thrust of beauty.

During the fourteenth century there was a great expansion of activity in the casting and hammering of bronze. In Italy the great doors of Lorenzo Ghiberti at Florence are a brilliant example of Italian technique. Among the great names of Italian masters, we find that Pisano, Donatello, Verrocchio, Cellini, Michelangelo, Giovanni de Bologna have all left their work in bronze as well as in marble and stone. In France, during the sixteenth century, Germain Pilon and Jean Goujon are the outstanding sculptors who left us their work in bronze. In England, many beautiful bronze objects and chandeliers date from the seventeenth century, and ever since the Middle Ages wonderful bells have been cast in bronze for the cathedrals and churches all over Europe. Without doubt some of the finest examples of bronze work are those of ancient China. There is a catalog of the renowned collection in the Palace at Peiping, consisting of forty-two volumes of data compiled in 1751. (And there are still certain Americans who think the only thing the Chinese do well is to run laundries!)

The Chinese regard their ancient bronzes as very rare treasures, as well they may—they are traced back to the Chow dynasty (1122–255 B.C.). The coloration of these Chinese bronzes is richer and more wonderful than that which we can produce today. The oxidation of chemicals and the aging of the metal buried for centuries in the ground results often in a gorgeous variation of brilliant greens and brown that add great beauty to the sculptured forms. The tooling of the surface is of the finest, and the forms have an aristocracy of design which has never been surpassed.

If bronze is the final material selected for the work, there are two methods of casting this metal: (1) The sand-mould method, (2) the lost-wax method. Nearly all the life-size heads and figures now in the Hall of Man, Chicago, were made by the sand process, in Paris and New York.

(1) To begin with, the founder has to study the plaster model to decide just where the joints of his metal should come. Then the model is cut. Around this plaster, in separate conical sections, are pressed the sand "pieces," each isolated from the next by a slippery surface so as to make it possible for the pieces to be removed and fitted together again when needed. These sand pieces are carefully pressed and pounded around the plaster until it is three-quarters buried in the sand bed. The top surface is then smoothed and dusted with a fine layer of talcum powder to keep it from adhering to the next surface. The model is now turned over, face down, and another set of sand "pieces" are pressed and pounded until the upper shell form is completed. The sand next to the plaster model must be compact and fresh; the outside may be filled in with coarser sand that has already been used for the same purpose. Into these sand moulds are cut the vents for air escape, and channels for admitting the moulten metal; then the plaster model is carefully removed, so that no edges of either the upper or lower section of the sand "pieces" are chipped off or injured. These air vents are of vital importance, for they carry off the combustion of the gases, which, if they do not have this escape, will explode and burst the mould into fragments. The channels for carrying the metal are so arranged that the weight of the liquid does not fall too suddenly on any part of the figure. A series of trails like the system seen in illustration are hollowed out of the finished sand mould, growing larger towards the entrance on top, which receives the full shock of the pouring. (See page 90, top.)

The making and placing of the core or interior lining of the mould is a complicated affair. The sand used for this is of a looser and more porous consistency, and does not hold together in such a compact, hard mass, thus allowing more circulation of air and gases. The canals in the core are made of "bougies" or strings of candle-wax on wicks, and a cage-like armature of crossed wires, which must be stiff enough to keep their shape when the sand core is pushed and patted in between all the interstices, so that the whole inside mass is both solid and porous, and swung on cross bars which extend out through the sides of the outer shell. When this core is completed, it is removed from the outer shell, and its entire surface, which is in one piece, is carefully scraped off for the thickness of about one-eighth of an inch. This slightly reduces the size and surface area and constitutes the thickness of the ultimate bronze. Piece by piece, the outer sand "pieces" and the complete "reduced" core are placed in the oven to be slowly dried and baked into very hard consistency at a temperature of 400 or 500 degrees.

The only space not solid inside this mass is the area of one-eighth inch thickness which is left between the core and the outer shell. It is this *empty* space existing at this point that eventually represents the work of the sculptor—and I can assure the reader that it takes the faith of "things unseen" to believe that months of effort in three dimensions has to pass through this stage of actual *non-existence,* before the ultimate result in bronze is born.

The empty space is left free to take the moulten bronze, which pours in at the top through the various channels until it overflows. At this moment the founder knows his cast is filled, and it is left to cool off. After a very short time the metal is set, and the outer shell is broken off. The air vents and entry channels have become bronze tendrils and look like a mass of wires and pipes. The bronze head emerges looking like the wrecked remains of a steel spider's web, with a head tangled up in the twisted metal. The sculptor breathes again as he recognizes his work in solid form, but feels a sense of dismay at the thought of having all the tangled accessories removed without destroying the surface modelling in any way.

The metal known as bronze is actually an alloy of copper and tin, the latter being mixed in at the last moment before the crucible is lifted out of the fire. This is a moment of dramatic tensity—all the men stand alert ready for instantaneous action. They wear leather aprons and heavy gauntlets of carpet on their hands and forearms, strips of carpet are lashed over their legs and feet—for tongs *can* slip and crucibles *can* break, and if they do . . . !

Thick, cloth-vizored caps are pulled over their heads, and absolute silence is the rule. Each man knows his cue and holds either the iron bar or the metal hooks which clasp around the center of the crucible. At a given signal from the head founder, the stirring of the metal is stopped, the chief steps forward and leans towards the glowing furnace, his face streaming with sweat and glittering red in the glow of the white-heated liquid. His cotton blouse is soaked over his back and chest. Swiftly and surely he lifts his tongs in both hands, grabs the crucible firmly, lifts the glowing mass, spluttering sparks over the edge of the open trough of fire. He sets it for an instant on the earthen floor. At this split-second the two next men holding the carrying bar slip the central ring of this bar up and around the crucible and help to lift it in unison and carry it deftly to the nearby waiting mould. The two men lift together, the chief removes his tongs, and they tilt the glowing crucible over, just enough to pour a strong, even stream of liquid fire into the opening of the mould.

In shorter time than it takes to describe it, the air is filled with flying bits of white hot metal and smoke. The snapping sparks fly in every direction, the mould overflows, the man with the poker swiftly knocks off the surplus metal before it hardens, and others stamp out the sparks on the floor. The excitement is over, and the silent dark spectres become once more a group of smiling workmen, pulling off their black mittens, and mopping their brows. The effect of these swarthy, dark shadows controlling the treacherous element of fire, illuminated by the glow of flames, is a sight seldom witnessed by outsiders.

The risks and dangers of such work are many. The number of burns and injuries received during years of foundry activity should be added to the unrecorded acts of courage and perfection of technique which go into the making of every piece of bronze.

I recall an incident in the Valsuani foundry in Paris when a heavy and valuable mould was being lifted by four men from the oven to an iron table. Monsieur Valsuani, one of the most conscientious of founders, was carrying the heaviest share of the load. He warned the men to take excessive care in setting the mould exactly over certain marks on the table edge, so that none of their fingers would be caught under the weight. Some one was indifferent to his warning and Monsieur Valsuani found that his own corner would not clear the table. Rather than risk any damage or sudden shock to the work, he said nothing and the mould was lowered to the table; the tip of his finger was crushed but no one knew it until the mould was safely balanced in its position. From that day he was known as *Maître Fondeur,* and when his son told me of this and other such incidents, he shuddered and added: "No one could guess what my father had to suffer to make the reputation of his foundry."

The first cast of bronze is generally called the "original." Actually, however, the only real original is the clay model, moulded by the sculptor himself, and this is practically always destroyed to make the first plaster. Numerous other replicas can be made, as long as the plaster model lasts, unless the edition is limited, and the model destroyed. Naturally, if the plaster is used too often, the crisp surface details become rubbed or worn, and then the "chasers" are called upon to "freshen up the bronze." This is a risky operation, unless one is absolutely sure of the ability of the chaser. In fact, at every stage of the work, there is risk of damage or complete destruction if any one along the line fails in his particular rôle. The miracle is that in nine hundred and ninety-nine cases out of a thousand the result is as nearly perfect as one could wish.

The final process, after the metal is assembled and the chasing completed, is the coloring. This is an art in itself, and curiously enough generally is neglected by modern sculptors and left to a few craftsmen with a knowledge of chemistry and a limited understanding of what a rich transparent *patine* can really do to enhance the beauty and value of a bronze.

The metal is heated by a gas-blower held in the left hand, while the right holds a brush and dips it in the various acids and rubs it

MARBLE PORTRAIT OF MRS. E. H. HARRIMAN

Photo. M. H.

JEAN DE MARCO PREPARING THE OUTER COVERING
OF TWO WAX MOULDS WHICH WERE CAST INTO
BRONZE AT M. H.'S STUDIO IN 35TH STREET, NEW YORK

THE BRICK FIREPLACE BUILT OUT AND TRANSFORMED INTO A FOUNDRY OVEN IN
WHICH WE MADE TWENTY-SEVEN BRONZES BY THE LOST-WAX PROCESS

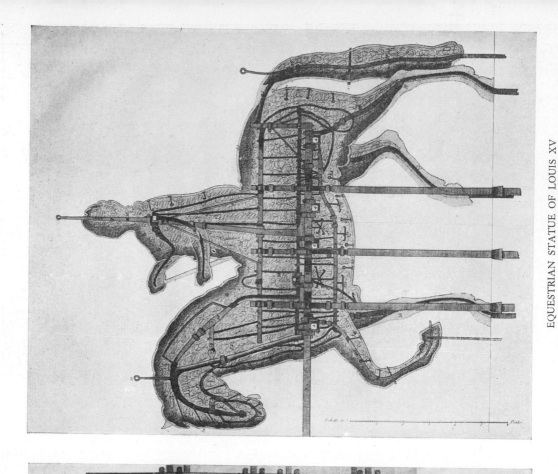

CROSS-SECTION AS SEEN FROM ABOVE

Transverse iron bars project outside the entire enclosed mass. Surrounding the core is a thin layer of wax. The outer plaster sections are built up around this, and keyed into

EQUESTRIAN STATUE OF LOUIS XV

Showing the iron framework to support the core and cast of this heroic bronze

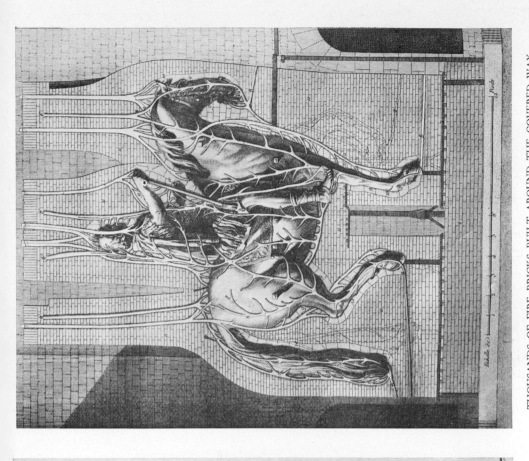

AIR VENTS MADE OF COPPER TUBING TO CARRY OFF COMBUSTION

Wax veins arranged so that the metal will reach all parts of the mould evenly. Over this forty coats of plaster and clay were applied

THOUSANDS OF FIRE-BRICKS BUILT AROUND THE COVERED WAX

Ending in four towers through which the metal entered the mould at the top, the wax having been melted and run out at lower exits from feet and tail and under the jaw of the horse

BENIN BRONZE

Collection Louis Carré, Paris

BENIN BRONZE

BENIN WARRIORS, HIGH RELIEF ON BRONZE PLAQUE

over the surface just after the flame of the blow-torch has heated the surface. This method really consists of opening the pores by heat, and pouring in strong acids that act on the hot metal and on each other in various intensities; then the metal is plunged into cold water to close the pores. The process is repeated an infinite number of times until the final desired result is achieved. Then the work is left to cool, and after twenty-four hours is carefully rubbed until all the transparent layers of color are brought out. The rich smooth surface should glow without the use of wax.

The sculptor who has not followed his "brain child" through all the stages of its creation must of necessity miss a great deal of the thrill of actually transforming his thought into tangible form. The curious thing is that once the dream becomes reality, it seems to break away from its creator, and belong to the world and not to the artist. The fact that we cannot correct our faults, once they are recorded in metal, seems to sever us from our work. It is the pliable, responsive quality of clay that brings our ideas to life, and as they emerge we are completely under their spell, and a sort of hypnotic slavery exists, until we see the ultimate result from which we cannot escape, try as we may.

(2) After numberless visits to the foundry to study the "sand process," I decided to have some of my models cast in the "lost-wax" process at the Valsuani Foundry in Paris and at the Roman Bronze Works in Long Island. The early Italian method has been gradually changed to adapt itself to modern needs and commercialism, but originally the process was the following:

Bronze, made of copper nine parts to one of tin, was used as an average compound, varying slightly in density and resistance. This proportion of alloy is still used. The earliest methods of *hollow* casting known were called the *cire perdue*—or "lost-wax" process. Benvenuto Cellini has dramatically described his struggles and triumphs with this method of casting his bronzes.

The artist prepared a core resembling roughly the contour of his proposed subject. The core was made of brick-dust and plaster, which was dried and hardened. On this, the sculptor modelled directly in wax, pressing the surface well into all the interstices of the core. He placed little metal rods at intervals securely through the core and projecting beyond the finished surface of his wax.

The outer mould was applied over the wax. This was made of liquid clay and plaster, and had to be very carefully applied so that no spot was left uncovered. The metal rods projected outside of the covering also, holding the three layers together. The mould was baked in an oven at the temperature of 500 degrees for 14 hours. The melted wax ran out, and then the liquid moulten bronze was poured in, filling all the space previously occupied by the wax. After the metal cooled, the outer shell was broken off and the core shaken out as much as possible, the metal rods removed. Chasing and tooling the surface completed the operation, and the result was a unique reproduction of the original, of which there was no other replica.

Today, the wax method consists of pouring the thin red wax into a negative gelatine mould, which has been made on the original plaster model. The outer surface of the wax is coated with the covering and mould, and melted out in the oven. After this the bronze is poured into the mould, and this process may be repeated as often as desired on the original model until it is worn out.

When I returned to New York from Yugo-Slavia, I decided to experiment and study the process of lost-wax casting in my own studio. With a young French assistant, Jean de Marco, who had had six years of experience in a Paris foundry, we transformed the large brick open fireplace into an oven, by adding in front a bricked-in section, and setting a grate of iron bars to hold the charcoal fire. The old chimney went up three stories, so there was a strong, steady draught. As the building had originally been built as a stable for ten horses, the construction had to be tested. It was found solid and adequate for our purposes.

We were able to bake four moulds at a time in the oven, but the difficulty was to keep these sufficiently warm when baked, while we had to rekindle a much hotter fire in the same grate to melt the bronze in a crucible which we set in the central opening, buried in the red-hot charcoal. The front of the oven had to be bricked up tight, with just a peep-hole left for us to see through. This aperture was only used occasionally to watch the fire and consistency of the liquid metal, etc., then it was plugged with clay. Of course, under such primitive conditions, we had a few accidents, but they were not serious, and it was these accidents that really were our best lessons. The fact that we had to keep the fire going for twenty-four hours steadily necessitated one of us being awake on guard all the time. The intense heat of twelve hundred degrees was rather an endurance test for the old chimney, which had originally been built for a stove-pipe, when the studio was a stable.

We had to use the enclosed courtyard, alias a box-stall, as a safe place to pour the metal, for the walls were of brick and the floor of stone; this obviated risk of fire. After three or four trials, we managed to control the heat steadily, and keep the moulds warm, and then we invited the clients who had ordered the bronzes to come to see the pouring of the metal. Mrs. E. H. Harriman, who had been the owner of the building for fourteen years, was our first guest. Her concern was not entirely for artistic reasons, but rather to supervise what was generally considered to be a most dangerous and rather wild performance. She was so thrilled by the experience, however, that she came each time that we had a "bronze pouring" throughout the winter—and watched the making of the cores and gelatine moulds and plaster moulds with as much interest and enthusiasm as if she were an ardent student. She was no doubt one of the very few art patrons who had witnessed every stage of the production of the sculpture she had purchased.

I kept the first experimental bronzes even though they were failures, for they demonstrated clearly just what occurred when the mould was too chilled, and the liquid metal therefore solidified too suddenly, leaving gaps in the casting. Another time, the air vents were not adequate, and this again caused blockage of the stream and spoiled the result. When I finally did learn this craft, I made twenty-seven small bronzes in a home-made fireplace, and from the clay original to the final patining with blow-torch and acids, I was able to feel that these bronzes were made under unique conditions and the personal supervision of the artist from start to finish.

While delving into libraries and the books of my friend, Eugene Rudier, in Paris, I came across a description of the casting of a bronze of heroic dimensions in one pouring. It was the equestrian statue of Louis XV made in France in 1757—"Le Bien Aimé," by Edmé Bouchardon, sculptor to his Majesty. The book was written in old French, and I translated and condensed the material from fifty to three pages. It was considered instructive and worth-while in the year 1757 to make a record of this gigantic piece of work by precise descriptions and by a series of sixty beautiful engravings drawn by a master-hand—four of which are here reproduced, as they give the best possible explanation of this complex and seldom understood process of sculpture.

This work is a tribute to all those who collaborated in this enterprise. To accomplish such a task, each man was inspired not only by the problem and difficulty of his work, but by a *love of his profession* which in all ages and all arts is a *sine qua non* for the achievement of any form of perfection. No set of instructions can ever be adequate to the undertaking of such a project as casting a bronze. From the clay model to the final result, the work must be done by artists and craftsmen of experience and conscientious ability. The risks and pitfalls are legion and the meticulous care and devotion of all the workmen are essential. A founder of repute, who has the respect and loyalty of his men, must know every branch of the work demanded of them. He must be in command, and able at an instant's warning to step in and replace any artisan in his employ. If he has proved himself to be an "ace" he can call upon his men to make any effort or sacrifice that, within human reason, is demanded during the execution of a work of art.

There is an unwritten law in this as in many other professions, which, like the Oath of Hippocrates, binds the moral allegiance of those who weld their individual strength into a common power of achievement. The description of the casting of Louis XV starts with the first operation of making a piece-mould in plaster on the clay model. When finished, this was removed and numbered piece by piece. The iron armature was now built by another set of workmen and set inside the plaster mould. The intricacies of this work can only be appreciated by studying the pictures on pages 104–5.

The armature of the core inside the bronze had to be strong and precise in position, all the parts thereof thoroughly in contact with the packing of the material which formed the core. The irons were strong enough to avoid all danger of bending, or breaking under the strain and heat of the firing at high temperature. They had to be so placed and joined that when the bronze was finished they could be removed from the outside piece by piece. As much as possible of the core material was cleaned out with wire brushes and hooks—for if this is left inside the bronze statue it gradually absorbs moisture and condensation, and when left out of doors for years often freezes in winter and causes the outer bronze to split or spread apart.

Later on the plaster mould was rebuilt from the ground in layers; the inner surface of these pieces was painted with oil to prevent the wax from sticking. To each piece was applied, with a brush, a covering of hot wax the thickness of the eventual bronze; then the next layer of plaster sections was built up and covered inside with wax, and so on, up to the top. The lower sections of the horse's legs were poured solid, full of wax, to insure strength for the support of the horse and rider in metal.

When the entire inside surface was covered to the necessary thickness in wax, the outer pieces of the plaster were removed; the wax surface now represented a complete and perfect reproduction of the original clay model. The plaster pieces were larger the further away they were from the wax, and were made with calculated precision to insure solidity and ease in the rebuilding of the mould. Brick-dust and plaster, mixed together, form the liquid core material which is poured into the mould of wax; it can harden sufficiently when dry to hold in place the weight of the *bronze,* which replaces all the spaces covered in the wax. The core was poured in after the armature was set in place, and a complete and entirely solid mass was now ready to be studied for the placing of air-vents and wax feeding-channels (see page 105, left). Long, solid lines of wax were fitted to the surface, leading like veins that carried the liquid metal to all the surface area; intersecting these at frequent intervals were the air-vents which served the same purpose as in the sand-process: to carry off combustion, and permit the free flow of the liquid bronze. These were made of copper tubing. When these were all in place and securely fastened, the final outer covering or mould was built up all over this amazing network of wax.

This covering was made of earth and water mixed with ground-up baked clay and cow-dung or horse-manure (or lacking this, the hair off the hides of cattle. It is this that is used in Africa by the Negro founders). It was carefully applied in thin layers all over the surface of the wax, until, in the case of this statue of Louis XV, *forty coats* were firmly laid over the whole group.

Heavy iron netting was laid all over this like a sling, which, by the extending edges and hooks, could be lifted without injuring the contents. These again were covered with a thick layer of the mould mixture, plus red sand, mixed into it. Against this was built a surface of thousands of fire-bricks to withstand the heat and expansion of the metal. The outside form of this mould tapered into four circular towers at the top, through which the metal was eventually poured. The entire outside was strapped with iron bands, strongly crossed and bolted together to hold the mould. When set into the oven, this mass of reinforced material was set on fire-brick blocks, and braced by the same, at intervals all around its surface, base, sides, and top, permitting the even and thorough circulation of heat to bake it throughout—and this melted all the wax, which ran out below, leaving the space to be filled by the metal. When the mould was sufficiently baked, the fires were let down, and the air-vents plugged so that no sudden draught of cold air could circulate inside the mould. If the fires had been left burning too long, the mould would have been burned and ruined.

Two weeks were given to this slow cooling operation before the metal was prepared and the fires started for the bronze casting. The entire court made a pilgrimage to the foundry to witness the pouring of the historic statue. From this point on, the pouring of the metal was similar to that used in sand-casting, which I have described in the preceding pages.

The first examples of this latter process are found in the gardens of Versailles. They were cast by the *fondeur* Keller. Many of the decorative fountain groups at Versailles were cast in lead. Recently, these have been taken apart and cleaned out and rearmatured at the Fonderie Rudier, as many of them were badly cracked and bent, owing to the corrosion of their inner iron framework and the remains of cores, which had not been cleaned out and which had absorbed the condensation through a long period of years and had caused the lead castings to split.

It was in 1935 that America had the first important exhibition, at the Modern Museum, of Negro sculpture and Benin Bronzes. The public was at first rather startled by the stark and primitive quality of this African art, but gradually they became more curious and interested, and it dawned upon them that these sculptures were something like opening an ancient tomb of forgotten treasures.

In 1871, the Kingdom of Benin, situated on the west central coast of Africa, was conquered by the English, and is now known as Nigeria. The discovery of about twenty-four hundred bronzes startled all connoisseurs. Their execution was so fine, the casting so perfect, that at first it was thought absolutely impossible that these bronzes could have been conceived and executed by Negro tribes. Such, however, was the case, and it is now known that the process used was the lost-wax method of laying the wax directly over the core and then covering it with a mould, into which the metal was poured, thus making each piece a unique example. About two-thirds of this collection is in the Berlin Museum, another fine group is shown in the British Museum, and various rare examples are found in the Trocadéro, and in our American museums. In Dahomey and other regions of Africa, the native Negroes often made bronzes, but they are far inferior in workmanship to these found in Benin. It was supposed that the founders of Benin learned the perfection of their technique from the ancient Egyptians, via the ancient kingdom of Yoruba and the Soudan. The archaic period of this bronze production dates back to the twelfth century. The portrait heads are believed to have been executed about 1500. The plaques and reliefs and conical-shaped heads in decorative hair coiffures date from the sixteenth to the seventeenth century. The serpents, cocks, and groups shown in London and Berlin, as well as the carved ivory tusks, date from about this same era or later. After the revolt in 1820, the art of their bronze casting fell into decadence, and hardly exists at the present time.

The collections of the best Benin bronzes certainly give evidence of a lost civilization of very high artistic quality.

Perhaps the most interesting discovery that I made during my many travels was the *instinctive art of primitive races*—the art that is not taught but comes forth from the blood spontaneously. When this instinct of decoration and artistic proportion has been developed through generations of memory-training and expert craftsmanship, the primitive carvers can exceed most trained sculptors and designers both in speed of execution and in their innate sense of scale. Their art has an inevitable quality that gives it great force, and the most primitive tribes have given us numberless examples of intricate pattern weaving and sculpture of great aristocracy and beauty.

We have but to examine the art of Pre-Columbian Peru, or the Melanesian and Polynesian collections in the museums all over the world, to be amazed at the fund of invention and decoration. If we study the best carvings in Africa and the paintings of our American Indians, we must surely be convinced that these instinctive artists, whose work has for many years been collected as ethnographical data, and placed in natural history museums only, will some day be better understood and ranked as genuine art productions worthy of highest praise.

III

THE STUDY OF RACES

Hunger in the Balkans

It was during my initial journey in the Balkans that I first became deeply interested in the study of races as represented by the types of each locality. It dawned upon me that certain people represented *race,* while others were merely individuals, and it was a source of constant adventure to discover just what did constitute their racial or *tribal* characteristics. Although I was sent on an official errand to inspect conditions and report needs, I could not help feeling that the artist in me was experiencing a more profound consciousness, that would strongly influence my future work.

In July, 1919, when I had finished my part of the work of installation of the Musée Rodin in Paris, I went to the office of Mr. Herbert Hoover, the Director of the American Relief Administration. Among other gigantic war activities he had dispensed the funds of the child-feeding centers of Yugo-Slavia. These funds had been collected throughout the colonies of Serbs, Croats, and Slovenes living in the United States, and from the generous Americans who realized the pitiful needs of the children in Yugo-Slavia, and who had organized the American Yugo-Slav Relief Society. As secretary of this organization, I had become familiar with all the complexities and difficulties of helping the Balkans to relieve their state of suffering. My conference with Mr. Hoover was brief but very illuminating. He was well informed concerning all my wartime activities, and wasted no time. As soon as I informed him of my willingness to go to Yugo-Slavia, he immediately led me to a large wall-map in his office. Pointing to the groups of black-headed pins in the various areas of the Balkans, he said: "These are the places where we have sent food and where the children are in great need of help. There are epidemics of disease where you see the red pins, and we need reliable information from all these centers concerning medical needs as well as reports on the child-feeding problem. When can you start?" He turned and went back to his desk. "In two days," I answered. "Will you be alone or have you some one who can accompany you?" he asked. "My friend, Marie Louise Emmet, is ready to go with me," I replied. "Very good," he said. "Tomorrow morning come here at ten o'clock and I will have all your passports and instructions ready for you.

"You must be careful about disinfecting water, and eat very simple food—the heat will be bad in August but you will not mind anything if you do the work well. Keep a written daily report and bring it back to me—take photographs—make drawings—ask questions—and above all, *don't get sick*. Every one I send there ends up in a hospital and I want you to come back here *well* and send me news all along the line. By the way, if you wear your Red Cross uniforms, don't do anything foolish or *get shot,* for that might involve those bronze letters U.S.A. on your shoulders in an awkward situation. Good luck and good-by. My secretary will see you when you come tomorrow."

The heat during the months of July and August in the Balkans can equal that of India in midsummer. It was not unusual to see the thermometer at 110 degrees in the shade. The lamentable conditions just after the war, the epidemics of disease, the absence of all sanitation, and of soap, medicines, plumbing-supplies, windows, door-hinges, or metal fixtures of any description, made this journey difficult, to say the least.

Many long trips, lasting sixteen to twenty hours, were taken in cattle-cars or dilapidated motors, which on occasion had their tires stuffed with straw, before we reached our destination.

During the long journeys by train we had plenty of time and opportunity to study the types of men who generally made up the trainload of 1000 to 1500 soldiers. Broad cheek bones and square jaws were always characteristic of these Yugo-Slavs. The men would gladly pose for drawings and photographs, and I filled many books with studies of these soldiers. A good supply of cigarettes and a few magic drops of Dakin-Carrel solution, which we carried to disinfect the stagnant water, were sufficient reward for any such services. When we would approach a trestle over a river, the train would stop, and the engineer would walk over to see if enough of the construction was left intact to carry us across. Then all the soldiers would sing some national ballad and we would hope for the best. Only once was the order given for the passengers to go across on foot, and then the train followed at a snail's pace. All the soldiers linked arms and put us, the only women, in the center of the line. This chain of singing soldiers was stronger than the swaying bridge, but we all cheered the thoughtful engineer when he drove his train on to "terra firma" and waved us to get aboard again. These dusty, rugged peasants were like children of the soil. One felt them at home behind a plow, but strangely out of their frame in war-uniforms.

The women of Serbia, who had been martyrs during so many years of war's horrors, had in their deep, dark eyes a look whose cause we knew without questions. Their suffering had added a sombre beauty to their faces and a new mystery for my artist's eyes to contemplate. War had left its scars on the entire generation which survived, and each face seemed to tell the same mute story of heroism and sacrifice.

While I was in Athens, the only time I was not officially occupied was between noon and three o'clock. During these hours of extreme heat, officials took their midday rest and siestas. It was at this time that I allowed my artistic self the privilege of studying the museums and the Acropolis. These hours revealed to me such beauty in architecture and sculpture that my strength seemed to stagger, as if under a series of blows. During one of these expeditions, I was suddenly aware of a strange band of pain that seemed to lift off the top of my head. I was just able to give the name of my hotel to a *fiacre* driver before everything went black. I realized I had a sunstroke. Five days in bed followed, with high fever. I was packed between ice-bags, and well cared for by an American doctor, under the kind and constant surveillance of our American consul-general, Alexander W. Weddell. The memory of everything I had seen seemed to be branded upon my mind indelibly. A good scorching fever can intensify our sensibilities to an amazing extent and become a valuable initiation to the mysteries that lie on the other side of pain.

While studying the wonderful collection of coins and medals at the

Athens Numismatic Museum, I had met the director, who seemed happy to show and describe his treasures to such an enthusiastic artist visitor "from far-away, friendly America." The sureness of treatment and the exquisite workmanship of these coins were a revelation to me; although of miniature scale they were fine enough to be enlarged to any size.

When I was taken ill and prostrated by sunstroke, this Greek scholar inquired as to why I had not returned to his museum. When he heard of my bad luck he made a little collection of twenty-four plaster replicas of those coins which I had most admired and mounted them on two stiff sheets of cardboard. These he brought to me at the hotel "as a consolation, and because they had been so warmly appreciated by me." So thoughtful a gift made me feel much better and certainly hastened my recovery, although I felt very prostrated for the following two or three weeks, and my mid-day art excursions were forbidden.

After I had recovered and when we left Athens for Salonika, Miss Emmet was bitten by some poisonous insect and fell very ill on the train, having to be driven directly to the Red Cross infirmary on arrival. We both felt rather ashamed of ourselves for falling ill against our chief's orders, but in a short time we were again able to travel and continue our nightly battles against crawling insects and mosquitoes.

Two cases of diphtheria were reported in one of the Macedonian relief stations. An urgent plea for ice was received in Salonika. Three heavy burlap bags were packed with ice blocks wrapped in newspaper, and we started off with these additional pieces of leaking luggage. The heat was so intense that by the time we reached the station only about a third of each bag was left unmelted. This we turned over to a Red Cross ambulance that was waiting for our train. Malaria was ravaging the population, and I shall never forget the prostrate yellow victims who lay in every abandoned position, propped against the sides of the railroad stations, their hollow cheeks and jawbones catching the highlights of the blazing sun and leaving the black hollows of their eyes like skulls set on bundles of sacking.

On one train journey of sixteen hours, which finally brought us to Nish, we had wounded soldiers in our third-class, wooden-bench car. The patient endurance of these men I shall never forget. They were suffering intense pain; some had lost a leg and others their arms, and one next to us had a terrible head wound as well as an amputated arm at the shoulder. As the hot hours of fatigue and sweat wore these men down, the bandages became soaked, and dark red stains slowly spread over them.

Although the Great War was over, they had been in some skirmish near the Bulgarian border, and were being taken to the hospital at Nish. We offered them what we had of disinfected water and some fruit and cigarettes. The nurse in charge gratefully accepted some of our compressed gauze bandages and the dressings were changed, much to the relief of the wounded men whose stoical behavior was a credit to their country. When there was no fresh gauze left, the bandages were simply removed and put on backwards, all surgical supplies being at a very low ebb, and almost unobtainable.

On our arrival at Nish, about ten o'clock at night, we assisted the wounded men off the train, and then drove in a flea-ridden, open *fiacre* to the hotel (?) called "Russki Tzar." Never shall I forget the ruin and filthy abandon of that shelter. Crouched in a dark corner on the floor slept a weary night-clerk; a sputtering jet of gas, behind a counter, was the only illumination. We woke the clerk and asked to be shown to a room with two beds. He yawned, stretched himself and nodded, then he lighted a candle at the gas-jet and we followed him up a creaking flight of broken-down stairs. Snores of formidable basso profundo and tenor variety came from all directions.

As there were no doors left on hinges anywhere in Serbia, the sleepers had hung their blankets or old pieces of carpets across the entrances to the rooms. Finally the clerk lifted aside a torn piece of Turkish carpet hanging over a rope, set the candle on a table, and left us. We lighted our own candles and turned our pocket torch-lights on the setting. His footsteps had faded into the general blur of snoring and mosquitoes.

There was a single iron cot with half a torn and filthy sheet thrown over the mattress. We were too tired to speak. We unpacked our linen bags, poured water into the chipped porcelain basin, disinfected it, and prepared for bed. There was no use complaining even when we lost count of the insects that crawled about us. It was the aftermath of war, and our next train left the following morning at six o'clock. Here life was too grim a battlefield for me to attempt any drawings —but every glance seared itself deeply into my mind.

At the time of our visit to Belgrade, King Peter was old and in retirement. He had been a much beloved monarch, and his son, Prince Alexander, was Regent of the new kingdom of Serbs, Croats, and Slovenes. He had been trained in Russia under the Tzarist régime. The political situation was in a state of confusion, and every one was speculating wildly as to what form of government would eventually be adopted.

The new kingdom, as a result of the war, had tripled its former population and more than doubled the size of the former kingdom of old Serbia. Belgrade, the capital, was a total wreck—the streets torn up, the houses abandoned; every piece of plumbing pipe or doorhinges had been removed when the city was sacked by the retreating and defeated Austrians.

We watched the seething crowds of Serbians, Croats, Turks, and tall, handsome Montenegrins wandering about the streets and crowding the cafés. Our hosts were Slovenians or Croatians. They all were unanimous on *one* subject at least—their profound gratitude to America for the relief work, especially for sending medical supplies and the huge quantities of food for the starving children. Hunger is sometimes stronger than national political platforms.

We were told that those striking tall Montenegrins were of the race of mountaineers whose code of honor and fidelity permitted any husband to shoot a man at sight if the latter were found casting an over-friendly glance at the former's wife.

Our days were spent visiting the food stations, tracing lost shipments of clothing or food or medical supplies and gathering reports on the existing conditions and most urgent needs. In Ljubliana, American food was being provided for 25,000 children, and in the whole country over 200,000 children were being fed by the American Relief Administration. The Rockefeller Foundation had already started activities under the leadership of Doctor Stampar, whose indefatigable efforts built up an amazing system of visiting nurses and general hygiene all over the country.

OUR FORD LASHED TO A RAILWAY FLAT-CAR ON THE WAY TO KOSSOVO FROM SKOPLIE

SAFELY LANDED AT KARLOBAC AFTER FIFTEEN HOURS OF DODGING FLOATING MINES
AND VIGILANT SENTINELS

Left to right: the engineer, the captain, Colonel Pribicevic, and M. II.

BRONZE PORTRAIT OF COLONEL MILAN PRIBICEVIC BY M. H.

(Metropolitan Museum of Art)

Showing type of knitted helmet worn by the U. S. soldiers in the Great War

Photo. M. H.

SOLE SURVIVING MONK AT GRACHANITZA, KOSSOVO

ONE OF THE MUTILATED SERBIAN VICTIMS OF THE WAR

We could not escape feeling that in spite of all efforts to pull the different factions and provinces together, there was a sense of impending tragedy and struggle ahead of this Yugo-Slav melting-pot.

The faces of the children in the cities and in the child-feeding stations haunted my memory. They were gaunt, hollow-cheeked, big-eyed, little victims whose deeply lined foreheads showed the strain of unnatural maturity and years of suffering. Over 125,000 of the war-orphans of Serbia wandered about in rags, not knowing what fate was ahead of them, having lost both their parents and their relatives. They were lost waifs, many of them pitifully deformed by rickets or by some form of tuberculosis. Their little stomachs were swollen and bloated with either no food or the heavy stale slabs of bread that they might find to eat.

When we motored from Belgrade to Bosnia we stopped overnight at Tusla, a small village where there were over 100 cases of typhus, and practically every child had chicken-pox. The wells had all been polluted and we were told that practically every woman had been violated by the retreating enemy and infected with disease.

When we arrived at ten o'clock at night in a drenching rainstorm, after motoring fifteen hours, we found a small hotel where the proprietor warmed us a pot of soup and beans, but informed us that as they had had no soap or disinfectants for months, he would not permit us to sleep in the beds, for whoever had lived there had either syphilis or smallpox and we would be safer sleeping in our motor out in the rain! Two young doctors overheard this converesation, which took place under their windows. They called down to us that they would let us have their cots for the night, and that they had a clean sheet! Our gratitude was unbounded, for Miss Emmet and I were completely exhausted. The next day we located the shipment of clothing which had been sent here by the American Red Cross, and this was distributed to the most needy.

To reach the child-welfare station at Kossovo in Central Serbia, we had to load our Ford on to a flat freight car to be dragged through a long railroad tunnel. About halfway through, the engine broke down, and there in the darkness the heavy, choking smoke soon made breathing a matter of desperate effort. Some man ran up to us with wet rags, which we clapped over our faces. By breathing through the damp cloth, we were able to last out until the engine started and pulled us into the fresh mountain air, which was so violent that it blew my black straw uniform hat into a ravine. For the rest of the journey I wore a Turkish fez of white felt.

The field of Kossovo is renowned for the great battle of 1389 against the Turks. Many are the tragic and heroic legends of this battlefield. "The Christian legions opposing the 'infidels' paid a high price, but the onrushing hordes were annihilated and Christian Europe was saved." So spoke the solitary monk of Grachanitza. Mestrovic, the great Yugo-Slav sculptor, has interpreted the legend of Kossovo in his marble "Widows," the wooden monument of the temple of Kossovo, and in many other statues.

We found the splendid edifice of the Temple of Grachanitza, with its frescoes still intact, a fine example of Byzantine architecture. The lonely old monk in charge gave us graphic tales of how his fellow monks had been massacred, and how he was the only man left alive when the church was attacked and the monastery destroyed by the Bulgarians. He took us up to the high altar and blessed two long candles made of home-made tallow, and asked us to carry them back to New York as a token of gratitude from the children of Kossovo, who had been saved from starvation by the American food-station. At five o'clock we saw the long line of Serbian children arriving from all directions with their tin cups in their thin little hands. Hot cocoa and condensed milk was given to each with a thick slab of bread. For this meal many of them had walked two or three miles daily. Others came at noon for their ration of American food.

It was no easy task to keep the candles safely during the next few months, but eventually they were placed on the high altar of the Cathedral of Saint John the Divine in New York and lighted at a special service of thanksgiving on June 15, Kossovo Day, attended by 5000 Yugo-Slavs and directed by the Reverend Howard C. Robbins, then Dean of the Cathedral, and one of the most loyal and devoted friends of Yugo-Slavia throughout the war.

The last area of our journey was the Dalmatian coast from Albania

up to Fiume. On this trip Miss Emmet and I were escorted by
Colonel Milan Pribicevic and his chauffeur. When we had collected
all data on medical needs and food supplies at Raguza and Split, we
found that the Italians had barricaded off our approach to Fiume and
Pletvitze. The sudden appearance of these totally different Italian
types was quite a shock to me, after having been completely surrounded by the strong-jawed and stocky, war-weary Yugo-Slavs for
nine weeks. From the anthropological point of view, not only their
appearance but their whole psychology was in sharp contrast to the
stolid, slow-speaking Slavic peasants.

We conferred with the governor of Dalmatia, and managed to persuade him to lend us his small yacht and his skipper, who had previously been a mine-layer in the Austrian fleet, but had deserted the
Austrian navy to join the Yugo-Slavs.

It seemed wiser to take along some one who knew where most of
the mines might still be lurking; so it was agreed that we should keep
our plans secret, and meet at the dock at ten o'clock at night in our
car. A section of the rail on the forward deck had to be removed to
allow the car to be loaded crosswise on the yacht. The boat was just
wide enough for the four wheels to rest on the deck. The front
lights and the trunk-rack behind extended well over the rail, but by
lashing it tightly the car was securely loaded. The governor sent us
flowers and hearty good wishes, and we cast off into the darkness.

No lights were allowed, and no smoking. I ventured to ask the
mine-layer whether there were any life-belts on board. He smiled and
said, "No, but we won't need any, if we keep out of trouble—and if
we *do* hit one of the floating mines, we surely won't need life-belts!
Just lie on the after deck and enjoy the moonlight; we will keep well
outside the islands and will hope not to be sighted by the Italians on
the coast. We should reach Karlobac by ten tomorrow morning. . . ."
And we did. By the mysterious means of communication known to
primitive races, word had been received of our imminent but secret
arrival. There were 1500 people collected on the shore to welcome us;
some had walked for six hours to reach the port in time.

Colonel Milan Pribicevic was the war hero of the "Brothers Pribicevic," a family known all over Yugo-Slavia. He had fought through-

out the war in the Serbian army and for years previous to 1914 against the Turks and Bulgars. When the Serbs were defeated in 1915 and their country devastated and looted, the staggering remnants of the army took refuge on the island of Corfu. This story is one of the tragic epics of the Great War.

Colonel Pribicevic, whose portrait I made in bronze, now at the Metropolitan Museum under the title, "Modern Crusader," had taken part in each step of his country's *débâcle*. He decided to go to America incognito and visit all the Yugo-Slav colonies there. He roused and inspired his fellow countrymen by his patriotic orations and enlisted a volunteer army of many thousand men. When America declared war, he donned his military uniform and returned to the Salonika front. The New York chapter of the American Red Cross equipped his legion with warm woollen clothing and knitted helmets, and our flag was presented to their standard-bearer by my sister, Mrs. Draper, at the Seventy-first Infantry Armory, New York. They embarked for Salonika where they were assembled with the Allied forces. Colonel Pribicevic was attached to the General Staff of the Drina Division of the Serbian Army, during the months that, step by step, each village of the lost territory was recaptured. When he reached Zagreb, as delegate to the National Council, the armistice was declared and he was carried on the shoulders of the populace through the streets of the city. After the war, Colonel Pribicevic was elected a member of Parliament, but soon retired from the political field, to take up the cause of the agrarian movement, and as an example to his beloved peasants became a farmer and writer on the famous fields of Kossovo (blackbirds), which are red with poppies and shadowed by the clouds of blackbirds that still fly over them.

At Karlobac, on the Dalmatian coast, doctors and teachers and local officials crowded about us on the dock. We were welcomed with shouts of *"Zivela America."* We all joined in with a group of gaily costumed peasants and danced the national *Kolo*. The roads were lined with cheering peasants for nearly a mile. Flowers were thrown into our car as we drove through the lines of happy faces, so different from the sickly, tragic victims of Macedonian fevers.

We found, as we travelled inland, that the people had been so cut off from outside help that their surgeons had been operating without anæsthetics for months, and there were no bandages or antiseptics of any kind. Amputations were made with ordinary carpenters' saws, without ether. The children were deformed, due to rickets, and tuberculosis was prevalent everywhere.

We bade farewell to our escorts and started for Fiume, where we were stopped by rifle-shots at a bridge leading from the adjoining town of Susak, with the news that D'Annunzio had declared a new war, and that all entrances to Fiume were barred by sentinels and guards who fired on all comers regardless of nationality or uniform. Even harmless artists would not be admitted. Our car made a quick turn-about and stopped. Two French army officers, in an official motor, were just ahead of us and were also fired at. They told us to lie on the floor of our car and ordered our chauffeur to follow them, which we did. They then agreed to lock us in a compartment with their army mail-sacks and escort us in this secret manner on a military train out of the war zone on to Zagreb in Croatia. We were not permitted to open the window or make any sign of life. About midnight the door was unlocked, and one of the officers very quietly handed us a bag of hard-boiled eggs and a loaf of bread. *"Vous n'avez rien à déclarer?"* he asked in a whisper, smiling. *"Non? Eh bien! Voulez-vous nous donner le plaisir de déjeuner avec nous à l'hotel à Zagreb demain matin?"*

"Oui, avec grand plaisir, et merci. . . . Est-ce que tout le monde dort? Où sommes nous?"

"Shsh . . . oui, et bientôt nous serons hors du war zone, *et vous serez libérées. . . ."*

We were a happy foursome at breakfast, having escaped with our lives from a hornet's nest of Italian fanatics, who carried their knives in their teeth while shooting at random over the bridges. D'Annunzio owes us our two railroad tickets from Fiume to Trieste, but we enjoyed the change of schedule, which ended happily.

From Zagreb we went immediately to Paris and turned in our lengthy report to Mr. Hoover and the United States State Department. The medical needs were reported to the American Red Cross. A supply was immediately prepared and sent to those hospitals which we had visited. My mind and heart were heavy with a mass of tragic human experience; I felt years older—the life of Paris appeared artificial and I found it painful to answer the many questions that every one asked. They all seemed to be so far removed from this recent world of smoking lava and victims of the bloody volcano of war, pestilence, famine, death—the Four Horsemen of the Apocalypse in ghastly reality, still ravaging the face of the earth. But where was the Angel with the flaming sword? Where was the answer to the prayers I had read on the women's uplifted faces—women beyond the realm of tears or pity, women who could not forget, whose hearts were locked forever in silent agony?

Africa

To transmute our personal experiences into some form of expression, and to find a way to interpret our dreams and aspirations is a slow and often disheartening process. The years following the war and my trip through the Balkans were spent in this continual mental struggle. Perhaps because I was one of the first to interpret the great contemporary dancers in sculpture, the idea seemed to attract attention and bring me success. In portraiture also, I had many very interesting sitters, and, considering the fact that I was entirely dependent on my own efforts for the development of my profession, I was unusually fortunate to be able to build up a good clientèle and obtain plenty of work in the various forms of sculpture.

After six or seven years, however, I felt the drag of continual routine and the imperious need of change and new environment. The wanderlust tempted me to search for something afar.

I have already tried to define the quality of restlessness, peculiar, I think, to the artist, that prompted me to leave New York in 1926. From a practical standpoint, everything should have tempted me to stay at home and capitalize my good start, but metronomic regularity has never appealed to me. The descriptions of Africa and the un-

MAP OF AFRICA SHOWING THE LOCATION OF AFRICAN TRIBES

Published by the Field Museum, Chicago

explored deserts, where time becomes merely a space between light and darkness and where definite, dated engagements were unknown, haunted me, and I fled New York and its vertiginous activities.

The tale of Ulysses sailing away into the uncharted sunsets has always held a great lure for me. The idea of finding a tiny island somewhere off the coast of Africa, where may be found the "fruit of the flower" which transforms life and changes past memories into future dreams, was enough, in 1926, to make me weigh anchor and set forth to find the island of the Lotus Eaters. On this journey, my sister, Sam, and I constituted our little party. After Africa, as I have told in earlier chapters, I went alone to study in Rome, and with Mestrovic in Zagreb.

The first impression of Africa was golden hills, set against flaming skies. The blaze of daylight staggered one; the heat of mid-day quivered and rose from the palpitating dust like zigzag patterns on a gauze screen. Through this we discerned the myriad types of humanity, swathed in voluminous folds of white. The dark-skinned Moors and Arabs, with their straight noses and eyes of ebony shining out under the turbans of gold and ivory, were silent and remote; their Oriental calm challenged our disturbing approach, in contrast to the bustling tourists in the northern cities, and the noisy tram-lines which were distracting reminders of familiar reality, and modern life.

The quivering sunlight blazed over the white city of Tunis. We threaded our way through an endless maze of shadowy, covered streets. Shafts of light pierced the shaded booths and fell on the crouching merchants, catching the high points on their displays of brass and colored silks. These lured one into the inner shops of soft carpets spread on the floors and folded in great stacks around the rooms. Up the walls the endless shelves of gauzes and silks were stored away by the clever merchant, who knew all the wiles of his trade. Hands were clapped, and a silent, bowing Arab boy appeared. Coffee and sweet cakes were brought in, and the visitor was charmed by Oriental hospitality. After that the art of salesmanship became easier.

We visited the Bardo Museum with its relics of ancient days—a delightful drive beyond the walls of the city—and the pottery kilns and the studios where garden-jars and tableware and wall-decorations in tiles are made by the native artists and sold throughout the world. The Arab manager of this pottery plant was a friendly soul and agreed to let me work in a corner of one of the studios. As he spoke French, we were able to get along easily. I procured some of his native clay and started to model in it, so that it would not have a totally strange, new consistency to cope with later on when I made portraits of African subjects. The Arabs taught me how to turn their primitive potter's wheels by foot, and how to apply the colored glazes. We made a number of big garden jars which I decorated. I also learned how the baking and firing were done. The artisans and painters were all interested in the activities of an American visitor, and gladly posed for their portraits. We seemed to understand each other in the language of fellow artists, and I was sorry to have to pack up supplies and take my leave for our southward journey.

Late one afternoon, before leaving Tunis, we made a pilgrimage to Carthage. Memories of the golden pen of Flaubert floated across our consciousness as we drove northward towards this historic city. The view over the cliffs across the bay to the lavender hills of Tunis evoked the panorama of ancient galleys, filing into the harbor below, returning from some triumphant war, and bringing back booty to the victorious ruler, Hamilcar, and his immortal daughter, Salammbo.

Today the temples and palaces of Carthage are in the dust, and the pageant of olden days has vanished. Only the ruins are left.

The evening sky and a new moon shed mystic beauty over the citadel of Byrse and the landscape beyond. The Cathedral of Saint Louis and the Archeological Museum are the only important buildings of recent times on the ancient site of this fabulous city. The museum guards the treasures from the excavations that were made under the direction of Père Delattre, and the Precinct of Tanit is now used as a cemetery for infants, small animals, and birds. *Sic transit.* . . .

Only the stark, gigantic arches of the Roman aqueduct remain, in defiant challenge to the passage of time. This triumph of masonry seems to stretch over the western plains into eternity. As Ruskin says: "They are like troops of shadowy mourners at a nation's grave."

The ancient port of Salammbo lies between Carthage and the sea. It is in the form of a circular lagoon, with a narrow channel to the

PORTRAIT OF OUR ARAB COOK IN COLORED CHALK
BY M. H.

STUDY OF MIXED TYPE AT THE POTTERY KILNS IN
TUNIS

"AS IT WAS IN THE BEGINNING, IS NOW . . ."

Biblical types of Jews reading the Talmud. Interior of Jewish Synagogue on the Island of Jerba,
off the coast of Tripoli

135

HEROIC–SIZE BLACK BELGIAN MARBLE
OF A SENEGALESE TYPE

(American Museum of Natural History, New
Field Museum, Chicago; Brooklyn Museum of

LIFE–SIZE BRONZE FIGURE OF SENEGALE
TOM–TOM PLAYER

This man was six feet three inches in height;
eet were perfectly flat, but he often ran for ei
hours at a time without touching his heels to
ground. (Hall of Man, Field Museum, and Ame
can Museum of Natural History, New York)

OUR HOSPITABLE HOSTS IN THEIR SOUKS IN OLD TUNIS—MERCHANTS OF RUGS
AND FABRICS

SUBTERRANEAN POTTERY "DUG–OUT" WHERE THE WALLS ARE MADE OF BROKEN
JARS HELD TOGETHER WITH CLAY

The potter turns his inevitable traditional water-bottle on a primitive wheel. Island of Jerba

THE UNBELIEVABLE CITY OF MEDININ, SOUTH TUNISIA

HOUM SOUK, THE CAPITAL OF JERBA

M. H. modelling a camel outside the Arab café where we lived. The glare from the white walls, roofs, and dusty roads was blinding and the heat at mid-day made working out of doors almost impossible

WOOD CARVING, "THE RABBI OF HARA SRIRA." JERBA

THE PORT OF SALAMMBO

The hills of Tunis are seen across the Bay of Carthage

FAMILY GROUP OF SOUTH AFRICAN KALAHARI BUSHMEN

Beside the mother are lying three ostrich-eggs in which she carries water. (Hall of Man)

WATER BEING POURED INTO THE SMALL OPENING IN OSTRICH–EGGS

No speed laws are known or needed here

MOTHER AND CHILD OF THE KALAHARI BUSHMAN TRIBE, SOUTH AFRICA, WAITING
FOR FATHER TO BRING HOME THE GAME FOR SUPPER

(Hall of Man)

Mediterranean. The effect of a crowd of poorly built modern villas
and cottages has entirely destroyed what might have been a picturesque
and beautiful town. But a small museum stands dignified and alone
at the edge of the sea. It displays the mysterious forms of Neptune's
gardens, with fine decorations by local artists.

On a high cliff overlooking the hills of Tunis and the Bay of
Carthage, stands a fairy castle, Sidi Bou Saïd, built without a blue-print
by Arab masons and decorators under the direction of Baron d'Erlanger. The marble floors of the inner courts are divided in the center
by a shallow channel through which runs cool, clear water, on whose
surface float occasional scarlet camelias and rose petals, dropped list-
lessly into this fairy stream by some unseen Nubian sentinel.

From the latticed balcony that surrounded this courtyard came the
sounds of a chattering male chorus. Ancient music had been studied
and taught to these Arab singers by our host. As we mounted the
wide marble staircase leading to the library, the pungent fragrance
of sandalwood filled the air. Intricately carved doors were pushed
silently aside by two ebony-colored servants in white native dress, and
we stood amazed at the beauty and intoxicating aroma of this library
of ancient manuscripts. The cases, each more exquisitely carved in
sandalwood than its neighbor, stood in rows in the center of the room,
with latticed openwork doors to let the soft air circulate throughout
the shelves and their precious contents.

At each end of this great gallery the wise architect had left huge
open panels to frame the views beyond. At one end the Bay of Carthage lay below us in limpid iridescence, reflecting a new moon,
rising over the hilltops of the opposite shore. The western window
framed an African sunset, fading into the evening mists that rise
over the endless desert; in the foreground the garden pool, a long,
narrow path of water between two walls of dark cypress trees, lay
placid as a mirror, while white peacocks made their stately way in
single file along the top of the garden wall, silhouetted against the
coral-pink sky. Slowly down the marble steps went these birds of
grandeur to the edge of the dark pool and drank their evening
draught, spreading their glittering tails in male pride and contentment.

Enveloped in a long black cloak, our host led us through the gardens and down winding paths, from one level to the next. We fed the young gazelles that trotted out unafraid, watching us with wide, dark eyes.

We felt completely removed from reality. Surrounded by exotic beauty and isolated from all suggestion of modern chaos, Baron d'Erlanger seemed to have succeeded in his desire to live apart from life and be at peace.

After a short stay in Tunis, during which I made five or six portraits of Arabs and Negroes in colored chalks, we procured a can of local clay, concentrated our luggage, and journeyed southward. Reaching Gabes, the last train stop on the coast line, we were so anxious to leave the hot railway carriage and explore the country, that my sister and I hurried to the platform and stepped off. A crowd of Senegalese soldiers were waiting at attention to meet a French officer. Sam was taking down the luggage from the racks inside the car, and as he started handing the bags out of the window to me the little train started off so swiftly that there was nothing to do but gasp and accept the awkward situation. There we were, my sister and I, with two bags, on a beautiful, tropical, moonlight night, alone on an endless, sandy space, surrounded by a glistening company of splendid black soldiers, who formed into marching order and started off ahead of us in a cloud of dust, their glittering bayonets flashing in the moonlight and their ebony heads capped with the snug felt fez. The French officer in command, seeing our dismay at being left alone without our escort or baggage, very courteously explained to us that there were two stops; one called Gabes Port and the other just Gabes—the latter at the end of the line—and that if we would join his company, which were to march to the barracks close to the hotel, we would meet our escort there, no doubt far more anxious than we were as to what the ultimate result of such a situation might be. As the little train reached the final village stop before we reached the barracks, my husband commandeered an Arab cart with two emaciated horses and drove with the baggage towards Gabes Port, where he had left us, meeting us on the way happily swinging along in step with our dusky escort, enjoying the adventure and feeling very much a part of this starry and radiant, nocturnal stage-setting.

I was deeply impressed by the sculptural quality of these Senegalese types. The planes of their great cheek bones and strongly marked jaws shone out in the moonlight like polished metal, and convinced me that my first work in Africa would be to study this race thoroughly, and model a head which might represent a synthesis of all these men that had introduced us so directly into the silent mysteries of an African midnight. It was not so simple, however, to secure the willing model to pose for his portrait, and my first encounter was a lesson of inestimable value for future work among Africans and other primitive races.

A French colonel in command of the Senegalese troops permitted me to attend a review and to select certain types that I found most sculpturesque. These men were then brought to our hotel and told to take off the fez. They were all startlingly impressive, and it was difficult to limit my selection to two especially fine specimens. The colonel then explained my needs and asked if they had any religious scruples that would prevent them from posing for a portrait, a clay reproduction of their heads. One of the two stated he could never return to his tribe if he allowed such a thing to be done to him. He was promptly excused. The second was called and questioned. He said he would submit on the condition that the "reproduction" would be immediately locked in a box and taken out of Africa, that his name would not be attached to it, and that I would never speak of it to his fellow tribesmen. As he lived some thirty days' journey away, I gladly agreed to this. We started work and he posed faithfully every morning until the head was completed. He occasionally entertained me with stories of his home-life and bemoaned the fact that his last wife had cost him five hundred francs—but she had two ready-made sons. The first three wives had been acquired for three hundred francs each. He could pose standing for hours without moving; his heavy eyelids would often fall into a dozing relaxation. He seemed to represent a sort of monumental inertia, the epitome of that lost art of occidental life—relaxation.

On our American calendar we noted that it was the fifteenth of

December, and for us this evoked the thought of snow-storms and bitter gales. It was difficult to realize that we were actually experiencing tropical summer. The azure sky and smooth sea seemed to tempt us to adventure, so we decided to try our luck. We pushed off in a flat-bottomed boat laden with a cargo of two camels and ten sheep, a few goats, and ourselves, in quest of the tiny island of Jerba. Three bronzed Arabs, stripped to their loin-cloths, sweating and straining in rhythmic unison, ran up and down along the rail of the boat and pushed off with long poles into the shallow sea. We managed to run the motorcar onto a sort of raft and lash it fast; this was attached by long ropes to our sailboat, and what with groaning camels and bleating sheep, we sounded and looked like a contribution to Noah's Ark starting out for lands unknown.

Luckily for us and for the motorcar, the sea was not too rough, and we soon discerned the waving palm trees outlining the golden coast of the island of Jerba and the low, white roof-tops of the port of Adjim. While exploring this island, I made many studies of the various local types and found two most interesting villages of archaic-looking Jews—Hara Kebira and Hara Srira. In one of these we visited the synagogue and persuaded the venerable rabbi to pose for his portrait. The walls of his synagogue were covered from floor to ceiling with gold and silver plaques brought by the pilgrims who come in masses every spring to pay homage to this renowned temple of their ancestors, where legend has it the tablets of Moses were at one time deposited. Every May, about 15,000 Jews land on this island, tie their little boats, pitch their tents as in Biblical days, and camp around the synagogue for about two or three weeks of prayers and feasting.

In Jerba I modelled a camel brought by his owner every morning to a shaded corner near our hotel. Swarms of flies and chattering Arab children soon gathered around us, and the work was completed under great difficulties and with many vituperations. I could never feel any real sympathy for the camel family. Whenever I happened to be in their vicinity they seemed to be suffering from some ancient grudge, and were forever watching their chance to lunge out and vent their spleen on any one who was near enough to be bitten. Lurid tales of their treachery and ill-temper were constantly being told us by the Arabs—how they chewed off the foot of a boy rider, how they bit off the hand that had fed them, and so on.

Whereas the ill-fated destiny that hung over the little donkeys of Northern Africa always struck me as cruel and unnecessary. These patient and indefatigable little beasts of burden trundle along the dusty, hot roads hour after hour—their slender legs looking totally inadequate to support the grotesque mass of material that is usually loaded on to their backs. Their great, flopping ears wave about in a dislocated and hopeless rhythm, while the mischievous and unfeeling Arab boy gratifies his sadistic desires by prodding with a pointed stick the open wound on the haunch of his defenseless victim.

In spite of the frequent reprisals we strenuously administered to these boys whenever we saw one stabbing his donkey, I fear the whippings and warnings were soon forgotten; once out of sight, we felt certain that this vicious habit was resumed, perhaps with a few extra jabs for revenge. We hoped that by some kind providence Nature had been able to dull the sensibilities of these unfortunate animal victims of human vices.

Returning to the mainland, we travelled southward beyond the end of railways, where little white cars are pulled by panting, syncopated engines until the earth grows too sandy for the rails, and the desert claims supremacy at last over the white man's machinery.

Camel caravans carry one along the road and over the oceans of sandy swells and endless lavender shadows. In the evening the moon in all its tropical radiance sheds such a glamour that one can easily read or write without other assistance of lighting. The length of a camel's shadow reaches such magnitude that fantastic murals are evoked by the changing patterns of huge scale, which stretch over the desert trail. A wisp of smoke rising in the distance is the only symbol of actuality. The evening fires of a resting caravan announce the death of day—but some keep on, forgetting schedule hours, swaying along the trackless space, growing smaller and fading at last into the distant mist, leaving only footprints of the camels in the sand.

My artist's soul was satiated and renewed during these journeys and I drank deeply of the peace and benediction of immensity. Oh, the velvet softness of tropical nights, when the glittering stars hung low over our heads!

Near the frontier of Libya we visited Medinin, a town so archaic and unreal in its architecture that it was difficult to believe that it was actually inhabited by the human race. The mud houses were often two stories high and had small holes which served for doors and windows; narrow steep stairs without rails, all uneven in their crude, unformed proportions, ran up the front façades of the houses.

In one corner of the village plaza an excited and noisy scene was taking place around a shaggy camel. Sharp cries from the different groups of Arabs that swarmed in a cloud of dust all over the market-place seemed to encourage an Arab merchant who was gesticulating wildly with a long stick, beating constantly across a huge load of olive branches and palm-leaf stems under which the camel was crouching on bended knees, with his grotesque head waving about in dumb protest to the blows which often fell on his neck instead of on the load of wood. We found that this dramatic method of auctioning off such valuable material as firewood, at fifteen francs a load, was quite a common procedure. The scarcity or complete absence of vegetation except at an oasis or along the banks of a river transforms a collection of dead branches into something worthy of dramatization, and the Arabs lose no chance to capitalize on their stock in trade.

On the reservation of Major Cooper, an English game-hunter, near the Ituri forest, a group of pigmies watched one of the men lock up a chest in which had been stored supplies of salt and chocolate. These commodities were considered a great treat, and as the key was left in the lock the little pigmies began to experiment as to how they could unlock the case. Apparently, they were incapable of turning the key; this motion of the hand was unknown to them, and they could not get the box open although they kept at it for days. When they finally gave it up and went away, two or three monkeys who had been watching the pigmies, swung down from the branches overhead, and in a few moments they had unlocked the box, removed the salt bars, eaten their fill of the other contents, and climbed back into their trees. Their power of observation and natural ingenuity had far surpassed that of the pigmies.

These little people resemble the Negritos in the Malay jungle, the Philippine Islands, and the Andaman Islands. Their crinkly, short hair is an easily recognized characteristic. They are not deformed as one might suppose, although they are sometimes only three feet eight inches tall, but generally the males vary from four to nearly five feet. They are stockily built and strong. I wonder if their pituitary gland system is built on the same principle as in Shetland ponies. These are also under-sized but in good proportion, and never grow up into real horses. Apparently the babies when born are normally proportioned, but after a few years their bones stop growing and they stay the size that a white child of seven or nine years might be.

Of course these Ituri people live on the meager regimen enforced upon them by the jungle: nuts, herbs, roots, occasional juicy morsels of small wild birds and game. When good fortune comes their way, the tribe settle down around the body of a dead elephant, killed by one of their diminutive tribal heroes, and treat themselves to a field-day of overeating until their little tummies swell up, and after a good deal of scratching and chattering the happy families fall asleep.

The mothers, when asked to bring their babies into the daylight to be photographed, would pluck great leaves and hold them over the heads of their infants, fearing that the sun's rays would be fatal. The children suffer seriously from lack of good nourishment during the first years of their life. Their bones do not grow hard enough to carry their weight, and the result is rickets and many other diseases that serve their primitive purpose of weeding out the unfit, and permitting only the survival of the fittest.

In Africa the natives can often be identified by the pattern of their scarifications. In fact, these designs are a means of communication, and record the fact that certain men have killed so many victims, or that they come from a certain locality or tribe.

Perhaps the most terrible example of physical deformation I saw was the slitting of the lips of the women in certain African tribes, the Ubangi for instance, where both lips are slit and wooden discs inserted, each year larger and heavier, to stretch the fleshy ring until discs of eight inches in diameter are carried with actual pride by these otherwise splendid physical types of women. This practice was believed to have been started when the chiefs, fearing an enemy might steal their wives, disfigured them in this manner as a defense. Later the custom became a fashion and a competitive beauty contest.

When I made the portrait of one of these women she pointed to my cigarette and showed clearly her desire to smoke. I looked at her heavy wooden discs and she read my consternation; laughing she drew a hollow reed of bamboo from her belt and deftly fitted a cigarette into the end of this tube. Placing it between the two discs and holding the end between her teeth she beckoned me to light it, and the operation seemed perfectly successful, though anything but attractive to the observer. We became quite friendly, however, during the sittings, and through the interpreter she reassured me and said one day that the discs really did not hurt at all and were very convenient for eating, as they served as the plate to hold the food, while she pushed in whatever morsels she might prefer with her fingers. The teeth, of course, and jaws, remain perfectly normal.

The year after I made her portrait, I happened to go to the circus in Mr. Ringling's box in New York City. As the procession passed close by, I recognized my discs girl with three or four of her village companions. We exchanged greetings and waving of hands, much to the surprise of the other guests in the box, who regarded me as "not a very nice person to know."

I frequently found most extraordinary skull deformations in Africa. The Mangbetu tribe has the most picturesque and unbelievable head-dress, which is woven into the hair with raffia strands. These strands are bound around the elongated and cone-shaped skull from the forehead upwards, and spread out wider and wider until a basket-like effect eighteen inches wide is achieved. The weight of this, after it is smeared with clay to stiffen it, is such that the neck muscles of those wearing it are abnormally developed.

Nearly three years later, when the Field Museum made its proposal to me, I realized how valuable all my African experiences had been in preparing me for this world-wide study of races. During the five

LIFE–SIZE BRONZES OF A FAMILY GROUP

Pigmies of the Ituri Forest in Central Africa. (Hall of Man)

A TRIBE OF 17
PIGMY WARR

MONSIEUR POIRIER AND
A PIGMY CHIEF, BEL-
GIAN CONGO

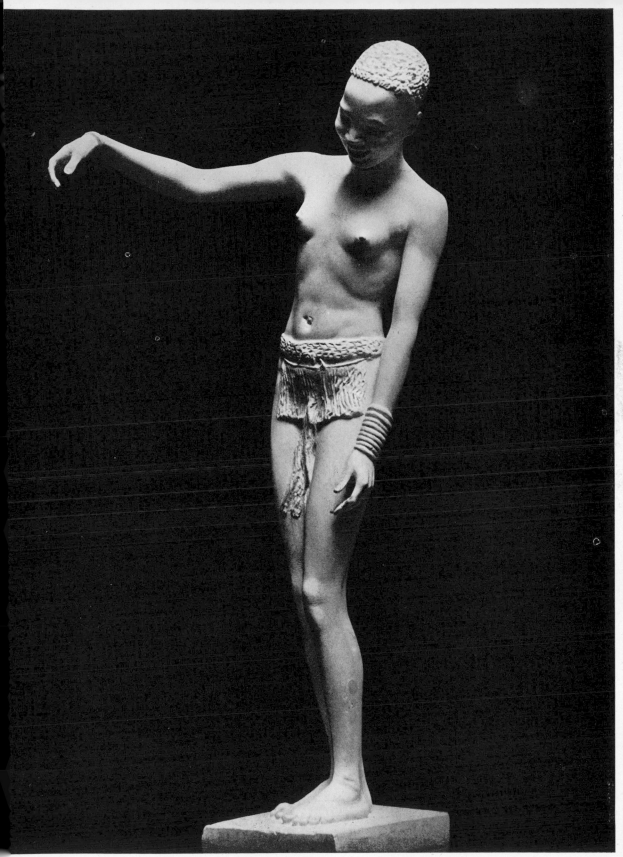

"DABOA," DANCING GIRL OF SARA TRIBE, LAKE CHAD

A life-size bronze of this subject is in the Hall of Man, Chicago, and in the American Museum of Natural History, New York

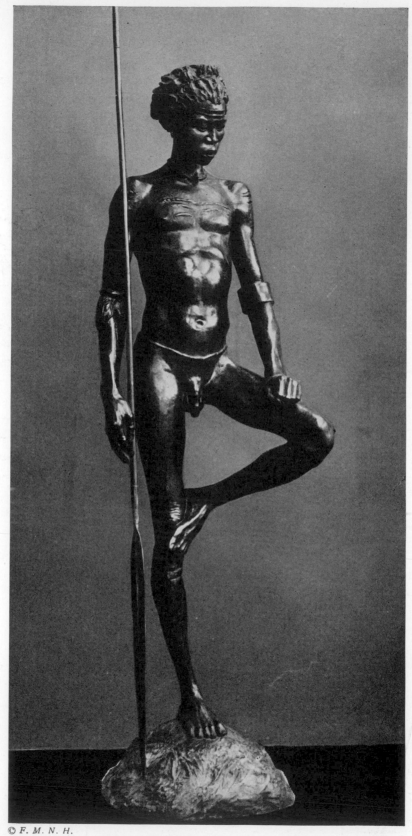

SHILLUK WARRIOR, NORTHEAST AFRICA
Life-size bronze. (Hall of Man)

Field Museum years, I often discovered splendid racial subjects far removed from their original homeland, and more strikingly typical of their own race than those we had actually seen in their native habitat.

Perhaps the most varied collection of African and Asiatic subjects ever assembled in one place was in Paris during the Exposition Coloniale in 1931. Through the courtesy and help of the officials, it was made possible for me to model many fine types from the various exhibits in my own Paris studio.

When the subject of the "Venus Hottentot" was first discussed, I confess that I came very near abandoning the whole project of the Hall of Man.

Examining the cast of the monsterpiece of female ugliness in the Musée de l'Histoire Naturelle in Paris, I grew very rebellious, and insisted that I be given artistic freedom to select at least the best possible representative of a race and not the ugliest, even if every anthropologist in the world preferred the latter.

I recall how shocked one of the eminent German professors was three years later, when, having listened to endless contradictory opinions concerning my group of Kalahari Bushmen, I told him very seriously that I had arranged to satisfy all the experts on the subject of the correct size of a Bushman woman's steatopyga development. (This, dear reader, really means "fat tail," or over-life-size "spankers.")

I told him that my model had been approved by the officials of the Cape Town Museum, as an average medium example, but that as some experts insisted on more exaggerated proportions, I had decided to have the buttocks of my bronze figure made in thick flexible rubber, which could be easily inflated or deflated according to which anthropologist was expected to visit the museum! He really believed me.

The Kalahari Bushmen of South Africa are good hunters, using a small bow and poisoned arrows. The primitive huts in which the Bushmen live open towards the rising sun and are hemidome-shaped. As game is very scarce and few vegetables available, families have to be limited, and the social rules are monogamous. If the children are born too quickly they are treated like kittens; the parents have to decide how many should be kept, and when the old folks grow helpless they are given a ration of food and permitted quietly to go to sleep and die. Otherwise they are a gentle, peaceful race, almost extinct. Their language is like no other tongue, but consists of quite a vocabulary and has a grammar of its own. Their skin is khaki color and falls in folds around their joints and in heavy wrinkles over the stomach, unless this happens to be distended after an extra good feast. Their hair is short, woolly, and crinkly, and their eyes and faces are pushed and in flat compared to other races. Although of very small stature, the Bushmen, like the Ituri forest pigmies, do not know fear even of large animals, such as elephants and lions. They are clever at making traps, and pride themselves on their hunting capabilities.

The buttocks of the women are often so over-developed that they are big enough for their husky babies to stand on when being taken for a ride. It is supposed that these pads of fat are nature's way of overcoming the lack of oil in any of their food. This same theory is sometimes applied to fat-tail sheep.

From the six-foot nine-inch Shilluk warriors, with all their virility and grace, to the woolly-headed pigmies or the seductive young maidens of the Congo, the races of Africa supply an endless field of variety for sculptural purposes. It caused me a pang of regret when I heard from Chicago that I must stop making any more types of the dark continent, and that I had already modelled more than were called for in our original scheme.

When I became engrossed, and under the spell of any absorbing problem, it was never possible to count heads and limit myself to any set program. Had I tried to envisage the entire plan after once giving my word to devote my whole time and energy to carrying it out, the enormity of it would have completely discouraged me. And so, after I had completed the Bushman and Pigmy families, the Shilluk warrior, the Senegalese drummer, the Sara dancing girl, the Mangbetu, Ubangi, Batwa, Abyssinian, Dahomeyan, Hamite, and Sudanese types, and many others, I had to call a halt on my African activities and turn my attention to the continent of Europe.

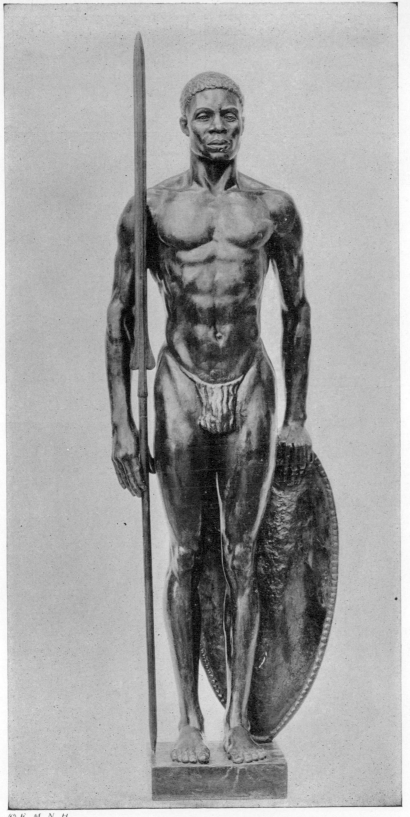

MASAI WARRIOR WITH TRIBAL SPEAR AND SHIELD

Black race of the central group. (Hall of Man)

MANGBETU TRIBE

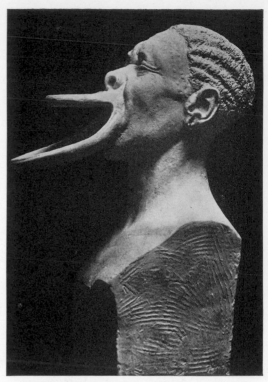

UBANGI "DUCK-BILLED" WOMAN

ZULU BELLE WITH CONICAL WOVEN HAIR AND
RAFFIA HEADDRESS

SUDANESE BEAUTY WITH FIVE SPIKES OF HAIR
AND CLAY COIFFURE

Europe and the Elusive Alpine

When the time came to study the Nordic, Alpine, and Mediterranean races, I was sent to London to work under the supervision of Sir Arthur Keith, collecting photographs of types at the Anthropological Institute and Royal College of Surgeons. He began his instructions by explaining the divisions of the Caucasian race in Europe.

The Nordic people are generally tall and well built, with rather regular features, fair hair and complexion, and heads rather longer than round. They live in the northern countries of Europe.

The central zone includes the race called "Alpine," living in the Alps, Carpathians, Pyrenees, and Russian steppes. Slavs, Bretons, Savoyards, Swiss Tyroleans, and southern Germans are also of the central zone. They are darker in hair and skin coloring than the Nordics, shorter in build, with round heads.

The southern zone is represented by the Mediterranean type, originally of North African origin. The type includes Italians, Southern French, Greeks, and Iberians.

I will leave the much-disputed subject of what is meant by the word "Aryan" to be fought out between expert anthropologists and Mr. Hitler. Perhaps the British and French diplomats of 1935 would gladly contribute their ideas on this subject.

When Sir Arthur was asked if he would pass judgment on my first models, he hesitated and said to Henry Field, who had introduced me, "But I never saw any of Miss Hoffman's work, how do I know she can model a head accurately?" Delighted with his honesty, I felt immediately that this slightly bowed head with keen eyes and gentle voice was a most sympathetic personality and an interesting type for sculpture.

"Well, Sir Arthur," said I, "if you would like to see me model a head in your presence before accepting the task of being my European censor, would you be willing to pose for me to make your own portrait? You must be quite familiar with the look of your own face, and able to judge of the likeness with accuracy."

"Oh! dear no," he answered, "I haven't any head for sculpture, and besides I really never have looked at myself."

"Surely once a day at least," I said, "for you certainly do not shave with your eyes shut."

This seemed to amuse him, and by a little teamwork with Henry Field we managed to persuade him to give me three sittings up in the loft of the Royal College of Surgeons. The weather was bitterly cold and damp, enough to freeze the marrow in one's bones. To add to my difficulties, the day of our first sitting produced one of the thickest of London's "pea-soup fogs." The sallow, yellow atmosphere was such that I had to rig up the stereopticon projector as an indirect top-light, by aiming it at the ceiling from a table placed beside the packing-case on which Sir Arthur was to pose. This powerful light burned through the fog sufficiently to enable me to start working. We huddled near the glowing coal stove, for the college has no steam-heat upstairs, and the *séances* were more a matter of endurance than anything else. Looking out over the dark streets, we could see the headlights of motors crawling about at snails' pace. Breathing was difficult. Sir Arthur was a patient and most entertaining sitter. When the portrait was completed, he agreed to be my guide, philosopher, and friend throughout the five years of the long undertaking, and now that the task is ended we are the best of friends and my gratitude to him is very sincere.

Doctor Malcolm of the Wellcome Historical Medical Museum was also a most helpful adviser and collaborator. He and I became great friends, for since 1921 I had always made pilgrimages to the Wellcome Museum to study its inexhaustible store of documents and models. During my first visit, I was so interested in drawing some wax and ivory figures of anatomy that I pretended not to hear the guard who quietly informed me that sketching without a permit was against the rules and that it was closing time. When he came back the third time, he very sternly asked me to accompany him to the director's office. I knew by his few well-chosen words that I was in for punishment. Closing my notebook, I very meekly followed him to Doctor Malcolm's office. When I explained that I was a student of sculpture and

PORTRAIT OF SIR ARTHUR KEITH, LONDON

(Hall of Man)

THE ELUSIVE ALPINE

(Hall of Man)

"GOD'S GIFT TO WOMEN"

Back of Nordic type. (Hall of Man)

had seldom found such a mine of information, he asked me to show him my drawings. They were of a series of embryonic models, and the section of a skull showing the pineal and pituitary glands and their surrounding neighborhood. He noted the name of Doctor Harvey Cushing at the side of a page with a list of questions to ask him. When Doctor Malcolm saw this, he closed the book and said "Are you a friend of Doctor Cushing?" I answered that I was. From that moment, the Wellcome Museum has extended to me the most cordial hospitality.

Sir Henry Wellcome, founder of the Wellcome Historical Medical Museum in London, selected the supplies and equipment for our travelling hospital kits; enough medical supplies were included to help many others on the long journey. He came over to Paris and spent the day at my studio, examining the plaster collection of my types before they went to the bronze foundry.

After our stay in England, Sam and I went to Hamburg, Berlin, Prague, Vienna, and Munich, studying in the museums and anthropological libraries and institutes of anatomy. Doctor Fischer, director of the Anthropological Institute, showed me over his modern installation at Dahlem and introduced me to a new race I had never heard of. "Do you know a Dinar when you see one?" he asked. "Oh, yes," I answered cheerfully, "Dinars are the currency we used in Yugo-Slavia." He looked at me quite horrified. "Dinars are a type of Middle European and I am myself a very typical example of this race!"

In spite of this break, we managed to discuss anthropology in German—mine was badly broken—and the fact that he was able to understand me and was amused at my mistakes made me feel more at ease. He presented me with his book on Hottentots and certain Polynesian cross-breeds, and gave me much valuable information that I needed.

In Prague, on my way to an appointment with a professor at the Anatomy Institute, I was deposited in front of a great doorway and told by my cabman, *"Da ist es."* I rang the bell, but no one answered. It was noon hour, and a group of fifteen or twenty young students were lounging about the steps laughing and smoking, and watching me curiously. Not wishing to miss my appointment, I pushed the heavy door and found to my surprise that it opened. I went in, and the great door slammed with a resounding crash behind me. Finding myself in an empty, eery hallway of gray marble, I called to ask if there were any one about—my voice echoed around the vaulted roof. I pushed another door and found myself in a room of death. Stretched out on marble slabs were a double row of cadavers, some half turned toward me, others with arms hanging over the slab, others in red-stained shrouds, twisted and contorted in death like some awful scene that one might visualize in a nightmare. It was the morgue. I was rooted to the spot and couldn't move; the silence was ghastly, there was no living soul anywhere.

When I could collect my dazed senses, I turned and walked to the entrance. Pulling the heavy door open, I went from the cloudy mists of the death-chamber into the harsh brilliance of daylight. The group of students must have noticed the pallor of my face for they all joined in a shout of laughter, mocking me for my mistake. Only the thickness of a brick wall separated this crowd of cynical youth from the silent rows of unclaimed dead. It was well, I thought, that their laughter could not disturb the company of pallid sleepers within the gates.

As I walked down the street, I noticed another building with many students coming out of the entrance hallway. This I found to be the Institute of Anatomy. The professor was waiting for me and I did not mention what had happened, for we had a long and difficult task ahead of us. His collection was most extraordinary and instructive, and I gathered a great deal of useful information for my work.

While in Vienna, after studying the collections at the museums and consulting with Doctor Weniger, director of the Institute of Anthropology, we attended a lecture by Baron Von Eickstedt on his recent travels in India and the Andaman Islands. We visited Madame Poller, whose late husband, a war-surgeon, had invented a very extraordinary process of casting from life in a material known as "Negocoll." This process enables one to make absolutely accurate casts without seams and therefore without retouching. We learned the technique of the process from Frau Poller, and later on in Munich from Doctor Strauss at the Anthropological Institute, who had been a collaborator of Doctor Poller's. In his laboratory, Doctor Strauss showed us how to make a cast from life of the complete head of a young woman who cheerfully submitted to the ordeal so that we might learn the method. Her short hair in permanent waves was completely covered as well as her face and ears. When the cast was made, the reproduction of the waves in her hair were as perfect as the features of her face. The process is used frequently in the Brain Surgery Institute of Vienna.

We stocked ourselves with a good supply of this material and took it with us all over the world, teaching staff-members of the various museums how to use it, in return for their assistance to us. This nearly always included space for a working studio, without which we would have been seriously handicapped. We never made any casts of heads, however, and only used the process to record the differences in foot and hand formation between the various races. These casts are exhibited in the scientific department of the Hall of Man.

The number of experts consulted on the subject of what constituted a pure Alpine type resulted in confusion and contradictions all along the line. Each anthropologist seemed to have his own pet idea about the elusive Alpine; so I put him at the end of my list and waited patiently until a consensus of opinion was reached three years later.

At last we decided upon a young man from the Bavarian Alps. His splendid strong physique had been admired by many Parisians and Londoners, for he was one of a troupe of dancers who travelled about with the operetta called "The White Horse Inn," which made a great hit in London and Paris. When I questioned my model about the medallion carved from an elk's horn, which is always worn on the chest strap that holds up the Bavarian *lederhosen,* he laughingly explained that this usually framed the photograph of the wearer's *bien aimée.* During the time that he posed for me, I noticed that the photograph was changed twice, and then omitted entirely. "For the sake of posterity," he mischievously remarked, "perhaps we better leave the medallion a blank!"

I had been most fortunate in finding in New York the man to pose for the Nordic type, for he had the best and most evenly developed physique that I had ever seen. His full-length figure in bronze shows his muscles in action on one side, with the right arm raised and fist clenched. The other arm is relaxed and the hand open, in contrast. When I asked him for his history he replied:

"Well, you see, I've won all the cups they offer for the best body proportions and physical development, so I decided to make a book of all the best photographs that have been taken of me. Now the book has such a sale I don't have to work any more. I live in Brooklyn and the girls call me 'God's gift to women.' "

"Well," I answered, raising my eyebrows just a little, "that would not be a bad title for my book, if I ever write one, on 'The Races of Man!' "

Maharajas in London

Before starting out on the world tour, it was arranged that I should meet the various Indian maharajas and princes, who were in London attending the Round Table Conference.

Through the kindness of Lady Reading, my first appointment was made to take breakfast with Colonel Haksar of Gwalior at the Savoy. His days were so full that the early morning was the only time he could see me. He was directing many of the activities of the conference, and was acting as regent *pro tem* for the principality of Gwalior. He took a great deal of trouble to assist me in every way. The son of this learned pandit of Kashmir was sent to me to pose for the statue of my "Praying Kashmiri." His handsome head and sleek, strong body were ideal for the purpose, although the cross-legged pose was rather an ordeal. The correct posture for meditation should give a perfectly straight line from the back of the head down over the shoulders and buttocks to the ground; the hands are placed together, one upon the other, over the solar plexus.

My appointments with maharajas were generally at tea-time, and although I had often to wait an hour before "His Highness" would

THE MOST NOBLE MARQUIS OF READING, VICEROY OF INDIA

Major-General H. H. Farzand-i-Khas-i-Daulat-i-Inglishia, Mansur-i-Zaman Amir-ul-Umra Maharajadhiraja, Rajesh-war Sri Maharaja-i-Rajagan, Sir Bhupindar Singh Mahindar Bahadur, G.C.S.I., G.C.I.E., G.C.V.O., G.B.E., A.D.C., Maharaja of Patiala

The premier Sikh prince and the ruler of the largest state in the Punjab. His subjects number one and a half millions, and his territory is some 6000 square miles in extent. A soldier, sportsman, and Imperial statesman. Served on the Staff of the Indian Expeditionary Force during the European War. Represented India at the Imperial War Conference and the Imperial War Cabinet in 1918. Also one of India's representatives at the League of Nations in 1925. Has been five times elected Chancellor of the Chamber of Princes

HIS HIGHNESS THE YUVURAJ OF PATIALA

Portrait made in Paris by M. H.

appear, they were always most cordial and surprisingly interested in the project of my visit to India to study the most representative types from the various localities.

My first encounter with an Indian prince was my meeting with his Highness, the Maharaja of Patiala, in his suite of apartments in the Savoy Hotel in London. An entire floor had been transformed into an Indian residence. Outside every door stood a bronze-faced sentinel in splendid native costume. I was conducted to his Highness's sitting room by his British military attaché, and invited to make myself comfortable, as I might have to wait some time for my audience.

After nearly an hour the door opened and a magnificent apparition in a mauve-and-silver turban and long coat and jodhpurs walked up to me. "Forgive my delay, but my conference with Mr. Lloyd George detained me—I could not get here sooner. Now we are free to talk."

His Highness had been informed of the purpose of my visit, and his own personal interest in the study of racial types was a fortunate background for me to work on. I tried to outline as rapidly as possible the plan of our proposed trip to India. My host listened attentively. We were both seated on a huge sofa. The situation struck me as slightly fantastic. His over-life-size eyes had a penetrating, hypnotic gaze; they never moved aside or noticed anything but my own, which seemed to be controlled by their intensity. My mind was busy detecting the signs of a new world called India, for in a single face one can often discover suggestions of a whole race.

"You know Sir John Woodroffe," I ventured as an aside, "or perhaps his *nom de plume* of Arthur Avalon is better known in India? He married my husband's sister."

My host leaned forward, instantly more human and un-selfconscious of his own power and importance. "Of course I do! What a brilliant mind he has! Where is he? How is he? I hear he has been ill. Tell me about him. I had so counted upon him to carry on a great work of translating ancient Vedic manuscripts. There are only two or three men left in the world who have such authentic knowledge of our people and our religion." To hear this Indian stranger speaking such fluent English was rather a surprise. The words seemed incongruous, coming from his extraordinary foreign mask.

The whole atmosphere had changed—we could now go on indefinitely; our mutual admiration of Sir John's accomplishments was an "open sesame." Hours slipped by. I had come at five o'clock; there were interruptions as the time went on; the British attaché would come in to announce that his Highness's guests had started to arrive—the banquet was announced for eight o'clock and it was now seven forty-five. A wave of the hand, a nod of the head dismissed the interruptions.

My host was now immersed in the idea of how to select the best representatives of his country—what itinerary we should follow in our travels.

"When you come to India, you must come to visit me at Patiala."

"With pleasure," I answered, rising to take my leave. "Your Highness has been generous today in giving me so much time and information. Is Patiala your country place in India?"

He looked at me, puzzled, but smiling. "Yes," he said, drawing his fingers over his silky black beard which was rolled tightly into a net under his chin. "But just what do you mean when you say 'country place?'"

"Oh, where you live in summer. May I ask what city it is near, so I may be sure to find it?" I said, apparently completely vague, but feeling that somehow a joke might ease off my exit.

"I think you will have no difficulty in locating me," he smilingly replied, "as my principality is one of the largest in India, and I happen to have over a million subjects under my rule."

"Pardon me!" was all I could say, "but your Highness must enjoy making any one feel as insignificant as I do at this moment. . . ."

"Not at all," my host replied, "you may enjoy the joke as much as I do, for as you walk down the hallway you can see the crowd of guests who have been kept waiting because I found the reason of your visit more important than my next engagement."

This gave me courage. "Your Highness will not forget to notify me if I may come to see you in Paris?"

"No, I promise, and what is more, I shall ask my son to pose for you. He is the best type of Sikh you could find in India."

And so we parted. Need I add that on my way out I *fled* past the reception hall!

Two months later the Maharaja of Patiala permitted me to make a portrait of his son, the Yuvuraj, while they were visiting in Paris. I motored over to the Crillon Hotel and fetched his Highness and two armed guards, who never left his side. The Yuvuraj was so tall (six feet four inches without his turban) that he had to fold up his height to enable him to climb into the front seat of my little Oakland touring car. He was only twenty-one years of age, so the adventure of being driven informally to an out-of-the-way corner of Paris (not even to be found on a map) amused him thoroughly. The armed guards sat in the back seat, and I confess that the responsibility of my precious passenger weighed rather heavily on me. To add to my concern, a light rain had left the streets as slippery as glass. As our little house makes the end of an "impasse," we always have to turn at the entrance to the blind alley and go in backwards to the garage under the house. On this occasion, however, I explained to my eminent passenger that instead of spreading red carpets or scattering jasmin flowers on his path, we would honor him by driving up to the studio "head first."

His Highness stepped out, laughing at the quaint aspect of the little row of villas and gardens. Tied to my neighbor's gate there was a shaggy little horse, harnessed to a two-wheeled cart. "This for 1931 is indeed an unusual sight," he said as he tickled the pony's ribs with his beautiful cane, which ended in an opal handle as large as a pear. My neighbors hung out of their windows at the sight of this magnificent visitor with a mauve chiffon turban the end of which stood up and waved in the air a foot above his head, and whose necklaces and earrings of pearls sparkled in the sunlight. After a two-hour sitting we had tea and a little American music to reward his patience, in the music-room of our house next door to the studio. Some of the characteristics I had noticed in his father's face were exaggerated in the young prince. At twenty-one his personality was clearly marked with lines which indicated the possibility of his future struggles and potentialities, both inherited and self-made.

A year and a half later, when we were in New Delhi, I had difficulty in recognizing my eminent sitter, for he had grown a short black beard and moustache which entirely changed his appearance. Both he and his father, the Maharaja, are *Sikhs,* a high caste in India, who never shave or cut their hair. In consequence they coil the hair under the turban and roll up their beards in a fine-mesh net which is suspended from each ear. This forms a round black mass under the chin, framing their bronzed faces very effectively, hiding the line of the jaw-bones and chin and concentrating attention on the eyes, which seem to have an unlimited range of expression in most of the Indians that I knew.

My neighbors in the Villa Chauvelot must have wondered at the constant procession of types from all corners of the earth that would constantly call at my studio: Chinese and Japanese, Malays, and Hawaiians, Indian princes and Nepalese princes and princesses, glittering Rolls Royce cars that fairly snorted their disdain at being obliged to enter such a modest neighborhood, and be forced to back out ignominiously, then turn around and back in again to await their owners, who would be quite willing to explore the garden and house and drink their tea by an open fire as informally as any simple traveller from our own home town.

Asia, Africa, and Oceania in Paris

During the months of the Exposition Coloniale in the Bois de Vincennes, we had many amusing adventures. Through the ministers and consuls of the different countries, passes and permits were procured which allowed me to select native subjects at the exhibition and temporarily kidnap them from their reservations, motor them to my studio at nine A.M. for a morning's *séance,* and return them at one o'clock to their village at the Exposition. This was strenuous work, for the Bois de Vincennes was at the extreme opposite end of Paris from where we lived. Luckily my old car knew the way so well that I could study my varied passengers during the journey and be sure the car would find its way home quite automatically.

At the Cambodian settlement I had many rare opportunities to study the Indo-Chinese subjects at first hand. Especially interesting were the visits to the dancing pavilion where the troupe of temple dancers would pose for me and show me all the practice steps of their dances and the unbelievable suppleness of their delicate fingers, which they could bend backwards and sideways at will in endless positions of grace.

The Dutch Pavilion offered me unusual opportunities of study; the Balinese dancers were only too happy to have the diversion of a visitor, and I was able to make many valuable studies of their dances. Through the kind interest and assistance of Mr. Loudon, the Dutch minister, permits for the Netherlands section were given me, and I selected a fine young sailor from the island of Madura to pose for me with his fighting cock. The next year when we visited the Dutch East Indies we met some of our friends from the Exposition, and by studying all these types in Paris under reasonable conditions, in my own studio, I was able to recognize characteristics and work much more surely and swiftly when I reached their native land than if I had arrived in these distant islands without any preliminary study and preparation.

One moonlight summer evening there was given at the African section of the Exposition one of the most dramatic and unusual performances I had ever witnessed.

A double line of white shrouded Somalis mounted on camels led up to the entrance gates of the French Colonial building. Going through this to the huge inner courtyard, the audience took their seats in a hollow square formed around a central raised platform. The earthen walls and high square tower made a remarkable African architectural setting to the scene—and above it all, the full moon illuminating a mass of floating clouds.

High up in the square tower the tom-toms began to beat their barbaric rhythms and African singers joined in a sort of chanting wail. In single file the ebony dancers came in from the second court-yard and took their positions around the high platform—spotlights illuminated the stage—the music in the clouds ceased and the musicians on the stage began their wild pounding and fanatical drumming. The black warriors jumped into the glaring light and each group outdid their predecessors in variety and agility of savage dancing. Spears flashed in the moonlight, shouts of wild ecstasy rent the air, and every one present forgot completely that they were in the heart of Paris.

For two hours those of us who had been lucky enough to be invited to this event knew that we had heard the pulse of darkest Africa, transplanted but authentic, a direct life-current from the jungle.

To describe the activity of a typical day at the Villa Chauvelot, let us choose a radiant morning in June during the Exposition Coloniale. Nine o'clock found me at the service entrance of the Balinese Restaurant. I presented my credentials to the manager and a boy, Number Eleven, was selected as my model from the island of Madura, north of Bali.

This slim little fellow, in white duck uniform, with a jaunty batik cotton wound about his head, climbed happily into the front seat beside me and was told by his manager, who fortunately understood French, that he was to go with me, to do whatever I asked, to stand still and, when I finished work, he was to return with me to the restaurant at one o'clock, not later. As soon as we started out of the enclosure of the Exposition grounds his excitement was intense. He chatted gaily in spite of knowing that I understood not one word. When we passed the Jardin des Plantes and were halted by the traffic, he obviously wished to climb out and explore. With one hand I had to hold him firmly in the car, while steering with the other, until we could speed up and cover the ground between the Seine and the fifteenth *arrondissement*. On arrival, I turned him over to Sam, who by gestures and signs managed to strip him of his clothes and make him feel at home by offering him one of his own native batiks for a loin cloth. A cigarette and a few smiles were all the preliminaries needed, before he was able to assume the pose of my figure, which

. N. H., photo. National Geographic Society.

COCK FIGHT. TYPE FROM ISLAND OF MADURA,
NEAR BALI, AND FROM BORNEO ON THE RIGHT

Two other figures from Bali and Java are with this
group in bronze. (Hall of Man)

CAMBODIAN DANCER OF ANKHOR
Gold bronze statuette by M. H.

SAMUEL GRIMSON, M. H., AND HIS HIGHNESS "KIKI" OF SIAM IN GARDEN OF THE VILLA CHAUVELOT, PARIS, JUST BEFORE THE TRIP ROUND THE WORLD

The tiles of black and turquoise blue we brought from Tunis, and with the assistance of an Arab mason lent to me by the "Mosquée de Paris," we built them into a wall-fountain. In the line across the front of the basin one black square was intentionally left out, as a good-luck symbol; perfection might attract the "evil ye." *Seulement Allah peut créer la perfection"*—so decreed my Arab mason

MADAME EAMES AS ELSA IN "LOHENGRIN"

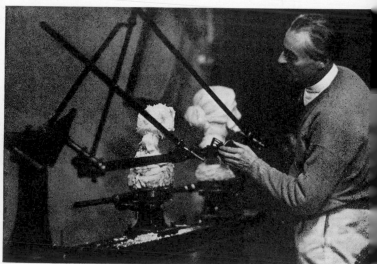

SAMUEL GRIMSON REDUCING A LIFE–SIZE HEAD TO ONE–HALF LIFE SIZE BY PANTOGRAPH

he studied from a small model, and most conscientiously held his position while he watched with sparkling wide eyes the progress of the life-size figure. This program was repeated day after day until the work was completed.

By the time I reached home again after safely depositing my charge with his manager, I found the afternoon model already waiting at my studio. A hurried lunch and then to work again. This time it was a Chinese student from Shanghai, selected by their embassy in Paris as being a very typical representative of the yellow race. To keep these ever-changing types distinct and separate in my mind, I had to develop a system of water-tight compartments into which each one could be locked away in my head and studied quite independently of each other.

By five o'clock, we all felt ready to stop work. Tea always revived us and an hour of relaxation was *de rigueur*. A motor would roll up to the door and our friend, Mme. Emma Eames, would come in to see how things were going. Her smiling and beautiful face always made life look better, and many were the peals of laughter that she could evoke by her terse and often vituperative remarks about the world's affairs and social doings, from which we were entirely cut off most of the time. Zarraga, the Mexican painter, often came to see us, and nearly every evening before seven, Mons. Rudier, the master founder, would come to report on the progress of the bronzes in his foundry. For many months there were sixty men kept busy in his establishment preparing the plaster-moulds, sand-moulds, casting the metal, assembling and chasing the bronzes and finally patining them, under my direction, to suggest the variety of tones and textures of all the races, so that monotony would be avoided in the final presentation of one hundred subjects.

After tea, Sam and I would usually go back to the studio, which was lighted by two great indirect reflector searchlights. He would continue the delicate and expert task of reducing the life-size plaster heads to half life-size, on a carefully adjusted pantograph machine, which demanded the utmost skill and patience to manipulate. During the silent, peaceful evenings, I would work from memory on the figures for which models had posed during the day.

This routine of concentrated effort was kept up month after month and year after year, both before and after we had made our several journeys over Europe, Africa, and around the world. It was necessary to work at "concert pitch" to accomplish the huge task, and the miracle was that we were given the physical strength to endure such continuous strain until the Hall of Man was completed and installed. We were often forced to overdraw our account of nervous energy, and I felt the premonition of eventually being declared a complete physical bankrupt. The mysterious power of recuperation must have come at night, through the benediction of sleep, and through the realization that our efforts were counted upon and believed in by those who had entrusted us with a great task.

IV

ROUND THE WORLD

Packing with a Vengeance

When we started on our "Round the World" trip in September, 1931, we crossed from New York to San Francisco, and sailed from there to Hawaii. The party in this expedition consisted of my husband, Samuel Grimson; Miss Gretchen Green, our secretary; and Jean de Marco, who cast my clay models into plaster.

Six months before we started on this world journey, I began to collect information about the best means of transportation and storage of our supplies. Luckily, I found in Paris a quantity of strong metal cans with metal covers and handles, left over from the war. These we filled with plaster of Paris, soldering a sheet of tin over the amount of material necessary to cast a single head or a one-third life-size figure; then we added this same amount on top of the tin and sealed the next compartment, so that it would not be necessary to expose more than a small amount of plaster at a time to the humidity of the tropics. In other cans we packed the clay and plasteline. In iron canteen trunks we packed the rolls of lead pipe, wire, rope, and lengths of one-quarter inch square irons for making armatures and reinforcing the plaster casts; bundles of hemp and rags; mechanic's soap; tins of green soap and oil; scrubbing-brushes and cans of disinfectants. All the necessary tools were included in the equipment.

The preparations for this last long journey necessitated, among other things, the concentrating of luggage into the smallest possible number of valises and metal trunks. There were twenty-seven of them with us as a constant burden of responsibility. These containers were light enough to be carried by one man, and two of them could easily be slung over a saddle-pack. Drawing-materials, cameras, and moving-picture equipment had to be hermetically sealed in metal containers to protect them from mildew.

Medical kits, which included a sharp scalpel and the disinfecting crystals used in cases of snakebite or poisonous insects, were our constant companions. The fantastic extremes of heat and cold and the unhygienic conditions of many of the countries in which we travelled made illness an inevitable part of our program which had to be accepted and endured. We can certainly consider ourselves most fortunate to have returned safe and well to our various homes, having penetrated into the fastnesses of many a jungle, where malaria and poisonous snakes might easily have put an end to our ambitions and activities.

The variety of experience and the general flavor of adventure throughout the past few years have created such a panorama of events that it is difficult to draw from this fund the "high spots" which might give the reader a consecutive and convincing impression of what "Head Hunting for the Field Museum of Chicago" and the interpretation of character by sculpture really comprises.

Representatives of Marshall Field & Company in Paris arranged through the American Express Company to ship the metal containers to the following ports: Honolulu; Yokohama; Taku, China; Hong Kong; Buleleng, Bali; Batavia, Java; Singapore, Malay Straits; Calcutta; and Colombo, Ceylon. They were to be held in a safe dry place until our arrival; in some cases the shipments were sent three months ahead of our departure from Paris.

In every port we found the Express Company eager to co-operate, and their services were invaluable both in handling the shipments and in securing for us reliable and intelligent guides and interpreters.

We travelled in more than forty types of ships, including ocean liners, oriental coast steamers, South Sea outriggers, canoes, and Chinese junks. We passed the nights in every variety of hotel, castle, palace, wayside inn, and thatched hut, sometimes sleeping on a carpet of tropical palm leaves, or on a seaweed mattress, or even in a broken-down motorcar. Having shared native baths, diets, and delicacies with our various hosts, we were initiated into many interesting and startling customs and were permitted to enjoy their unfailing hospitality and protection.

Hawaii—Sailing Westward to the East

Moonlight, flowers, and cordial hospitality welcomed us to the island of Oahu. Our good friends, the James Wilders, helped me to find a suitable studio. This may seem an easy matter to one who does not know the awful handicaps of modelling in places where the light constantly changes, or the sun suddenly strikes the clay head and transforms it into a mass of glare and dark shadows.

We motored from one end of the town to the other, visiting every one who might suggest a possible solution. Being a tropical resort, Honolulu is built for protection from heat, with the usual low overhanging roofs to give shade to the verandahs and half darkness to the rooms within—all quite impossible for the purpose of a studio. The modern office buildings where space was available were so filled with glare and heat that these also proved useless.

At last, after trying even palm-leaf huts with "lean-tos" at the rear, I went in desperation to a painter who had a small studio with a corrugated iron roof and one good big window. He very kindly accepted my bribe to move out and take a holiday for two weeks, and I moved in and began my studies of Sargent Kohonomoku, the younger brother of the renowned "Duke," who had won the world championship at the Olympic games for swimming and surf-board riding. The five brothers of this family are all remarkable types of physical prowess. David was chosen by a certain scientist as the best specimen of Polynesian, to be represented in a collection of anthropology. His experience, however, had left him and his brothers bitterly opposed to ever submitting themselves again to any visiting "museum artists"!

David had innocently agreed to allow himself to be cast into plaster from head to foot, and when he was halfway buried in this rigid, hardening and hot mass, with only his chest and head left exposed, the casters had gone for their lunch hour and told him to be patient and not move or crack the mould! By the time they returned, he had made up his mind that he must keep to his contract, but also fight for his life. When the plaster covered his strong chest, he cleverly took deep long breaths before he felt the plaster hardening and in this way broke the inner wall apart while it was still soft, thereby giving his diaphragm the necessary leeway to expand and contract inside the mould. One can easily imagine the gruesome impression such an experience would leave on the mind of a Hawaiian athlete, and in fact on any one to whom he related his story.

Every effort to lure any member of his family to my studio failed. Finally, I decided to take a few swimming lessons on Waikiki Beach, to be nearer the surf-board riders, for I was sure that the pose of one of these men would be my choice for representing a fine type of Polynesian.

The scenes on this much advertised beach would make good copy for scenario writers of the era B.C. (Before Censors). The outrigger-canoe club also supplied plenty of picturesque material.

While chatting with the "beach boys"—the bronzed Apollos who seem such a menace and lure to the pale-faced visiting ladies—I was able to meet Sargent Kohonomoku and talk with him about the technique of swimming and surf-board riding. He consented to do all his best aquatic stunts for us. Moving-pictures and stills were taken, and after reassuring him and his brother David that my purpose in asking him to pose included a guarantee that no plaster-casting was to be even mentioned, much less resorted to as a means of recording his bodily conformation, we began work at once and the result is to be seen in the "Bronze Surf Rider" at Field Museum.

As I stated before, we never did make any casts on heads or bodies of my models, except in the special cases of hands and feet and ears of the varied races, to show the physical differences, and to make records of "mudras," hand-gestures, and the curious effect of tree-climbing on the feet of aboriginal tribes. The most extraordinary formations of toes and muscle development result from constantly gripping the rough tree trunks. These casts and many others of different races, showing the use of the hands in eating, sewing, the use of chopsticks, etc., are displayed in the adjoining room in the Hall of Man together with the collection of transparent colored photographs of racial types on glass taken by my husband.

With the helpful collaboration of the Bishop Museum of Honolulu,

HAWAIIAN SURF–BOARD RIDER, LIFE–SIZE FIGURE, HALL OF MAN

Skimming over the foam on the long swift currents of Waikiki waves, surf-board riders develop an
amazing sense of balance and acrobatic agility

THE FIVE BROTHERS KOHONO-
MOKU OF WAIKIKI BEACH,
HAWAII

BRONZE PORTRAIT OF SAMOAN WARRIOR WITH HEAD-
KNIFE OVER HIS SHOUDER   (HALL OF MAN)

TYPICAL HAWAIIAN SWIMMER OF SPLENDID PHYSIQ
"IT'S TOASTED"

I was able to study a great variety of local Polynesian types, as well as Chinese, Japanese, and Samoans, for the population of Honolulu consists of a very mixed collection of nationalities.

One of the surprises of Hawaii was to find, at the remote end of the island of Oahu, a great stone temple dedicated to the Mormon religion. The adjacent villages were entirely made up of Samoans transported from their home island in the southern Pacific and converted to this sect. Some of the men of this Samoan community were the finest specimens of physical development that I found in any part of the globe.

A young Samoan posed for me with his ancestral war knife, which had a big hook at the end, with notches to represent the number of heads cut off. His father may have added a notch or two to the family heirloom, but he himself was outwardly, if not naturally, a peaceful, industrious member of the large Samoan colony at Laie. He performed an extraordinary war dance, during which he whirled this knife in the air, jumped under it, and caught it behind his back. Sam was able to get a fine movie of this performance.

To find this colony of transplanted Polynesians living in the shadow and under the influence of Mormon missionaries, gave one a sensation of incongruity not easy to describe. Their women wear the traditional Eve-destroying cotton dresses, like the Hawaiians, passed on by the wives of our early New England "uplifters." The Samoans live in native grass huts, raised up from the ground about three feet on wooden posts. The walls are of palm-leaves which allow air circulation. They sleep on straw mats and eat chiefly taro-root and raw fish.

In view of the fact that polygamy is *not* now practised by these transplanted Mormons of Hawaii, it was amusing to hear that the most famous King of Hawaii (*non*-Mormon) was named Kamehameha the First, meaning "lonely, lonely man!" and that he had married eight times, perhaps trying to live down the suggestion of his name!

In the trail of wandering missionaries, one finds in certain South Sea islands as well that the female natives all wear these most appallingly ugly cotton dresses and "swing-clears." Tuberculosis in the

South Seas has resulted in alarming proportions, for the frequent rain-showers soak these cotton dresses, and the natives have to let them dry on their backs as they continue their daily tasks until the next downpour. In certain seasons, showers occur six or eight times a day. The naked natives have grown accustomed to the exposure of the skin, through many generations. They derive strength and energy from the sunlight, and in most cases have kept their race alive by this natural force and hygiene of the elements. In one group of South Pacific islands I was told by an explorer that the race was almost extinct owing to just these causes.

The native Hawaiians have a general diet of raw fish, which they catch by standing on rocks or canoes and throwing spears into the water. They then dive in after their catch or pull back the spear. which is attached to a light rope.

One of the delicacies of the island of Oahu is the section of tentacle of the octopus known as "squid." The squid is caught by the Hawaiians by hand; the man grabs the octopus under the water and holds on until the tentacles are wrapped around the arm tightly. When the pressure is sufficiently intense, he lifts it out of the water and sinks his teeth into the head of the octopus just between the eyes (this being the one vulnerable spot), which instantly kills the beast, and the tentacles relax their deadly grip.

This specialty adds variety to the usual food regimen, which consists of bread-fruit and endless quantities of *poi*—a pounded, soggy sort of dough, the charms of which none of us could understand or enjoy. Local pineapples, however, are so luxuriant and splendid that one can indulge in this refreshment beyond any established medical limitations, without any ill effects. They are as different in flavor and tenderness from what we usually know in the eastern States as "pine-apples" as sunshine is from a London fog.

While in Honolulu we met an eminent member of the Maori race of New Zealand, who was willing to pose for us in native costume consisting of a grass skirt and a huge flat war-knife carved from a heavy slab of jade, about fifteen inches long and guaranteed not to bend when used to crack the neck of your opponent.

There were some fine specimens of racial types from the island of

Tahiti, who also submitted to our camera and measuring compass. All these "slow-motion," big-eyed Polynesians have no idea of time or of keeping their appointments, so endless delays and difficulties beset our path, which was laid out on the "American plan" of high-pressure production.

Included in our instructions, however, was the wise counsel of Doctor Laufer in Chicago: *"Do not try to hustle the East."* The general impression of Honolulu is a sort of transplantation of mid-Victorian New England traditions, horse-hair sofas, rocking chairs, clothing, and mental point of view. One senses in the Americans, as well as in the Hawaiians, the absence of any appreciation or need of art in any form. Nature has been so lavish in the beauty she has bestowed upon the island that the gorgeous flowers have taken the place of painting; birds and waterfalls supply enough music, and rocks very adequately take the place of sculpture.

The last five years only have seen an awakening consciousness of the fact that Art is possibly the record of a people as well as of their feather caps, but the missionaries have destroyed all the idols, gods, and other carvings of the former natives. It is, therefore, all the more to the credit of one of the most important families, headed by the Dowager Mrs. Cook, that, single-handed in the face of great apathy, they have designed and built the Academy of Art and stocked it with their own beautiful art possessions. They are adding to it constantly, and the impression given is one of great discrimination for beauty and distinguished presentation.

Japan and Hokkaido

Long before our arrival in Japan, Doctor Laufer had written to his good friend, Count Hyashi, who was attached to the Imperial Council. This distinguished person, who knew of the scientific collections and activities of the Field Museum, was eager to render us all possible assistance. Having ascertained from our embassy that we were expected to arrive on a certain day, and knowing that our luggage would include many metal cases of rather mysterious supplies, as well as valuable scientific equipment, Count Hyashi dispatched his personal representative from Tokyo to meet us on board our steamer before we landed at Yokohama.

This suave and polite gentleman appeared as a complete surprise to us, knocking at our cabin door at seven A.M., just as we were docking. There were plenty of war rumors and alarms, and we had many qualms as to how we were going to pass our twenty-seven trunks through the Japanese customs. The preparations for war between Japan and China were quite evident, and we had been warned in Honolulu of probable complications for our proposed travels.

Our unexpected but most welcome visitor turned out to be a high official in the Japanese navy. We formed in line, each one of us packed into a rickshaw with as many bags and bundles as he could carry. The little procession followed our Japanese leader, passing all the other mere travellers at a quick trot and stopping at the customs office. Here the notice read that the bureau would not open before nine A.M.—and it was only seven-thirty. The cold, damp wind was blowing a sharp mist into our faces and the outlook was not too cheery. Our leader, however, produced a magic key, opened doors, returned with bowing and obedient clerks carrying great seals and ink pads. These were stamped on all our bags and trunks and, with much bowing and smiling, we were ushered to a waiting omnibus and comfortably transported to Tokyo—bags, trunks, and all—in the best Japanese manner.

Arriving at the Imperial Hotel, we were informed that the peculiar low-swung ceilings and dark, narrow hallways were specially designed to withstand earthquakes, and that this hotel was one of the few buildings that remained standing after the great earthquake in 1927. To be sure, on entering the dining room one had a slight feeling of *mal de mer,* for the floor rises in waves and swells, giving the tables a rather cockeyed appearance, which to newcomers is slightly disconcerting. After a while, however, one is grateful for small favors in these zones of upheaval, and so long as the earth remained quiet one was thankful not to be obliged to put storm-racks on the tables.

The first days in Tokyo were spent meeting the American and Japanese officials. Luckily for us, the director of Saint Luke's American Hospital, as well as the chief nurse, were old friends of my sister, Mrs. Draper. The atmosphere of real human interest in this great institution was very extraordinary, and both Sam and I are deeply indebted to members of the Japanese staff for most expert medical and surgical care, for we both were in need of it.

I managed to pick up some of the unemployed oriental microbes, and by good fortune and the work of X-ray specialists was prevented from what might have developed into a much more serious infection and the probable loss of my left arm. All's well that ends well, and after five weeks of treatment the microbes decided to give up and move to some one else who might give them a more friendly habitat.

During our entire stay we were enabled to study types under the guidance of Doctor Rudolfe Teusler and Miss Christine Nuno of Saint Luke's Hospital. Groups of subjects were collected and our needs explained and interpreted to them in a most helpful manner. The operating room in the unfinished building of the new hospital was fitted up as a temporary studio. By nailing boards around the allotted space and installing a stove and a charcoal brazier, we were able to keep out most of the bitter cold, but the high winds whistled through the cement hallways and shook our improvised partitions. We made careful studies of the various models. There were Japanese ladies, doctors and scholars, sailors, coolies, and every age of local resident. Many were the amusing incidents that occurred in this improvised shelter. When I could not work on the life-sized portraits, we made "Negocoll" casts on the hands, feet, and ears of the various victims to show the variations of form in the different races.

The first evening introduction to Japanese methods of living was a personally conducted dinner-party to a typical Japanese restaurant. The weather was cold and penetrating. Our host omitted to warn us of the local custom of removing shoes when entering the house; so that when we arrived half frozen at the remote little restaurant, it was the last straw to be forced to abandon our footgear at the entrance and glide over the ice-cold, highly polished floors in thin silk stockings!

Upstairs we went, through courtyards and around balconies into a private latticed chamber where a diminutive and beautifully gowned little Japanese waitress bowed and bowed and invited us in sign language to seat ourselves on chilly grass mats on the floor. The low black table was only a foot high and there were no chairs or foot-warmers in sight! The curious meal was prepared before our eyes, on a charcoal stove, and we felt immersed in the Orient.

Our host had lived so long in Japan that none of these details impressed him as unusual, but a few furtive glances of amazement were exchanged between Sam and myself. Hot *sake* we decided would be our only salvation; so after we had tried every conceivable position of folding up our cramped and congealed legs under ourselves, with small success, we indulged in enough of the hot national beverage to anæsthetize the pangs of our discomfort. The next day we both had bad colds and felt pretty rocky, though glad of our initiation.

After this experience of "live and learn," we never left our hotel without taking a pair of extra woollen socks in our pockets, which we stealthily slipped on after the inevitable doorman removed our shoes. At certain temples, a pair of straw mules or old cotton bags were sometimes supplied to assist the visitor in his long wanderings over damp floors and endless outside courtyards and stone steps.

We felt thoroughly transplanted and isolated from all other races except the yellow . . . when one evening we were astonished to find ourselves completely surrounded in the hotel dining room by darkest Africa. There was a delegation from Ethiopia in full native regalia, solemnly talking over the political situation in English and Ethiopian. Their handsome ebony countenances glistened in the candlelight and made the Japanese hosts appear like pallid ghosts from another planet. Perhaps the Kings of Kings was foresighted enough to establish useful contacts in Japan in case of future needs. It was evident that there was a very cordial and solid *entente* between the representatives of Japan and these Ethiopians, who had the unmistakable dignity and aristocracy of an ancient race.

In the late afternoons we would drive about the city, and one day I visited the Omon Gate of Tokyo, which has watched the long procession of oriental beauty weave its way to endless nocturnal revelry throughout the years. "Abandon all hope, ye that enter here," for most of them walk in never to return to the same life that they have left behind, and no one knows how much blood it costs. The girls of Japan are brought up by the severe rule of their parents, and when the family income threatens hunger or privations, the girls are often sold by their parents to the proprietors of the "Houses of Pleasures" on the other side of the Omon Gate. The average price, I was told, is equivalent to one hundred and fifty American dollars, if the girl is attractive.

In Yokohama, the Yoshiwara is a famous rendezvous of night lovers. I was told that their "lovely ladies" were generally bought from farmers living in the north of Japan and that the best time to acquire female beauties—known as "Jupus"—at low cost, was after an earthquake, when thousands of homes and habitations had been wiped off the map. This was the first time I had ever realized that earthquakes had business advantages. "It is an ill wind," indeed, "that blows nobody any good."

The whole idea of women being slaves to the men is accepted by every one as an inescapable and everlasting tradition. Self-sacrifice is looked upon as essential in women, just as bravery is considered an important quality in men.

The inmates of these *Kashizashikis* are forced to submit to a weekly medical examination. I was informed that seven per cent of each one's earnings is turned over to the police; sixty-five per cent is taken by the proprietor. A monument was erected after the earthquake of 1923 to the memory of all those "slaves of pleasure" who had perished in the terrible fires that destroyed the whole district of the Yoshiwara in Yokohama.

The education a girl needs to become a Geisha-girl includes the arts of social behavior, the technique of the traditional dances, the arrangement of flowers in the house or on the table, the make-up of her masklike countenance, the tricks of elaborate hairdressing and costumes, and finally the learning of a repertory of songs which she should be able to sing when some eager client is willing to pay an extra fee for entertainment at the tea-house. The ritual of serving tea often makes a mere foreigner feel very awkward and rather like a "bull in the china shop." It is a ceremony which often assumes the dignity of a religious performance, and the passing of the fragile bowl of tea from one hand to another is done with almost as much reverence as if it contained a sacrament.

When we had completed our work in Tokyo, our courteous friend, Count Hyashi, came to lunch with us and asked what we would care to see before leaving the city. We expressed a desire to attend a ceremony with the priests at the Buddhist Shogun temple—and be permitted to take a moving picture of this ceremony! This was immediately arranged, and we were driven with official escort to the temple. There the long procession of shaven-headed priests and nuns marched across the courtyard, led by the high priest in saffron robes, with a white silk handkerchief folded around his neck. It was almost impossible to distinguish the nuns from the priests.

Tributes were paid to the Shogun's last resting-place, one hundred feet beneath the ground, in a well with a stone and lacquer shrine covering it. During the ceremony inside the temple, the priests and nuns formed a hollow square, chanting and murmuring their prayers in unison. The high priest before the altar sifted incense into the braziers, and made cryptic signs with a little wooden wand in his hand. As the clouds of smoke rose and enveloped the gilded statue of Buddha, the chanting grew louder, and the ritual terminated with us all kneeling and bowing low before the great Deity of the Orient.

Suddenly the high priest turned towards us and beckoned us to come up to the high altar. Rather astonished but obedient, we went through the ranks of monks in single file. When we reached the high priest, he pointed to the bowl of incense and motioned us to make our own burnt-offering to Buddha. We did this with great solemnity, bowing our way backwards into the smoke-filled semi-darkness of the great temple.

After the service, the procession filed out of the doorway and we waited, kneeling on our hard straw mats, wondering what was going to happen next. The high priest and his first assistant returned smiling and bowing their heads in a most sociable manner. We rose and followed them into a screened-off portion of the temple, where there were more golden altars, and incense burners gave off their pungent aromas. Here we were invited to partake of the sacred cup of tea in fragile jade bowls, while the priest through his interpreter asked us questions about America and our travels. He signed his decorative autograph across a picture of the temple and then posed immovably, holding his bowl of tea, and framed between the panels of a golden screen, while I set my camera on the floor, and took a time-exposure.

During our journey in Japan, as in other countries, by special request of the museum we collected many samples of human hair. This was one of the trickiest games we had to play, for the latent instinct of Sampson to defend his own locks as symbols of strength seems to have been inherited by most of the members of the human race. In certain places, to avoid too much insistence, we had to let the local barber into our secrets. When our subjects objected to giving up a lock of hair, he would often trim the unsuspecting native a few days later in his shop or crouching on the roadside, and then slip his locks into an envelope for us, with the name, age, etc., and nationality of the former owner, and, incidentally, we avoided the possibility of having whittled tiger-whiskers put in our food, which seems to be a favorite form of revenge, frequently practised below the equator.

Our next problem after Tokyo was to brave the elements and travel northward to the island of Hokkaido, there to study the race of Ainus, who were the original inhabitants of Japan. This exiled race is now forced to live in a few isolated villages on a bleak seacoast and gain what living they can by fishing and hunting. They have heavy overhanging brows and deep-set eyes, and the men generally wear long hair and beards. They suggest the type of Russian *mujik* rather than any Mongolian ancestors.

No first-class trains run to the northern end of Japan, as tourists seldom visit this part of the empire. Therefore we joined a crowd of orientals in a second-class sleeper and spread our blankets like the others on the benches which line each side of the car. Within half an hour all the passengers took off their shoes, the smiling porter having placed a pair of leather mules beside each of us. Our fellow-travellers paid little attention to us and curled up in every manner of position, after changing their business suits for kimonos. All such matters as dressing or undressing were attended to in the aisle, quite unconcernedly. The Japanese seem to take a national pride in their heavy knitted woollen underwear, a recent importation from the western world.

The countryside grew a bit more colorful as we left the dreary suburbs of Tokyo. The little farmhouses, with low, thatched roofs and paper walls, gave a picturesque effect, and submerged fields of rice made us realize that we had left the Europeanized city, covering an area of thirteen miles, for the farmland of cultivated fields and landscapes studded with pine forests. Chrysanthemums and fruit-laden persimmons trees added their charms to the outlook. As night fell, the paper windows of the little houses were illuminated from within, and colored lanterns were hung at the entrances.

In the railway-car, chopsticks soon fluttered in and out of the little lacquered boxes or metal bowls containing strange and highly seasoned concoctions, including raw fish, the particular secrets of which I am thankful not to have been forced to fathom.

The train seldom reached a speed of thirty miles, and by five-thirty A.M. we were dressed and anxious to escape into the cold air—almost any kind of air would have been a relief, as the over-heated car was filled with oriental vapors and smoke.

At last we reached Awomori, a drab and dripping town of small, stark buildings, railroad offices, storehouses and a wharf—a good place to leave without delay. Thousands of fur-coated soldiers marched past us and packed themselves away on steamers. Suddenly, we were aware of great military activity, of a smooth organization with formidable strength. Memories of 1914 flashed across our minds. A hardy-looking ferryboat bound for the island of Hokkaido or "Yezo" took aboard about sixty passengers, including two foreigners, my husband and myself, who, wrapped in blankets, promptly assumed a horizontal position. The northeast gale took charge of the rest. The Pacific Ocean tries to get into the Japan Sea, and the Sea tries to get

YOUNG WOMAN OF TOKYO, WHOSE PORTRAIT I MADE IN THE OPERATING–ROOM
OF ST. LUKE'S HOSPITAL

JAPANESE PRIESTS OF-
FERING A PRAYER
DURING A "HOUSE-
BUILDING" CEREMONY

The nervous reactions of
these young Japanese swim-
mers are so instantaneous that
within one or two strokes
they easily pass the heavier
build of competitor. **Their**
usual light diet of rice enables them to keep in fit
condition, and they are difficult rivals in the art of
swimming

A SLIM YOUNG JAPANESE ATHLETE WHO DEMONSTRATED

HIGH PRIEST OF THE SHOGUN TEMPLE IN TOKYO

Photo, taken while we were having tea after the religious ceremony. He wore a saffron robe with white silk kerchief; the gold
lacquer screen in background and green jade bowl made a beautiful
color-scheme for a painting

Photo. Galloway.

BABIES ARE SNUGLY WRAPPED AND STRAPPED TO THEIR
MAMMAS IN JAPAN WHEN TAKEN OUT FOR AN AIRING

Photo. de Con & Galloway.

CHERRY BLOSSOM DANCERS AT KYOTO, JAPAN

Photo. Suito.

DANCING STEPS AND ACCOMPANYING MUSICIANS IN JAPAN

MAKING WOODEN SHOES JAPANESE STYLE

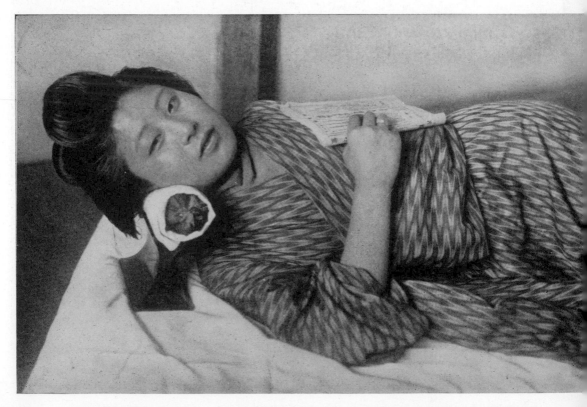

WOODEN PILLOWS WITH A SILKEN PAD TAKE THE PLACE OF OCCIDENTAL FEATHERS

OUR JAPANESE HOSTS IN TOMAKOMAI

In the center, three full-blooded Ainus including Miss Yai Batchelder. S. B. Grimson at the extreme right

AINU MOTHER CARRYING HER BABY IN A FIBRE BAG HUNG BY A FLAT ROPE OVER HER HEAD

THE "RARA AVIS," A BEARDLESS AINU

Photo. Burton Holmes & Galloway.

VENERABLE AINU OF HOKKAIDO, GREETING A NEIGHBOR

Photo. Burton Holmes & Galloway.

AINUS DRINKING FROM THEIR *SAKE* BOWLS, AND USING THEIR MOUSTACHE-LIFTERS
(CARVED WOODEN STICKS)

A TYPICAL AINU

Life-size bronze portrait, in the Hall of Man, made by M. H.

THE LONE AINU FISHERMA
ON A STORM–SWEPT COAST

The Ainus depend upon fish an
wild game for their daily rations
food

A FULL–BLOODED MALE AIN

Life-size bronze figure by M. I
in the Hall of Man

into the Pacific. They fight it out in the Tsugaru Strait. These hours at sea were a sufficient test of endurance to make one realize why more first-hand information is not available concerning the aboriginal Ainus and their wind-swept habitations. "If they are worth *this trip,* they must be a great race," I noted in my diary.

At last we reached the fortified zone of Hakodate, the southern part of Hokkaido. On the pier an American missionary stationed at this lonely outpost brought us the greetings of Doctor Batchelder, the venerable British missionary at Sapporo, who has given his life to studying and helping the Ainus.

After a long day of railroad travel, to our intense relief we were met at our final destination by the representative of the Oji Paper Mills at Tomakomai, Mr. Yamakata, to whom we had a letter of introduction. We were presented to a black-haired, dark-eyed woman in native costume, who, to our utter amazement, greeted us in English. "We heard that you were coming to study the Ainus, so Doctor Batchelder sent me, Yai, his adopted daughter, to welcome you. I came from Sapparo this afternoon and bring messages of welcome from my father." Actually seeing and talking with so gentle-voiced a member of the aboriginal race filled us with dismay. Miss Yai's sense of humor, however, enabled her to enter into our astonishment with hearty laughter and a sensitive and charming understanding. We looked for the traditional marks of blue tattooing over her upper lip; these were seen on most Ainu women, but they were not on Miss Yai.

On our arrival at 10 P.M., the storm had ceased and the air was cold and brittle, and the streets through which we drove were covered with ice.

At last we stopped at a gateway which opened into a small garden filled with shrubs and dwarfed pines. Pushing aside the panelled doorway, which shook a garland of bells, our host welcomed two enchanted and weary travellers into a miniature haven of golden screens and floors covered with padded matting. A group of bowing maids and a man-servant waited at the entrance, ready to remove our shoes and substitute soft felt slippers. A red-hot stove gleamed in every room with hospitable reassurance of warmth.

This modern Japanese house included two rooms fitted with European tables and chairs. The native rooms, however, contained no furniture; the walls consisted of sliding rice-paper panels, framed in black, which concealed various cupboards and shelves. On the east wall hung an ancient proverb, brushed on parchment and mounted on a dull silver mat. On a richly carved, red-lacquered pedestal was a bronze Buddha, and on each side of the statue were chrysanthemum bushes and dwarfed oaks. It would be difficult to imagine any scheme more simple and restful.

Here one realized that the Occident ceased and the Orient was in full bloom, and one called to mind Kipling's lines, "Where east is east and west is west and never the twain shall meet." What we in America consider vital necessities—complex and expensive types of hangings, elaborate furniture and tiled bathrooms—are considered quite useless in Japan.

Our inexperience created much amusement, for when we slid the wrong panel we found ourselves in some one else's domain. Among the first native customs to which we were introduced was that of bathing in a steaming tub of polished wood, six feet long and five feet deep. This sacred ablution is performed in a special room with no other furnishings except the tub and rough towels with which to rub one's self down after being submerged to the neck in a steaming hot well. Result? A delicious sense of refreshment, in spite of all one's former ideas that hot water lets one down or brings on a chill. In Hokkaido it strengthens and protects one. A delicious dinner, specially prepared for us, was served in bowls and, much to our host's delight, we ate with chopsticks. Many cups of hot *sake* added a gay note to our evening.

Miss Yai and I retired to a corner in the Europeanized sitting-room (for in this room there was an occidental table and two chairs). Here I am afraid I exhausted the poor girl, for I asked innumerable questions about her Ainu relatives, and made notes of all she could tell me of their general attitude and and social habits. It seemed too good to be true that up in the wintry wilds of Tomakomai I should be comfortably chatting in English with a full-blooded Ainu who proudly announced that she had been to England and had held the hand of the Archbishop of Canterbury, and had visited Westminster Abbey and knew London better, no doubt, than I did—for her adopted father, Doctor Batchelder, had taken her back with him when he visited his home country some years ago.

She was really very happy to show us over her Ainu country, for she said we and the Lindberghs, who had landed in their plane at Nemuro on the northeast coast of Hokkaido, were the only Americans that her people had known. She spoke of the visit of Doctor Montandon, the French anthropologist, and of Doctor Berthold Laufer of Field Museum, but she had not personally known the latter.

On retiring, we found our bedroom transformed. In the center of the floor were two mountains of silken quilts, much glistening white linen, and dark bamboo baskets containing brocade kimonos lined with soft blue-and-white cotton under-wrappers. Everything shining and perfect in its austere and oriental fashion.

The night treated us to one of the earthquakes that occur about every fortnight. Afterwards there was a severe thunderstorm, and in the hours of dawn a rough northeast gale that almost took the quivering little house with it.

Before we had finished breakfast, we heard footsteps and, looking out, saw on the garden path a group of Ainus with their guide, the postmaster of the village of Shirawoi, which is near a large Ainu settlement. Service? Could the unattainable be produced more quickly even in New York?

We began at once to measure and examine the models. After we had completed our preparation for the day's work, we started off on foot over the frozen clay roads.

We visited the local hospital and were given the use of the operating room as a studio. We were disguised in surgeons' aprons and caps. The Ainus were very shy, and objected rather violently to being asked to disrobe for us, until it was thoroughly explained that if they would do this we would give them healing ointments and whatever treatment they might need for skin diseases which, by reason of no washing, are very prevalent among these people.

Everything possible was done to help us examine our models and take their photographs. Finally we returned to our host's house and I modelled the portrait head of an aged Ainu with the traditional long beard. He posed on the covered, open-air verandah, which was the only place where I could find enough light by which to model.

During the next few days we made trips to Shirawoi and other villages, continuing our search for types and our studies of Ainu life and lore, under the indispensable guidance of Miss Yai Batchelder, who preceded us into each dwelling, greeting the inhabitants in their own tongue and explaining the reason for our visit. Her tactful friendliness won for us what would otherwise have been quite impossible to obtain. We took many moving-pictures. A young Ainu riding past on horseback, with the sun gleaming on his bronzed face, reminded me of an American Indian with his square jaws, high cheek-bones and black hair.

The Ainu women mend the roofs of their huts by replacing the worn tufts of thatch. One woman sits on the roof while another tosses up the bundles of straw from the ground. The desolate, wind-swept land on which the Ainus live makes farming a great struggle against the elements. The men build boats and catch fish, when the bear-hunting season is over. We came across a few black bears, which had been caught and caged in heavy wooden crates. These animals are fed and fattened for the Bear Ceremony, in which they are offered as sacrifice. Their cages are set on a raised platform three feet off the ground, within a few yards of the living quarters of the Ainus, and the unlucky beasts howl out their four-foot misery between the bars of six-foot prisons.

It was reported to us that on the seacoast during the winter there were frequently seen crowds of great sea-lions climbing over the rocks. Their roaring is heard for many miles about. This sound, added to the northeast hurricane storms and frequent eruptions, gives one a good idea of the charms of winter in Hokkaido.

The Ainu hunters use a curious, primitive form of spring-bow and poisoned arrows to hunt the bears. Great is the rejoicing if a bear cub is captured alive and caged in the enclosure near the house. He is petted and played with by children and adults, and fed until the day of sacrifice—for the Ainus have an animal-cult which regards certain animals as deities, such as bears, wolves, raccoons, and martens, and they are worshipped and offered as sacrifice. Throughout the months from December to March the bears withdraw to their caves and sleep. In the early spring the hunters go out with dogs, and when a bear's den has been located the men light a fire over the entrance-hole and try to smoke out the inmate. If this fails, one of them often wraps his head and face in thick cloths and crawls into the cave, believing in the tradition that a bear will not kill anything in his own den. He keeps a sharp knife in his hand, and if his encounter is successful, he manages to drive the bear into the open by pricking him with little sharp sticks.

Once the bear is in the open air, the other hunters shoot with their poisoned arrows, which soon take effect. The bear is sometimes able to put up a fierce fight before succumbing to the arrows, and it is considered a brave act to run up to him as he stands, roaring and rearing on his hind legs, and rush into his embrace, striking the blade of the hunting knife into his heart at the moment that his front paws hug the hunter too closely. The man who takes this long chance of being crushed or scalped is looked upon with envy and admiration.

When the spring-bow is set, the arrow is released by a touch and, being barbed at the end, cannot be torn out of the flesh by the bear himself. The pieces of flesh reached by this poison are carefully cut out and buried; the heart is the organ most affected by it. The body is divided among the hunters, the head and breast and viscera being given to the man who actually killed him.

A feast is always arranged to celebrate the return of the brave hunters, and the deities are thanked and worshipped with gratitude suitable to the Ainus' totemistic beliefs.

The eating and sacrifice of animals is an occasion of great rejoicing. The Ainus seem to feel that they are giving their victim a great send-off and are communing with him in the closest possible religious ecstasy by eating his flesh and blood. The old men and young dance about in a frenzy of delight, and after the party the skull of the bear is spiked on to the top of a post and left to dry in the sun. Sometimes dozens of these heads are seen in rows in all stages of decomposition. They are supposed to contain the spirits of the bear or divine preserver from harm.

The cubs are brought up to be so tame that it is the custom for the women of a village to form a circle around the cub and suckle it at their breasts, passing the little fellow from one woman to the next.

Another form of worship among the Ainus is the snake-cult. The association of evil with the serpent is the cause of much dread concerning this reptile. Ainu women are very much afraid of snakes, as they believe the serpent has a special spite against women. Snake-worship is practised in the temples of India and Burma, and in ancient Persia and Mexico the serpent has figured as a very omnipotent deity, as well as in certain African tribes, such as the Danhglive in the serpents' house at Dahomey.

Among the Ainus, images of snakes are made of straw or sedge and bound with strips of cloth. These are worshipped like fetishes and are in some way propitiated to lessen the perils of childbirth, and much *sake* is drunk during the ceremony. The custom of eating snakes is Japanese, not Ainu, and in Japan the snakes are often given as medicine to the sick, or served as a great delicacy. They are supposed to add to one's strength when digested! Surely the idea alone ought to be considered a test of endurance.

Other fetishes, known as *inao,* are carved sticks about four feet long. These are planted in the ground, accompanied with much *sake* drinking, and are taken very seriously as guardians of the village, being carved to represent eagles or eagle owls. These spiked sticks are used to mark graves and drive away the demons of disease. When a funeral procession follows the body to the burial-ground, the mourners put on their coats wrong-side-out and upside-down to symbolize the reverse of death to life, and the fetishes or *inao* are frequently supposed to have spirits which link mortals to their deities. In cases of extreme illness, the *inao* is often stuck into the ground of the hut and prayed to for the life of the invalid.

Wood-shavings serve as "good omens" and are carried by medicine-men, and tied to the fishing boats.

The huts of these hardy aborigines are about as uncomfortable and stark as could be imagined. The roofs are sometimes thatched well, but the walls and floors are not constructed solidly enough to keep out the freezing-cold winds of winter. Dried and rotting fish is hung from the beams, and the smoke from the continual fire causes eye diseases. The houses swarm with fleas and insects. It is not rare to see snakes sunning themselves in the thatch of the roofs, where they find good hunting for mice and birds' nests. Two windows, consisting of openings in the wall, have rush-mats hung over them on the outside, and these are lifted up or tied down, according to need. There are no chimneys; the smoke rises through a central hole in the roof. The rooms are lined with matting hung on the walls.

When bears or deer are brought home to be eaten, their carcasses are always pulled through the east window; it is considered a holy place, and I was warned not to peer inside through any east window. I frequently hit my head on the door frames as I went in and out of the huts, for they are only about five feet high.

In one house Miss Yai went ahead of me and found a very old man sitting on the floor in silence with hands folded and eyes closed. She spoke gently to him in his own tongue. He told her, in broken gasps, that he was dying, that he would have to sit here waiting only a few days more, but that she could bring in her friend and show her his house. He hardly opened his eyes and seemed to be living in another world remote from ours. I could not help feeling awed at this simple acceptance of death, as if he waited for a friend to take him home.

The native costume worn by the Ainus is of elm fiber, made from the inner bark of the tree and woven into long kimono pattern coats, decorated with a complicated and effective design. Each district has its traditional patterns and different ones are used for men's clothes than for women's apparel. In winter, snowshoes, made of wood, over five feet long and seven inches wide, are worn.

Sympathetic magic plays an important part in the habits of the Ainus, who resisted our every effort to obtain samples of their hair. They believe that it is most unlucky to allow a hair of their heads or even the paring of their finger nails to get into a stranger's possession. Their hair could not be cut unless as a sign of mourning. A widow must have her hair plucked out or closely shaven. Until recently this was done with sharp shells or flints, which must have been very painful. There is a legend in Ainu folklore which states that in matters of love the little bird known as the water-wagtail assumes the duties of cupid, and his feathers are kept as charms wrapped up in *inao* to keep the lover in quest of his mate.

The Japanese have so subjugated the communities of Ainus that they have been forced to work out a form of village government under the control of Japanese authority. Crimes and thefts are punished severely. The offenders are well beaten up with war-clubs, and robbers generally have their noses and ears lopped off so that they will carry the stigma of their offense throughout their lifetime. For murder, the tendons of the feet are severed close to the heels, making the wretched man helpless for life, or he is banished to Siberian ice-fields.

If we compare the methods of healing the sick in the Ainu villages with those among other primitive peoples, we are struck by the similarity of their procedure, although the Ainus seem to remain in the crudest state and most of the cure is left to the gods. There was one detail that struck me particularly when I questioned the Ainus about their methods. They feel that illness is the possession of the body by demons. These demons hate certain *smells,* so the Ainu medicine-man seeks out what he feels will be most odious to their sense of smell. Certain wildflowers (one of them is the convolvulus root) are chewed and then spat out over the unfortunate invalid. The "doctors" rush about howling and spitting this evil-smelling root, waving swords, and generally doing their best to terrorize the demons of disease, and I should think scare the patient into a state of collapse. The result must often be successful, for the custom persists, and this form of exorcism is repeatedly resorted to in all corners of the globe.

Certain symbols are tattooed as a religious signification. In Hokkaido the blue moustache is tattooed on the Ainu woman's upper lip as a style of beauty, and frequently the hands and arms are covered with tattoo. But in Japan the idea of tattooing is looked down upon by the better classes, because for many years it was forcibly inflicted upon criminals. It is still secretly practised by certain individuals, although it has been officially forbidden by the Japanese Government since 1868.

FINE TYPE OF MALE AINU, STANDING IN FRONT OF HIS THATCHED STRAW HOUSE, AND WEARING HIS BEST ROBES

AINU WOMAN IN NATIVE COSTUME, WITH FINELY DRAWN BLUE TATTOOED SMILE

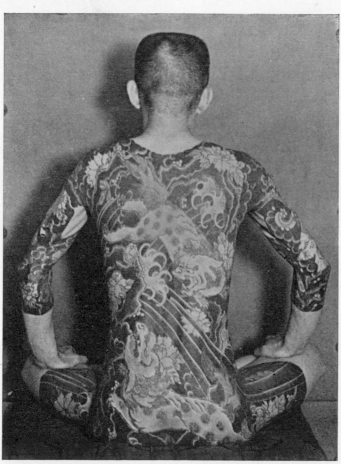

A REMARKABLE EXAMPLE OF COMPLEX JAPANESE TATTOOING

Covering almost the entire body, and necessitating many years of painful self-imposed ordeal for the wearer

JAPANESE WOOD–CARVERS WORK ON THE FLOOR, THE ONLY PLACE WHERE SUFFICIENT LIGHT FALLS

THE SEATED GODDESS IN THE NUNNERY AT NARA

A masterpiece of awe-inspiring beauty

KWANNON, BODHISATTVA OF COMPASSION, HOR-YUJI, NARA. 6TH CENTURY A.D. CARVED IN WOOD AND POLYCHROMED

One of the most serene and aristocratic statues in the world

The Thracians, twenty-four centuries ago, were found by Herodotus to puncture their skins, as a mark of high rank or noble lineage. Tattooing has been used chiefly as a means of identification, but it has also been a means of alluring the opposite sex, and in many countries has been developed to an excessive degree. Very often, as a test of endurance, the process was continued until great surfaces of the face and body were covered with intricate designs. In the Bushman tribes of Australia, the deep scarifications cover the whole body and legs, and the cuts are rubbed with earth and certain plants to raise great welts. The design, instead of being colored, is literally carved in relief. Even the women of these tribes have many of these so-called "decorations."

In the Polynesian islands the boys at the age of puberty generally indulge in tattooing to make their appearance more manly and ferocious, as these are the two qualities most admired by the savage brides. It is considered a disgrace for a boy to pass the age of seventeen without having tested his endurance by tattooing.

Eskimo mothers tattoo daughters' faces at the age of eight, and later on the girl is dragged by her hair out of her tent by her future husband—(just an old Alaskan custom).

According to my own observations and those of Doctor Montandon, who is one of the few scientists to have studied the Ainus in their own land, the Ainu people are similar in build to the Mediterranean types, and often are like certain Alpine subjects in their bodily proportions. Their profuse growth of hair is more wavy than the above European races. Doctor Montandon states that the Ainus are a distinct people, evolved from some primitive proto-Nordic race of the Paleo-Neolithic era. The popular idea of the Ainus represents them as descendants of dogs and covered with hair. This is a gross exaggeration, for in examining many subjects and consulting Doctor Batchelder's records, covering a period of fifty years of observation, I found that the Ainus do not appear to be as hairy as the Todas of India, or in fact many Europeans. As for the dog's being their ancestor, it is merely one more legend added to the long list, probably invented by the imaginative traveller with a good sense of what attracts curiosity and helps to sell his book of daring adventures. The

Japanese word for dog is *inu,* and this may have given rise to the legend of the Ainus "going to the dogs."

"The true origin of this isolated race remains unknown, but they may have been in Japan since the beginning of creation and that the race is not Mongolian is clear." This view of Doctor Batchelder's is generally accepted as fact by any one who has compared the features scientifically with the other Asiatic races.

In my regular weekly report to Mr. Stanley Field of Chicago, President of the Field Museum, I wrote:

The Ainus were very shy about undressing for anthropological photos, but Sam has taken many types, in stills and movies, of male and female Ainus of practically all ages. . . . All that now remains to be done is for us to go to the delousing station and then re-enter the social life of Tokyo. Please tell Dr. Laufer that although I really try to follow his last words of instruction "Do not try to hustle the East," the only sign in English in these Japanese trains is printed in large letters in the washroom: "Please hurry; others may be waiting. . . !"

Before leaving Japan we visited Nikko, Kyoto, Kobe, and—best of all—Nara, the evergreen forest where, throughout the centuries, ancient treasures of Japanese and Korean art have been hidden away behind the dark, wooden walls of the temples. Doctor Niiro, the Director of the Museum of Nara, showed us his collection, and we then persuaded him to come with us to the Treasure Houses of Horyogi. None of us will ever forget, I am sure, the excursion across country to these sanctuaries of other days, where, because of the darkness of the inner shrine, it was often necessary to light candles or use flashlights in order to see the paintings and sculpture.

In the temple of Horyogi Doctor Niiro very kindly asked us to visit the "studio," another wooden temple in which a group of silent, busy sculptors were engaged in making a copy of the beautiful and famous Kwanon. The gracefully draped figure was lying on its back with an exact copy beside it. The delicately designed nimbus which serves as a background to this figure had also been reproduced with such accuracy that we could detect no flaw. Only the coloring of certain details still remained to be done, and then the copy was to be sent to the British Museum. In 1933 I saw this copy in place at the British Museum and marvelled at its perfection.

The methods of the miniature craftsmen were of the greatest interest to us. They use their tools in quite a different way from western carvers, drawing their planes and chisels towards their bodies instead of pushing outward. They squatted on the floor on straw mats. On account of the overhanging, thatched roof, the only good light fell very low. There were no benches or lathes, or any modern devices; clever hands and heads and swift, sharp blades did all the work. The result was perfection, contentment, and constant employment. Have we progressed so far in the last hundred years—in art —in technology?

At Kobe we boarded a small Japanese steamer, which carried us through violent midwinter storms and northeast gales on the Yellow Sea, to the port of Taku. From there one goes to Tientsin and thence to Peiping. Wild reports of impending war and risks of landing were circulated each day as we approached China—the land of bandits and bloodshed, according to Japanese opinion. Our little ship was heavily loaded with Japanese cavalry horses, and all the open decks had been boarded up and made into narrow stalls, in which the unfortunate beasts were slung in belly-bands to prevent their being thrown down and having their shaggy hides rubbed off on the rough boards. Flapping tarpaulins were slung over the front of the stalls to keep out the icy spray. The continued pitching and rolling made the animals so miserable that the passengers were ashamed to complain of their own discomforts, which were, after all, not to be compared with the fate of these patient dumb creatures out of doors in such cruel weather.

Cruisers escorted us into the harbor, and we tied up to the dock. The cargo of shaggy ponies lifted their distended nostrils and filled the air with whinnyings and shrill cries of relief as their hoofs felt the solid ground at last. Their riders looked like Russian bears—great bundles of fur coats and helmets. It was a very cheering sight to see an American officer coming in our direction, sent by our consul in Tientsin, to facilitate our landing and passing the customs with our mysterious canteen trunks and heavy metal containers.

China

The Great Wall of China hides the secrets of the ages and envelops the race in a shroud of remoteness—China, that vast land of unexplored eternity, little scraps of which our Western writers have attempted to set down in words. How futile all such efforts seem!

We followed our long line of padded, gray coolies, each one carrying cans and crates and valises. We packed into the railroad car with our twenty-seven pieces of luggage. The train was fourteen hours late coming down from Manchuria and crowded with Mongol refugees. The journey to Peiping served me well for making a close-up examination of various types under dramatic conditions. Moving from one group to another, I tried to recognize the principal division of the race: the stark, rugged northerners, taller, strong, and more remote from the southerners; the Mongolians, hidden away behind their fur collars and their own great cheek bones, their faces mask-like, unsmiling and determined; their voices thin, serious, and high pitched.

The journey from Taku to Peiping gave us a dramatic introduction to the military ethics of the Chinese army. There must have been a thousand or more soldiers on the train. Soon after we left Taku the young officer sitting next to me, wearing a heavy sword at his belt, was suddenly surrounded by three or four excited Chinese soldiers. These men were showing him a passport and certain mysterious papers which they had discovered in the possession of a terrified young recruit. They evidently agreed that the papers were forged and that the passport did not belong to the present bearer. Without further formality or warning the victim was pushed forward and thrown down on his knees at a yard's distance from me, and the officer dealt him a series of violent blows on the face which raised red welts on his cheeks and drove the tears in streams over his pallid and terrified countenance. Sam, sitting opposite me, gave me a warning look which said: "Keep your brakes on!" He then remarked to me not to forget that we were strangers in a strange land, that this was China's war and not ours. The infuriated officer ordered the soldier stripped and searched, and after taking from him a few silver coins, tied up in an old handkerchief, and finding nothing else, kicked the wretched man, who begged for mercy, until he fell sobbing on the ground. He was told to dress, and at the next station he was taken into custody by the local police, dragged to the platform, and marched off to his doom.

I confess that this incident gave one rather an ominous feeling as to oriental military discipline. But, war is *war*.

When we finally reached Peiping after fourteen hours in the train it was evening, and we were bundled into the taxi rickshaws and trotted along Legation Street to the Grand Hotel. As we passed near the Japanese embassy we heard a loud explosion on the other side of the high walls. Our coolies merely gave each other an eloquent look and kept right on at a quicker pace. When we reached the hotel, the hospitable clerk seemed quite concerned as to just what route we had taken from the station. "Why do you ask?" I said. "Well, we have just heard that the Japanese embassy was bombed ten minutes ago, and we thought you might have been near enough to give us some interesting information." This matter-of-fact way of accepting war conditions was contagious and rather comforting. From that time on we never felt any further qualms.

In Peiping we were joined by Miss Gretchen Green, who had left Paris after we did, travelling eastward to China to meet us. She had made felicitous contacts which everywhere proved of great assistance to us. When she had reached Shanghai in early December, the railroad trains had been temporarily discontinued, owing to a student uprising and political upheaval. The cars had been pushed over on their sides and the tracks were completely covered with the thousands of students who milled about the railroad terminus day and night.

Miss Green, nothing daunted, went to the Chinese aviation field. There was one small mail-carrying plane going to Peiping, but no passengers were permitted to travel on this. She managed to prevail upon the two young pilots to smuggle her into the postal department and, carrying her hat-box in one hand and a teapot in the other, she crouched under the low canvas roof and reached her destination safely. The week before, the plane on this route had crashed into a mountain hidden by fog and had killed the poet, Hsu Tse Mou, who had been a passenger. Miss Green's plane was the last one to make this trip for a long time, and her courage and *sang froid* were the topic of conversation at our hotel for many days.

The rugged experiences of our trip from Japan, the violence of the Yellow Sea, and the scenes that ensued on the railroad, were in sharp contrast to our first evening in Peiping, when we were introduced to a large group of foreign residents by Mrs. Calhoun. This was an astonishing banquet. The effect of thirty guests in full evening regalia, illuminated by candles and standard lanterns, was rather a revelation to us. We had been travelling so long that evening parties seemed a great treat. We had never seen a Chinese house, and the rows of colored paper lanterns, throwing their light over the snow-covered courtyard, was breath-taking. Silent, bowing servants, in long satin coats, stood like sentinels, guiding us through the labyrinth of courts and inner rooms. I met Doctor Davidson Black, famous the world over for his part in the discovery of "the Peking Man." The next morning, when we went to the Peking Union Medical College, where Doctor Black had been director of the anatomy department, we found a studio and work-room set aside for us. With the assistance of Doctor Paul H. Stevenson, who has since taken over the direction of the department, we plunged into our task of studying and selecting representative types of Mongolians, Manchurians, and Chinese, who differ as much in appearance and bony structure as if they belonged to separate races. After a few days of careful observation, we learned to pick them out at sight when we walked through the crowded streets of Peiping.

The fact that martial law was in force during the time that we were in Peiping made little difference to our daily program. In fact, it added many incidents, all of which helped us to study and understand the Chinese temperament and character. The temperature was twenty degrees below zero, but the sun was bright, except when extinguished by the "sand storms of the Gobi desert," so-called by visitors, but which consisted chiefly of the dust of all the streets and unpaved *hutungs* of Peiping.

At nine o'clock each morning I started work at the Peiping Union Medical College, working until the late afternoon and enjoying frequent visits from Doctor Davidson Black, who was always accompanied by his "Number one boy" carrying a tray with fragile bowls of steaming Chinese tea. With his assistance and that of Doctor Stevenson of the anatomy department, we were able to study every type of Chinese, male and female, both in good health and in the hospital clinics and wards. The following quotation is from my letter to Mr. Field after examining an endless procession of bald or shaven Chinese heads:

The box containing samples of hair colors and eyes (glass!) arrived safely from Germany. They look extremely scientific and anthropological in every sense, but between you and me and Doctor Laufer and God I'm not worrying about the use of these much, as there is trouble enough in our camp without trying to match celluloid platinum blond curls to the shaven heads of my oriental victims. Nevertheless we all remain respectfully, seriously and energetically yours. . . .

P.S. You might like to know about the WAR in Manchuria. I believe it is going on and forms an interesting topic for the cocktail reunions which are all the rage between six and eight P.M. As we do not attend these reunions, I cannot tell you much about the war. See New York papers.

The "studio" which I fitted up with modelling stands and an improvised throne, made of a packing case, on which my sitters posed, was situated halfway between the "morgue" and the "mouse-house," where thousands of white mice were serving their time as experimental material for the study of diseases. This place was the only free space available that had a good north light and which was not filled with all kinds of laboratory equipment. If the sitters were not led to the door by an attendant, they might accidentally open the wrong door and find themselves in the presence of various sections of human cadavers laid out on tables for the anatomy students, and the effect of such a mistake would occasion such commotion that the *séance* was rudely interrupted. To open the other door into the mouse-house was almost as much of a shock to the olfactory nerves.

A constant procession of models would come to my improvised studio, ranging from eminent scholars and merchants to the lowliest coolies and impoverished beggars. One most unusual case that I studied at the hospital was the tea-eunuch of the late Empress's court. He was a most gentle and friendly patient, who recounted for our benefit the story of his life as an imperial eunuch. Miss Green, our secretary, with her natural sincerity and kind heart, easily overcame any obstacles of shyness or fear on the part of her "victims," and I was not surprised to learn that she had, through an interpreter, been able to persuade this eunuch to unfold the secrets of the tea-ceremonies in the late Empress's palace. It was interesting to hear that the six books of Confucius were the basis of their education, and that the eunuchs were expected to be well versed in history and geography as well, and able to teach the ladies of the court and to entertain them with music and poetry. There were over two thousand of these eunuchs in the court of the last Empress, and it was considered a great honor to be one of her royal household.

This long list of qualifications demanded of imperial eunuchs recalls the advertisement which appeared in one of our New York papers: "Wanted, an expert governess to teach children. Must know four languages, must be able to teach piano, mathematics, history, literature, etc. Must be one with Jesus and eat with the servants."

Jean was busy every day at the Peiping Union Medical College, but was slightly afflicted *à la française* by the miasma of combined white-mouse stench and embalming fluid in which his labors were accomplished. He said that taken separately they are not fatal to life, but together they were worse than a gas attack. Miss Green was busy taking the measurements and histories of the models who posed for Sam's photographs.

One of the most remarkable records made by Sam during our stay in China was the series of seventy-eight photographs of the *mudras* or hand-gestures of the Tibetan religious ritual. The Mongolian priest, who was an old friend of Doctor Lessing's, agreed to give a scientific record of each and every position of the hands during the religious ceremony. At the appointed time, the priest and Doctor Lessing arrived, accompanied by bearers carrying chests of costumes, altar-cloths, thunderbolts, bells, lotus-bowls, and other accessories. The incantations were spoken in Tibetan; these were translated by Doctor Lessing into German, and from German into English by Sam. The

THE EVER CHEERFUL RICKSHAW COOLIE OF CHINA, IN SUMMER OUTFIT
Life-size bronze by M. H. (Hall of Man)

Photo. S. B. G.

YONG TA SEN, OUR RICKSHAW COOLIE IN PEIPING, IN
WINTER FUR HELMET AND EAR–MUFFS

Photo. S. B. G.

MRS. DAN, A MANCHU BEAUTY OF RARE CHARM

Photo. Buxton, Oxford.

WOMAN OF CENTRAL MONGOLIA

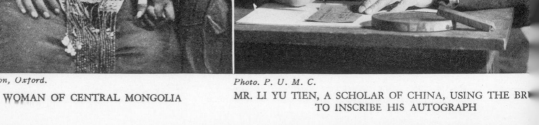

Photo. P. U. M. C.

MR. LI YU TIEN, A SCHOLAR OF CHINA, USING THE BRUSH
TO INSCRIBE HIS AUTOGRAPH

MONGOLIAN DANCER

Turquoise-blue bronze statuette by M. H. With ancient bow and gorgeous costume of blue brocade.
The hat, covered with eyes of peacock tails, surmounted by a crystal ball, was acquired by the artist

Photo. Dr. Hannon.

PEIPING UNION MEDICAL COLLEGE, WHERE I HAD MY STUDIO WHILE IN PEIPING

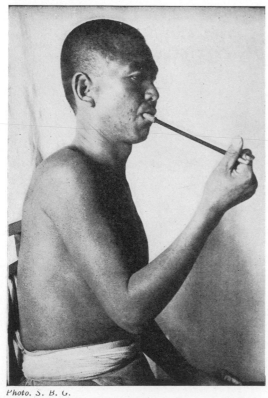

Photo. S. B. G.

ONE OF OUR RICKSHAW COOLIES WITH HIS
CHINESE PIPE

Photo. S. B. G.

SECRETARY TO THE LIVING BUDDHA OF
OUTER MONGOLIA

Posing in the courtyard of Owen Lattimore's house
in Peiping

226

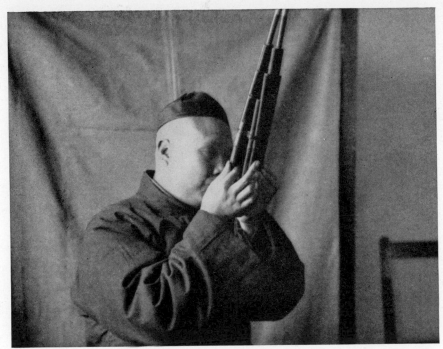

Photo. S. B. G.

BLIND MUSICIAN PLAYING THE SHENG

A Chinese musical instrument

INSERTION OF FALSE TEETH AND EYES. LATEST METHODISTS.

眼補牙鑲 記富德信

補 鑲

眼 牙

ONE OF THE RESULTS OF MISSIONARY WORK IN CHINA

Photo. S. B. G.   THE ABBOT OF A MONGOLIAN MONASTERY WHO MADE THE

© F. M. N. H.   PORTRAIT IN BRONZE OF DOCTOR HU SHIH

Left: THE LIVING BUDDHA OF OUTER MONGOLIA, ON THE TERRACE OF HIS ABODE AT THE
LAMA TEMPLE, PEIPING

The green-tiled roof and red copper bowl gave a rich setting to the dark brown folds of his cloak and
crimson brocade robe with golden cuffs

Right: THE QUILTED WINTER–COSTUME OF A CHINESE WOMAN

The pointed felt slippers protect the bound feet, still often seen trotting about the streets of China

CHRISTMAS DAY CAMEL RIDE TO THE TEMPLE OF THE CLOUD
Owen Lattimore, Gretchen Green, and M. H., just outside Peiping

LAMA PAINTING, KNOWN AS *MANDALA*

Designed and colored by a priest in Peiping. Owned by M. H.

Photo. M. H.

DOCTOR LESSING ON THE RIGHT AND THE SECRE-
TARY OF THE DALAI LAMA OF TIBET ON THE LEFT

symbolic significance of these *mudras* is complex and difficult for the occidental mind to grasp.

Sam also made a series of pictures showing Chinese musical instruments as played by blind musicians. These musicians have for generations been attached to the Imperial court and, as it was considered by the Emperor to be more discreet not to have eye-witnesses to many of the entertainments, the musicians selected for the court were always blind ones.

We also visited the shops, where we acquired a very rare Tibetan priest's costume, entirely carved out of human bones. This is worn on very special occasions over a brocaded silk robe. The head-covering is a delicate, carved crown of bones with a circle of skulls about two inches high. From these falls a fringe of carved bone beads which cover the eyes and entirely disguise the face of the wearer.

In both China and Japan we made a study of the physical culture schools to record the differences in muscular development between the athletes of the two countries.

Our experiences in Hawaii had initiated us into a few of the inside "tips" on how to make others take our expedition seriously. We had hit upon the idea of having letter-paper printed with large, official-looking type: "Expedition for the Hall of Man. Field Museum of Natural History, Chicago. Members of . . . etc. . . ." This was useful in many ways, and permitted us to recover slowly from writer's cramp, caused by writing these same words at least twenty or thirty times a day; for each visit, please remember, had to be explained and our reasons for barging into the private offices of high dignitaries had to be couched in terms guaranteed to overcome every type of psychological resistance.

In Tokyo a second idea had struck us—to go to a printer's office and have a set of visiting-cards made for each of us, printed in English on one side and in Japanese on the other. They were really the "life of the party." We were then able to meet the Japanese social-custom experts on their own ground and exchange visiting-cards as rapidly as any Oriental could desire or expect. As the Chinese characters resemble the Japanese (to a New Yorker's eye)—*printed* characters, I mean, not speaking anthropologically in any sense—I made some rather alarming social blunders later on in China with our visiting-cards. I had a double supply of these now, for we had not used up our Japanese supply and I could not bear to throw them away. Their cryptic importance seemed to add such dignity to the mere name and address in English, and as for "Representing Field Museum, Chicago" —in Japanese it was simply a "wow."

When we were in the early stages of breaking down the wall of China's social remoteness, I inadvertently presented one of my Japanese cards as an introduction, having been definitely instructed in Tokyo NOT to bring up the subject of Sino-Japanese relations, unless it was necessary (owing to a state of war). I soon realized my mistake and with much bowing and rather forced smiling, I solemnly asked for my card to be returned, and exchanged it for the Chinese one— "change the lily for the lamb," as Ruth Draper would say. The smiling then became quite natural on both sides, and the incident served its good purpose after all. I remembered Rodin's remark to me one day . . . *"Il faut attraper les accidents, et les convertir en science. . . ."*

To obtain photographs of models for the library of anthropology was a complicated matter, and my husband was obliged to collaborate most tactfully with the directors of art schools and other institutions. However difficult the work was, we always found the Chinese officials and other acquaintances more than willing to offer their assistance. Especially were we indebted for friendly co-operation to Mr. Engert of the American embassy, to Doctor Philip Fugh—a great friend of Doctor Laufer's and of many other social acquaintances, who put us in the way of meeting interesting and distinguished Chinese—and to Doctor Hu Shih. The latter, who is considered the leader of the modern intellectuals, posed for his portrait while we were in Shanghai. He is a writer of distinction and a philosopher. During the summer of 1933 he came to Chicago and other cities to give lectures. His portrait in the Hall of Man is placed beside that of his great friend, Doctor Wong Wen Hau, whose brilliant mind keeps watch over all the archeological researches and discoveries that are made in China.

Twenty-six degrees below zero was an average temperature during our visit. The population knows well how to dress for the intense cold of winter, but the occidental traveller, especially if one comes from Hawaii and its tropical weather, finds it difficult to adjust himself to such extremes of temperature and often falls ill as a result. The little quilted box-covers to the rickshaws are a great protection, and through the square of glass set into the front curtain one may see the most exquisite miniature compositions of this most wonderful city of Peiping.

Trotting over the snow-covered roads and crunching the ground under his padded feet, the faithful coolie drags his passenger cheerfully from dawn till eve. Never complaining, always cheerful and alert, these millions of men give their lives to the *profession* of running between shafts, from one generation to another. It is not an unusual sight, in the early morning, to find the frozen body of one of these coolies curled up on the ice at the side of the road. Having fallen exhausted at night, the weary sleeper sleeps on, never to awaken.

It is often in the everyday activities of life that we find the most strikingly characteristic symbols of a race—in the ceremonies of marriage or burial, or in the signs that denote the nature of a merchant's wares, such as we find in profusion in the fascinating streets of Chinese cities. Colors have their own important meaning and manifold significance. The constellations control a palette of their own, and the complexities of hieroglyphics have been unravelled throughout the ages to interpret the mysteries of Egypt's language of symbols. Perhaps to many the factual truth of a certain sign is more convincing than the metaphorical symbol, but the horizon of the latter stretches into infinity and in its very abstraction includes a wider range of meaning and suggestion. It was in China that I was the most impressed by the majesty with which their symbolic life is invested— the worship of their ancestors, the evocation of the dead by a symbolic tradition that has defied all the powers of destruction.

If we study the trades and crafts of China, we are entranced by the decorative quality of their emblems. The cake-seller, with his golden discs ending in a tiny vermillion wisp of color; the noodleshop and the rice-cake baker—each has his charming insignia hung outside his shop. The color-grinder and the painter have their unique signs. The latter is curious indeed, for it is the bladder of a sheep in which the lacquer is kept. The old custom of painting by dipping cloth into the color and rubbing it over the walls is still practised. The use of painters' wide brushes has not yet been adopted by the Chinese; they prefer to rub and daub the color on the surface, letting a generous portion flow over their hands and arms during the process. This form of waste is encouraged by the manufacturers of colors and dyes.

It is the quaint custom in Peiping to have all the shops that deal in certain specialties crowded into a single street. The Street of Lanterns is one continuous and colorful array of every conceivable shape and color of lantern, from the most ordinary paper cylinders to the most expensive and ornate painted horn lanterns which are made for special ceremonies and high potentates, and reach the prohibitive price of five hundred dollars apiece. The Street of Jade is perhaps the most perilous place that one could visit if one must avoid serious inroads upon one's financial assets. Here one can go into one shop after another crowded to the windows and ceilings with delicious little brocade boxes and trays containing every shade and quality of jade—white, smoke-color, or green; in plaques, beads, boxes, delicately carved and polished to tempt every taste and buyer. The other public menace to the pocketbook is the open-air market, where everything from ancient seals and bronzes to modern toys and gay lacquered trunks and chests, decorated with splendid brass locks and corners, can be bought for amazingly reasonable prices.

The district of fur shops does a brisk and profitable business, for the icy weather is enough to drive any winter visitor to wild extravagance in acquiring baby-leopard coats and divan covers made of soft, tawny wildcat pelts and lined with one's choice of brocaded Chinese silk. After visiting a number of these fur merchants and seeing their huge stores of skins, one marvels that there are still enough leopards and other wild animals alive to keep the breeds extant.

The bound foot of Chinese women has always been a subject of severe criticism and certain mystification to the western mind. While studying in China, I had frequent occasions to examine cases of foot-binding. This practice causes many painful diseases of the foot and knee, and often results in the necessity of amputation. It is a custom of fashion, and although now forbidden by law, there are numberless examples still to be seen trotting about the streets in tiny pointed shoes. They are often called "The golden lilies," and are supposed to have certain phallic significance; if a woman is known to have exposed her bound foot to a man not her husband, it is the cause of violent jealousy and severe punishment. In any of the fine Chinese paintings the bound foot is always concealed under many folds.

In 1899 there was a report issued by the Tien Tsu Hui (Natural Foot Society) which quotes the extraordinary fact that although male members of a family may object to this cruel disfigurement of their wives, the women would not dare submit themselves to social ridicule and shame by not adhering to this custom. This slavery to fashion on the part of women seems to be international and eternal.

I noted the curious fact that certain Europeans who had lived a long time in the Orient and had married either Chinese or Indo-Chinese ladies, had grown to look extraordinarily like these races. "The twain" do meet, in spite of Kipling's poem. Their faces had undergone a complete transformation of expression, and I could almost say that the outer corners of the eyes had lifted slightly and the nose had flattened. In any case, their general appearance, although originally they had been typical Frenchmen, struck me as more oriental than that of their Indo-Chinese or Chinese wives. There certainly is something in the saying "more catholic than the Pope," and it was rather amazing to me to find nature transforming the actual European physiognomy and character into an exaggerated oriental one.

A curious coincidence occurred in Peiping when Miss Green received a note asking her if she was the same Miss Green who had at one time been in charge of prison work in Boise City, Idaho. "For if you are," said the note, "I am the western boy who came with my mother to consult you there, and I would be so glad to renew the acquaintance. I am now a Buddhist monk, living at the Lamaist Temple with another American friend, who is also a Buddhist." Miss Green answered at once that she was the same person to whom he alluded, and the next day we were interested to receive a visit from these two "searchers for spiritual truth."

At Christmas time we asked the two young Americans, who had

left their homes in our Middle-West to become Buddhists, to lunch with us. They had spent two years in Japan and had recently reached Peiping, where they were spending a hard and bitterly cold winter in a stone cell within the walls of a Lama temple courtyard. Living as the monks live, on the charity of the passerby or of friends, these two men were sallow and sunken-eyed, but strong in their spiritual conviction that they had found the way to their souls' deliverance. It seemed strange, indeed, to hear the unmistakable western voice and accent coming from these saffron-robed, sandal-footed followers of Buddha, but it was most gratifying to see their enjoyment of a square meal, served on a white cloth, with a few American specialties to make them feel at home.

Another interesting luncheon was given to the abbot of a monastery and two Mongolian priests. These friends of Doctor Lessing, the erudite Sinophile, had come to see my husband, and as I was suffering from rather a severe fever and infection of my sinus and had been kept in bed by doctor's orders for ten days, I was only permitted to receive the guests for a few moments before their departure. Doctor Lessing acted as interpreter, and the element of friendliness and humor in these Mongolians was a delightful surprise to me. Their faces seem like immovable masks until they smile, and then the mask breaks into a series of expressions; their eyes twinkle, deep lines accentuate the emotional reactions, and their remote and impersonal appearance is entirely changed.

Apparently the only English words known to the Mongolian abbot were "mamma sick," so he stroked my hand most sympathetically and kept repeating in various inflections and crescendos: "mamma *sick,* mamma sick sick, *mamma.*" Finding a warrior's costume flung over the end of my bed, the abbot suddenly decided to dress up and amuse me. He looked resplendent in the metallic armor and peacock-feathered helmet. Raising a gilt cup in his hand, he strode about in dramatic poses, much to the delight of all of us.

To celebrate my recovery, my husband engaged a troupe of Chinese puppet actors to show their skill behind the travelling stage and screen. About five o'clock of a dark wintry afternoon, the players arrived at our hotel, bundled up in blue-and-gray quilted robes and ear-tabbed fur hats; they were swinging lanterns, and were carrying their theatrical properties in great bundles and baskets swung on poles. There was no way to give them any instructions, as they understood no word of English. They seemed quite able to transform the hotel room in their own fashion. The poles were set up, the sheet stretched over a framework, and all lights extinguished except the candles behind the screen which cast the translucent shadows of the puppets in brilliant colors. There were strange gutteral conversation for the male characters and high, piping voices for the ladies of the cast. Tiny gongs were struck and melodies of flutes occasionally were heard.

The dramatic performance included mounted warriors, waving pine-trees, architectural settings, and costumed characters of every walk of life. We left the doors of our rooms open so the room-boys could peek in and enjoy the surprise party. When the drama ended, the puppets were carefully packed into their baskets, the stage and frame rolled up, and the lanterns lighted. The smiling performers filed out, and the fairy tale was completed.

A three days' snowfall ended the night before Christmas, and the heavens were aglow with stars and radiant moonlight. We drove out to the white marble bridge which spans the lake of the Winter Palace, and there at midnight watched the few skaters who ventured out on the untrodden snow and ice. The silence was holy, and the crystal clarity of this moonlight scene was a revelation of beauty never to be forgotten.

The following morning—Christmas Day—we and the Owen Lattimores, who had explored Turkestan and had written extraordinary books on their journey, mounted a string of Mongolian camels that had been thoroughly brushed and "fly-toxed" for our benefit. These camels had carried coal but never human beings, so we were wondering, as we mounted, just what their behavior would be. We crossed the glittering snow-fields, and rode out from the walls of the Forbidden City to the Temple of the Cloud. The motion I found not at all unpleasant, and far more agreeable than the diagonal and rotating slinging-about that one experiences in the howdah on an elephant. The Taoist monks at the Temple of the Cloud wear their long coiffures in circles on top of their heads, held in place by high skull-caps of black cloth without crowns.

This camel ride introduced us to one of the methods of transportation of the Far East. We were eager to taste of as many local customs as possible. To be initiated into the ceremony of a Chinese banquet, one must be courageous and ready to partake of any strange food that may be offered, from sharks' fins and birds' nests to snake soup and eggs from fifty to one hundred years old. These savory dishes are accompanied with endless other oriental dainties, the provenance of which I preferred to leave unknown. In Japan we had learned the art of eating with chopsticks—a difficult task—but even this becomes simpler after a few glasses of potent hot *sake*. A boy is in constant attendance behind one's chair and as soon as the glass is empty the boy fills it with hot *sake* again and again, until the mysterious meal is ended and Nature is left to her own devices as to how you can reach the next day in safety and be at work with a clear mind at nine A.M.

While looking over certain records of local customs and medical history, I found that in 1879, in China, there were recorded many examples of filial piety. In the Province of Chihli honors were given to those children who had part of their liver cut out to make broth for their sick parents! The Chinese believe that determination and decision proceed from the gall bladder, that anger makes it expand, and that it is symbolic of bravery. Rice steeped in the gall of a fearless criminal is supposed to add courage to the consumer. There are cases in certain South Sea islands where the adrenal gland is cut out of the captured victim and eaten by the warriors, who believe in its strength-giving qualities—merely a more direct method than the modern injections of glandular extracts by hypodermics!

I was told that in Indo-China, knives were not used at table because of the violent differences of opinion that often arose between the diners. Chopsticks are considered adequate, and safer. If one wishes to despatch an enemy slowly and secretly, the clever device is used of mixing poison with food in graded portions, so that after a few weeks of illness the patient quietly dies.

During our stay in Peiping, we spent an evening listening to a band of celebrated blind musicians at Mme. Lauru's. She is the

Photo. S. B. G. ARRIVAL AT THE GATEWAY OF THE TEMPLE OF THE CLOUD

Mrs. Owen Lattimore, Jean de Marco, and M. H. on the camels. The emerald-green tiles on the roof and wall glittered in the sharp winter sunshine

BRONZE FIGURE OF THE WOMAN MUD–CARRIER OF HONG KONG (HALL OF MAN)

LAMA PRIEST WORSHIPPING A SACRED INCENSE–BURNER IN THE LAMA TEMPLE, PEIPING

This sect is headed by the Dalai Lama at Lhasa, the Forbidden City, in Tibet

daughter of the oldest European inhabitant of Peiping, Lady Bredon, and has written several books, one a travel guide for Peiping and another called *The Moon Year*. Her husband brought some of the musicians to be photographed by us the next day. Her mother had a "pig-tail" servant, which is so rare a sight these days that the unfortunate boy was obliged to stay in the compound to avoid being stoned or mocked in the streets. She gave us permission to take pictures of him.

Doctor Hu Shih, the philosopher, gave a reception for me at the Returned Students' Club, with only Chinese as guests. There were over thirty of the most eminent men and distinguished women that Peiping could produce at the moment; it was an honor not vouchsafed to every foreigner. Sam, Miss Green, and I were the only "Whites." It was amazing how well they all spoke English and how conversant they were with American and European ideas of progress. I was more and more impressed by the fact that the Chinese have become suspicious of the foreign worker to such an extent that unless you can break down barriers and show you are working in good faith, it is absolutely impossible to make any headway whatever. Doctor Mei Lan Fang was present at the tea. He told me that as a result of his first trip across the United States of America he lost over one hundred thousand gold dollars on the venture. I considered him full of optimism to attempt such a journey again, as he was hoping to return to America in 1932 if his project materialized. It never did.

When I asked this distinguished actor to explain to me why occidentals always depicted the Chinese with sharply rising eyebrows, he told me that the masks and colored reproductions of many theatrical favorites, who had always made up their eyebrows in this exaggerated manner, had probably flooded the market and influenced the occidental mind, so that gradually the belief that all oriental eyebrows shoot upward had become firmly established.

One of the favorite masks used in processions and festivals in Tibet and China is the huge lion's head carried on a pole. Curiously enough this same lion mask is often made by the Tyroleans and Slavs who carry it about in their folk dances and festivals. If we study the use of masks in the Japanese theatre we find that it is the principal characters in the Nō plays that wear the finely carved wooden masks. The oriental sculptors have so keenly observed their own people that they have succeeded in making a synthesis of the facial expressions in these masks—each one depicting a definite emotional mood—with the least number of strokes and the simplest accentuation of the forms.

One cannot describe Peiping without paying homage to the gorgeous architectural masterpiece of the Temple of Heaven. The altar was the sacred terrace where the emperors offered their annual sacrifices at the time of the winter solstice. This mathematical phenomenon is located just outside the southern suburbs of Peiping. It is built in three circular terraces two hundred and ten feet in diameter at the ground. The upper terrace is made of marble slabs in nine concentric circles. Everything is arranged in multiples of nine.

To mount these marble terraces of vast and awe-inspiring proportions makes one realize the latent power that has made this country of China stronger than the powers of destruction. Wars and plagues and famines rage over this land of poverty, politics, and treasures. Centuries have unfolded but a few pages of China's history. What is yet to be discovered will take centuries to come, and only after living in this country can one realize how it is bound up in Eternity, and how its people have, by this very fact, grown to be an ageless and enduring race.

While studying with Doctor Lessing in Peiping, we were fortunate enough to acquire a very beautiful example of Lamaist painting, made by a monk and interpreted by Doctor Lessing. Lamaist paintings are not considered primarily as works of art. They are rather the expression of religious emotion of some priest or devotee who follows certain rigidly established rules but may, within these limits, enrich and add to his conception to the extent of his artistic ability. These decorative religious pictures are symbolic of the mystical concepts of union with certain gods or deities. The same may be said of the sculpture and architecture of the Lamaist.

The "Mandala" is actually a mental picture. The one shown in the illustration was painted in 1931 and is very brilliant in color and delicate in its complex ornamentation. It is in water color and about fifteen inches in diameter. According to Doctor Lessing's translation from the Tibetan text, this painting represents the Palace of Yamantaka, the powerful and terrible deity who was able to conquer even death, and who is shown in the sculpture of the Chien Lung Dynasty clasping the goddess "Shakti"—his energy—close to his body, identical and not different from him. They are represented in mystical union or the state of Highest Bliss.

Many scientists agree that there are striking similarities between the monuments of the Asiatic Buddhists and those of Central America. Surely the migration of symbols is one of the most fascinating routes by which to trace the ancient history of the human race. With the slightest variation, a well-known pagan symbol becomes a Christian one. The Solar Wheel becomes the Wheel of the Law. Cosmic signs were used as actual language; they were often the expression of prayer or glorification. Behind these symbols lie the secrets of the past and the roots of tomorrow.

Travelling through many lands, I noticed the infinite variety of designs used by the different races in their carvings, weaving, and religious ceremonial paintings. It was a constant source of surprise to find the same symbols repeated in widely separated locations. One finds the elements of lightning and thunder represented by nearly every nation. The Greeks used the eagle who held the thunderbolt in his talons. This became the symbol of Zeus. In the East-Indian form, the trident suggests lightning and the thunderbolt is formed of a double trident bound at the center and used by the Hindu sects as well as by the Buddhists, who carried it to China and Japan. This symbol is used by the Lama priests to drive out demons and to bless the holy worshippers.

Our departure from Peiping was something like a movie scene that began at ten A.M. and did not cease until the train drew out of the station at five P.M. It seems to be a charming Chinese custom to give presents to departing friends and to call at any off-hour during the last day and settle down to the inevitable cup of tea and a chat. Sudden decisions of baggage-agents, refusing to check our plaster in metal cases or insisting on special kinds of strapping and handles and locks being put on our luggage at the last moment, caused a great deal of extra commotion. The number of final gifts included fruits, costumes, books, pictures, seals in cases, ivory brushes, all of which necessitated additional baskets to carry them, but they gave us a delightful sense of being spoiled by kindness. The Engerts of the American embassy motored us to the station where more friends awaited us, including Doctor Davidson Black and the Lattimores. Doctor Black was really all that any friendly person could be, but he rebuked me soundly for leaving before I had modelled a complete hall of *China,* for in his opinion Java, India, and other countries are of no importance whatever in comparison. I could have had any type I wanted to model for the next six months.

By a stroke of good fortune the Wagons-Lits Company had just added a new sleeping car to the Nanking route, so we were able to enjoy the clean accommodations—a rare and extraordinary privilege. The rest of the long train was crowded with soldiers. We had armed guards at both ends of each car, because, only a short time before, this train had been held up by 700 bandits and every bag and piece of clothing taken from the passengers.

We realized that life was only a matter of chance here. The whole country was a smouldering volcano of unrest. From day to day Japan crept up a little nearer, and slowly the situation grew more and more tense and desperate. We were seriously advised to make a safe and quick exit, while the lines to Shanghai were still in operation, so we were trundled along at the national rate of fifteen to twenty miles per hour across endless miles of frozen khaki-colored fields and wastes, where only a few clumps of trees occasionally sheltered the mounds of ancestral graves and relieved the desert-like flatness of the scenery. Distant mounds and hills, cultivated in terraces of winter wheat, suggested the existence of human beings but, except at the railroad stations, where blue-padded and fur-capped crowds clustered about the platform, one saw no living sign of the population.

Our arrival at Nanking at eight A.M. was a bleak and exhausting experience. The icy, damp air of twenty degrees below zero whistled about the station, and the news that we would have to unload our twenty-seven pieces of baggage on coolie back to a ferry and then go twenty minutes across to another station before we could continue our train journey to Shanghai was poor news.

Could this really be the present capital of China? It seemed incredible as we were crowded and pushed down a long, creaking gang-plank like a herd of cattle on to a windswept wharf, where we waited until the marrow of our bones had been thoroughly congealed. Finally we settled into the second train, which appeared from nowhere, wheezing and coughing asthmatically. Going southward, we managed to get some hot tea and this helped to reconcile us. The countryside grew more human; there were clusters of trees along the canals, and groups of happier people; the long rows of winter wheat (no rice in ten winters here) covered the fields as far as the eye could see. At last we felt we had left the lands of floods and desolation and that a more hopeful, fertile country lay ahead of us.

On our safe arrival in Shanghai we felt very bucked up by the fact that our train reached its destination without mishap and had passed through rows of Japanese armored cars bristling with soldiers at Tientsin and other stations—for that very day the Japanese occupied the town.

In Shanghai, under rather dramatic circumstances, I made a portrait of our friend Doctor Hu Shih, leader of the Chinese literary renaissance. It was in January, during the celebration of the Chinese New Year. The noise of myriad fire-crackers exploding in the streets and courtyards was to be expected during this festival, but occasionally we could distinguish a different sound—the rattle of the machine guns of the approaching Japanese. In my hotel room I had no equipment, and it was necessary to work rapidly. I took the drawers out of the bureau and piled them one on top of the other to make a modelling stand. I placed Doctor Hu Shih on a chair on my steamer trunk. A pair of compasses was improvised out of a two-foot rule hinged in the center, and points made of hairpins were fastened to the two ends of the rule by adhesive tape. The plaster head of the Chinese scholar was dried on the radiator and carefully packed in the wicker basket. The next day the bombardment became so insistent that we were forced to assemble our luggage and catch the night boat to

Hong Kong. We learned later that the hotel in which I had made Doctor Hu Shih's portrait was completely sacked just after our departure.

While in Hong Kong we enjoyed the cordial hospitality of Professor and Mrs. Shellshear. Doctor Shellshear was Professor of Anatomy at the University of Hong Kong. He assisted us greatly in securing many fine models, and escorted us on a trip to the walled Hakkar city of Kam Yin, New Territory, which has but one small gateway for entrance and exit to the outside world and is locked away behind heavy grilled gates. This is situated northwest of the New Territory. The inhabitants wear wide, flat-brimmed straw hats. Around the brim's outer edge hangs a ruffle of black cloth six inches deep. This acts as an umbrella or parasol, as the need may be. Their long, black hair is coiled on top of their heads.

On this excursion we tracked down a fleet of water gypsies, near Castle Peak, New Territory, and prevailed upon them to land and let us photograph them. These hardy river-dwellers are born and live their entire life on flat-bottomed boats. They fish and sail and spend their days between the shores of the Yang-Tse-Kiang, and are a race by themselves.

In wandering over the site of an ancient civilization, about twenty miles north of Hong Kong, we unearthed many pieces of authentic prehistoric pottery, decorated with the swastika design. A picnic lunch on the rocks overlooking the river was a jolly intermission. Doctor Shellshear entertained us by throwing Australian boomerangs in an expert fashion.

I happen to recall that while we were climbing over the hills and fields hunting for fragments of antiquity, a crowd of water buffaloes started bellowing, and when I called out to ask Doctor Shellshear what we should do, he said: "Keep quiet—and above all, *do not talk English*. These Chinese buffaloes hate the sound of the English language and may surround and charge you. Talk Chinese!"

I confess that I was thoroughly frightened and never realized so poignantly the value of learning an oriental language!

In Hong Kong I modelled one of the most interesting types I found in China—one of the female mud-carriers who transport heavy baskets of earth for the road-makers. These baskets, weighing sixty or seventy pounds when loaded, are slung one at each end of a stout bamboo rod, balanced on the shoulder of the carrier. The look of dogged resignation on the faces of these women recalls Pearl Buck's peasants in *The Good Earth*.

When one hears that the island of Hong Kong, when turned over to the British by the Chinese, was a barren waste, mountainous and rocky, it seems hard to believe. Now the hotels are first class, the city modern and well policed by smart Indian Sikhs; there are marvellous motor roads for hundreds of miles, forests, gardens, parks, ports, and good sanitary conditions.

Miss Green had stopped here on her way to Peiping, so our short stop was greatly assisted by those who expected us and were forewarned of our many needs. We had brought with us the box containing samples of hair colors and every shade of glass eye. Our instructions had been repeated: to match these colors accurately to our models and to note just which shade of hair and eyes they happened to have. I wrote Mr. Field the following rather insubordinate note:

The glassy, scientific eyes are looking at me with accusation, but I have to confess that, although they may be very useful to science, they are soul-destroying to art, and although I brought them along with me, I am not able to use them. Surely they would be more useful in Germany, where the anthropologists would have all shades of blue eyes and "Aryan" hair with which to match these samples for a Nordic world. Forgive me, but I am returning them to Chicago.

If the visitor to Hong Kong is seeking a change from noisy city life, he will do well to motor over the high mountains back of this busy commercial port and stay on the inland curve of Repulse Bay. If he has the added luck, as we did, of driving there under a clear, sharp moon, he will realize how well the British know how to make themselves comfortable in the Far East, in a fine hotel with delightful wide terraces and gardens. *L'art de vivre* has certainly been tested out by the colonial service experts. Here on this placid bay one looks over a maze of islands. The beauty of the sunsets and of the moonlight is dazzling. One is removed from all confusion and noise—an oasis of rest.

I went down to the beach, and on its flat, smooth surface traced the outlines of camels and elephants with a cane, by cutting deep into the sand and using the bright moonlight to accent the relief. These "sand carvings" incised on the beach gave the illusion of stone bas-relief in the moonlight. I would lie on the soft, warm sand and watch the tide creep up and wash away the procession of elephants.

It was on that beach, under the moon, that I felt the first symptoms of serious fatigue, after my two rather unpleasant illnesses—a sort of warning that from then on the strain would be increasing for us all on account of tropical heat and shorter intervals between our "movings" from place to place. Paris, the United States of America, Hawaii, Japan, the Ainus, and two months of China had drawn heavily on all our funds of intensive energy and enthusiasm. I remembered how, in the war, the British had calmly remarked to the new recruits, "Cheerio, the first seven years are the hardest." I tried to laugh it off—"Why worry? It may not happen!" But the sense of responsibility would run down my spine in sickening shivers at the thought of what we had undertaken. I never dared to count how many "heads" were still ahead of me! Moments of apprehension looked up and grinned at me like the "Big Bad Wolf." The other members of our party were well but tired, and I felt that I had put them under an abnormal and too constant strain. Perhaps if the three little pigs would have started their reassuring national air of "Who's Afraid of the Big Bad Wolf?" my qualms would have vanished—but the three little pigs had not been born in 1931!

At frequent intervals the task I had undertaken seemed quite impossible, but I dared not confess my doubts. The germs from the dust of Peiping seemed to form a secret alliance with those which were already "in residence," and as a result of this combine a constant sinus pain was troublesome enough to wear down the most congenital optimist. Our activities did not allow us time to relax too far. This would have been as fatal as it is to the tired cab-horse if he is once taken out of the shafts!

In the evenings, sipping cool drinks on the terrace of the hotel and watching the moonlight creep over the dark flanks of the mountains, one thought of the floating world of night on the other side of those dark barriers. One had but to go to the high ridge overlooking the river to see the myriad floating pleasure-houses with their colorful garlands of twinkling lanterns. For in Hong Kong, as in other river ports, the night-life is carried on to a great extent in boats. If one goes closer, one can hear the strains of a lute and singing and occasional laughter floating over the water. These are called "flower boats," and I heard that the parties generally start on the big boat and then after a good quantity of opium and liquor has been imbibed, the revellers go off in couples, each to their own smaller boat. These float down the river, and one by one the flickering candles in the paper lanterns burn out and darkness closes over the scene.

Our exit from China seemed to close a door on an important chapter of our existence. The strange power of this land is only suggested in such words as "oriental atmosphere," "ancient culture," or "elemental influence of air and earth," and yet . . . when once the lure of China has seeped into your veins you are left with an eternal yearning to go back and refresh yourself at its fountains of ancient wisdom.

Boarding a Dutch steamer at Hong Kong, we began our southward voyage via the Philippines, Borneo, and Macassar to Bali.

Although we spent only a short time at these places, they each held its own particular flavor and interest. Between ports I worked constantly, finishing the subjects I had almost completed on land (in the one-third life-size figures or life-size heads), or drawing colored chalk portraits of the cabin-boys and certain native travellers who, more from curiosity than any other motive, were willing to pose for me.

The Philippines

The native class of passengers on oriental steamers sleep on the decks, surrounded by their baskets and bundles. These groups of cheerful, chattering comrades and members of the crew have a habit of collecting nightingales and other songbirds of brilliant plumage. Colored lacquer cages are hung all along the framework which supports the canvas roof over this section of the ship—and what a fantastic galaxy of song comes from these full-throated messengers of spring! It is, however, often mixed with the usual cargo of grunting pigs and squawking ducks.

It was in Manila that we felt the first real sultry heat, after our Chinese winter. The year had already given us two summer seasons, one in Paris, one in Hawaii in October, and from now on in the South Seas and India we knew the thermometer would rise constantly. The renowned mountain resort of Baguio, frequented by Americans and visiting tourists, has been so over-capitalized as having an ideal climate that we decided to be unpatriotic and did not go there. The wild beauty of the mountain scenery is certainly vast and dramatic, but Manila itself struck me as so over-Americanized that it lacked any real interest. The pier was undeniably the longest and the "best ever"; the main street was hopelessly straight and wide and had more calla lilies than I ever wish to see again. Everything appears exactly as it is advertised.

The native tribes which live on the main island of northern Luzon are the Bontoks, Igorotes (one of which I modelled), Ifugaos, Kalingas, and Apayaos. These stocky little warriors are believed to be descended from Malay stock, and it would seem easy to believe that they drove the aboriginal Negritos, or woolly haired pygmies, up to the mountain-tops where they have stayed ever since. The Igorotes must have been busy on the terraced hillsides for over a thousand years, for there exists a system of rice-terraces greater in scope than anywhere else on earth. The Igorotes worship the God of Sun and Fire, and their deity is known as Kabunian. Since the advent of outside control and missionaries the pastime of head-hunting has gone almost entirely out of fashion. These tribes are now industrious farmers, having splendid physiques and alert minds. The Moros who live on the southern island are more warlike in disposition. They have broad, powerful shoulders and thick shocks of straight black hair. Living in a state of suppressed revolt, they give the Americans plenty of work to keep them in order. Long training has made all these natives expert spear-throwers, and to finish off their combats they used to swing a head-axe at arm's length. At present, however, they hunt only the animal kingdom with bows and arrows, and work in rice-terraces, except at odd intervals when some of them quite naturally go native.

A local industry, the making of thin gauze dresses, embroidered by Philippine girls, seems to do a lively business with all the tourists who visit Manila, for from this point southward one recognizes them on every shape and size of globe-trotter, from the stream-line débutante to the ever present octogenarian lady, who prefers to stumble down the gang-planks rather than permit the long-suffering Cooks' guide to take her arm, and who prides herself on knowing everything when it comes to postage-stamps or the minimum rates of tipping.

Perhaps one of the indelible shocks that a globe-traveller should be prepared for, at about this latitude, is the sight of one's fellow-country-men and other tourists in "shorts"—and stockingless legs! The first days in the tropics produce a collection of weird "passenger birds" that appear to have lost all their feathers! The wearers of khaki shorts are generally pale and unsunburned, so that their bare legs have a look of pallid nakedness. They strut about the decks with a sort of defiant pride, and I often felt like crawling into a dark corner and wrapping myself in layers of blankets.

Pith helmets or topees are other articles of complete disguise, but these are indispensable if one is exposed to the sun, and are generally flattering to the wearers, as the wide brims come down over the ears and neck and throw a dark shadow over the face.

A small canvas swimming-pool is often found rigged up on the deck of the coast steamers. The water is so heavy that if a light sea shifts the boat about, the sides of the tank bulge and the water splashes over the deck, making a most unattractive entourage for the rest of the passengers who are unwilling to risk the perils of such a crowded community bathtub. As the days go by, the shoulders, backs, and legs of the determined "sportifs" start peeling and blistering—there would seem to be some primitive urge that drives these deck-bathers to burn themselves into a state of fever, and brick-red skin color. Many are the aches and pains that help to keep the ship's doctor occupied!

Having been forewarned of all the infections and deadly diseases that we would most probably contract in the course of our travels, we had submitted in Paris to the unpleasant but quite indispensable practice of vaccination and inoculation against typhoid, diphtheria, smallpox, and other ailments. Thus, armed with an impressive collection of malaria preventatives and anti-plague serums, presented to us by our good friend Doctor Simard, in Paris, we started off with a clean bill of health, feeling that we would be immune to all the powers of destruction, including poisoned arrows, cobras, lightning, or any other menace which might loom upon our horizon.

As we moved from port to port, however, changing currency, climate, clothing, and language, and growing ever more weary with cumbersome bags and boxes, the one burning question presented itself . . . how could we lighten our luggage? The illnesses that I managed to contract never seemed to be the ones we had prepared for! Whenever we could find a fellow traveller in need of quinine or castor oil we were only too delighted to give him a large enough supply for an overdose and thereby reduce our travelling drugstore in bulk.

Tropical showers of the wettest variety greeted our arrival at the Port of Macassar. When the sudden downpours ceased, the shafts of sunlight glittered over the network of shrouds and halyards of the sailing-ships that were nudged one against the next, laden with cargoes of grain and spices. Over their decks and above the wharves swarmed the little bodies of native crews and dock-hands, dragging and lifting endless sacks in teams of four or six, depending on the weight of their loads. No noisy derricks here to shorten hours or lighten the labor of sweating humanity. The beauty of muscular strength, the young stream of energy flowing from one body to the other in a synchronized smooth rhythm! Here the young men were as agile and surefooted as panthers; there was no sound of effort, the work seemed to flow along with an inevitable pulse, like life itself.

We were fascinated by the unfurled nets and sails swinging out from the masts to dry their faded colors in the blistering sunlight.

When Sam had taken his movies of the scene, we proceeded to the market-place, where every age and size of native crowded under the shade of palm-leaf shelters and bartered their pungent fruits and condiments to every passerby. My appetite for fresh bananas "on the branch" started at about this time, and has never yet been satiated or equalled, I am sure, except by Sam's inordinate appetite for fresh pineapples as discovered in Hawaii.

Gretchen Green and I wandered off, exploring the neighborhood, while Sam disappeared on his own quests. When the time came to return to the steamer, we could not find him, far or near. At the market-place we boarded a rattling carriage and made a tour of the village, stopping at occasional shops to inquire if an Englishman in a pith helmet and long trousers had been seen. (This description generally excluded most of the visiting tourists, who wore shorts.)

Finally, to our amazement, we caught sight of Sam in a music store, sitting on a table chatting happily with a young Macassar girl, and smoking a pipe, as if he had every intention of missing the steamer. He was listening to a Kreisler phonograph record for which he had hunted all over Europe in vain, and which he had found here in Macassar by one of those accidents that suddenly reduce the size of the world to unbelievably small proportions.

Bali

A handful of earth in a boundless ocean! We stood on the deck and scanned the seas as the heat of the midday sun subsided into the lavender afternoon mists, and the straight line of what seemed to be an endless horizon suddenly showed a break, a darker and more definite edge, that drew the mariner's eye and quickened the heart-beat. I dared not look again, lest the thread had broken and the long-hoped-for reality had vanished into a dream—this sudden possibility of fact after so many months of fancy and imagination! Was it not tempting nature, asking a bit too much of life, to produce the evidence of much fiction?

The sea was calm as glass, and the distant shadows took on the glow of opalescent reflections. Bali—the "Enchanted Isle"—was outlined by its mountains, and the dark groves of palm-trees, crowded on its flanks, waved their rhythmic wands over the lowlands down to the sea.

The excitement of seeing living creatures astir on the beach made us impatient to land. There was no dock or tender to transfer the passengers from the steamer, but a fleet of wooden canoes, rowboats and outriggers, manned by bronze-backed natives, swarmed out to meet us and, encouraging the boys to carry our twenty-seven pieces of luggage, we climbed into the little boats and pushed off on the wings of adventure, to taste of tropical mysteries and delights.

On landing we were fortunate in procuring a diminutive Malay guide, who also acted as chauffeur and drove his Buick touring-car with ease and ability. His brown, bare feet gripped the clutch or brake with a firm, prehensile hold which soon gave us confidence, as he climbed the wooded hills and turned the hairpin curves that carried us from the sweltering heat of sea-level up to the chill and cloudy heights of Kintamani, the peak of the volcanic ridge of mountains forming the backbone of the island.

Evening with its seven veils enveloped the fairy-like landscape. As far as the eye could see the hillsides were terraced in flooded rice-fields, varying from the limpid, glassy surfaces of water to the tender, new, pale green of myriad rice-blades pushing their tips above water-level. Between these lakes stretched little paths of dark earth, and along these the rice-workers strolled homeward, like glittering gods delighting in their ecstasy of strength and beauty, outlined in gold against the setting sun. Darkness fell, and whispers of evening filled the air—or was it laughter mixed with moonlight? We recalled the subtle music of "L'Île Joyeuse" of Debussy, and realized how vividly he had suggested this rippling woodland ecstasy by his poetic harmonies.

Threading our way slowly through forests and palm-groves, we listened to the sylvan symphonies of wild birds and waterfalls, passing, now and again, single files of radiant natives carrying flowers and fruits piled high on their heads to celebrate some local festival at a shrine. They never turned their heads to notice us; they sang on serenely, unconcerned in other people's affairs. Swinging along the dark roads the women carried, on their hips, poles ending in flaming torches. These threw an eery light over the groups and ignited our minds to wonderment and awe. A new moon found its way into the picture, and yokes of white oxen, with gilded horns and garlanded with brilliant flowers, blocked the roadway. They too were celebrating the Harvest festival, and each pair of these beasts of burden carried a huge wooden bell swung between their necks. The bell was often three or four feet across and a foot thick. As we pulled aside to let the frequent groups pass by we became more and more aware of the mysterious pungent aromas of a tropical night. The distant vibrations of a gamelon orchestra filled the air, growing louder and more intense. These orchestras consist of a group of instruments made of metal strips hung on a carved wooden frame. These strips are of varied tone and are struck with small hammers, alternated with gongs. Through a grove of tree-trunks in the glow of flaming torches we saw about fifty natives squatting about the players, young girls practising their dancing steps and marvellous gestures of the hands. All had serious faces, intent on perfecting their technical skill. At one point, the roadway was cut off by a crowd. The space cleared for the dancing performers was marked out by four great, painted wooden animals, mythical beasts with black and golden bodies, pulled on platforms and laden with scarlet and white garlands of hybiscus and jasmin.

The native host of the evening had his woven straw couches brought out to the edge of the dancing arena and invited his guests to recline and enjoy the performance. A youngster of eleven years, arrayed in golden costume and glittering headdress (his huge, dark eyes giving him the look of a surprised fawn) stepped into the torchlit square and challenged all comers in continual succession from nine o'clock until two or three o'clock in the morning.

During the performance a silent crowd of natives gradually filled every available space of ground. Three or four hundred men, women, and children were packed together, shoulder to shoulder, in solid rows—the babies held by the young children seated on the ground, the youths next, and banked behind these the men and women of all ages, their slim hips wrapped in multicolored batiks with belts of vivid orange and green and scarlet. No one spoke; the eternal chewing of betel-nut kept them quiet and contented to let their eyes drink in the beauty of this midsummer-night's dream.

Through the efficient service of Minas, the American Express Company's agent, we secured lodgings in a small hostel, "The Satrya," where the regular tourists seldom came. This permitted us great freedom for working, and the enclosed courtyard served as an open-air studio. Our "chambermaid" was a "fuzzy wuzzy" pure-blooded Papuan, named Made, with a bone through his nose, black as darkest Africa, with a gentle, high-pitched voice. Every morning at six-thirty he would come silently into my room, draw back the mosquito netting, and place the tea tray beside me on the wide, flat bed. There were never any sheets provided to cover one—it was too hot to care —and the Dutch wife (a cylindrical pillow under our knees) was one's only solace. The doors were of netting or, if of wood, never closed. The room where one bathed had a concrete floor and a tank of water from which one ladled out in tin dippers what was poured over our bodies.

Another not-far-away experience was the visit to the sacred forest, where hundreds of monkeys of all descriptions seemed to know that no harm would befall them. They gathered in crowds, chattering in the branches, darting in and out of the thick underbrush and mischievously snatching the bananas offered by the occasional visitors. They seemed rather shy about being photographed, but in spite of this Sam made a fine movie record of them.

Frequent showers of torrential rain fell at odd intervals during the day and added their steaming moisture to the tropical heat, which only abated for a few hours between midnight and dawn.

THE TEMPLES OF BALI ARE A MASS OF NATIVE STONE–CARVING

The soft gray stone is highly colored with patches of green moss

Photo. Bernes Maroteau.

BALINESE WOOD–CARVING (18 INCHES HIGH)
MADE BY A BOY OF SIXTEEN

Photo. S. B. G.

THE STAR DANCER OF DEN PASAR, BALI, PERFORM–
ING IN THE SHADE OF THE PALM–TREES

Every gesture of the supple fingers has a definite meaning
and significance

BALI AFTER THE TROPICAL RAIN, WHICH FLOODS THE PADDY FIELDS AND FILLS THE
AIR WITH MISTY CLOUDS THAT HOVER ABOUT THE VOLCANOES IN THE DISTANCE

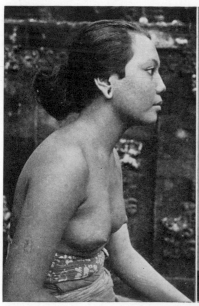

Photo. S. B. G.

NI POLOG, DANCER OF BALI,
WHO POSED FOR M. H.

GOLDEN BRONZE STATUETTE
OF BALINESE DANCER BY M. H.

© *F. M. N. H.*

LIFE–SIZE PORTRAIT OF NI POLOG
BY M. H.

(Hall of Man)

THE TOWERS OF THE DEAD AT A CREMATION CEREMONY IN BALI

Note the figures of the boys climbing to the top of these bamboo and *papier-mâché* structures

PARTICIPANTS IN THE HARVEST FESTIVAL STOP BEFORE THE VERANDAH OF OUR HOTEL SATRYA

The bullocks are resplendent in gay-colored head-dresses, gilded horns, and wooden bells that hang from their necks

THE PAPUAN BOY POSING FOR HIS PORTRAIT WHILE IT WAS 105 DEGREES IN THE SHADE,
UNDER THE CORRUGATED IRON ROOF

The portrait in pastel is shown at the right

TWO LEADING LADIES OF THE BALINESE BALLET, BEDECKED IN GOLD AND RED BROCADE,
AND GILDED HEAD–DRESSES

One evening we were invited by the only four guests at our "hotel" to attend an open-air dancing party, provided by the generosity of Mr. John Ford, of the Fox Film Company in Hollywood. He warned us to carry our own chairs, as there were no seats provided, and so we all filed out of the dining-room carrying our chairs on our heads, until we reached the enclosure of the Satrya Temple coconut grove.

There were so many bats flying about in our dining-room that I preferred to wind the table napkin into a turban. As we approached the temple we could see the torches flaring between the trees, and heard the sound of myriad waters—or was it the gamelon orchestras tuning up?

Grouped around a hollow square, lighted by moonlight, were the golden-costumed girl dancers, wound tightly into their beautiful costumes, the shimmering fan-like head-dresses sparkling in the flame-light from the resin torches. They were intently following the ever-present priest who, seated in one corner, was chanting his prayer before the ceremony could begin. Squatting on their haunches, the sleek little figures of the musicians were dotted about in groups of twelve or sixteen players, the leader in the center, swinging from side to side as his thin, dark arms darted out over the glinting array of metal strips, striking them with a hammer in unbelievable rapidity and giving the rhythm to the other players.

The front rows of the audience were crowded with children and babies. Most of the latter had fallen asleep in the arms of their sisters, who seemed hardly old enough to stay awake themselves after six o'clock. Many of these interested youngsters would follow the dancers so attentively that their own little hands and arms would imitate the gestures almost subconsciously in their instinctive desire to be a part of the performance.

To Mr. Ford's amazement, a crowd of three hundred or more Balinese natives had come from far and near to enjoy his party. He had difficulty explaining why he and his guests should have the front row seats, but when the situation was finally explained by an interpreter the crowd cheerfully made room for us and the signal was given to begin. Without warning an occasional coconut would drop from the top of a sixty-foot tree and split itself open on the ground, just missing our heads.

With a jangle of gongs and gamelons the skilled musicians filled the air with their strange, alluring music.

The first dance was performed by a group of twenty men wearing long, black, false moustaches and white cotton gloves, their batik saris wound about their sleek brown hips and legs. These men shouted and jumped about in a frenzy of excitement, piling up on each other in geometrical patterns like acrobats—sometimes four or five men— and working up to a wild climax of whooping shouts and gesticulations. As far as we could tell, they were shouting: "Go die! Go die!" and the chorus was: "Bow wow wow! Bow wow wow!"

Mr. Ford, being accustomed to the technique of entertaining his performers in Hollywood, invited as many of the troupe as the hotel manager could crowd into the one main dining-room and entrance hall. Soft, cool drinks and sweet cakes were enthusiastically consumed, and the meaning and symbolism of many of their dances were explained to us amidst a continuous ripple of laughter and gaiety.

The difference between Bali and Java is very striking. The former, by its isolation and lack of accommodation for the casual tourist, and because of the wise policy of the Dutch which has left Bali for the Balinese, has retained its individuality and primitive character. The people are taller and rather lighter in skin color than the Javanese. Their features are less sharp and their manners gentler. They seem more like unspoiled children of Eden than any other race I have yet had the opportunity of studying. Surrounded as they are by a garden as beautiful as an earthly paradise can be, these creatures of sunlight and music exude a mellow satisfaction of life that seems too good to be true.

Bali is an island where gods still sanctify existence by their presence, and the people live their religion instead of preaching it. Brahmanism is practised throughout the island; the Balinese migrated from Java in the ninth and sixteenth centuries and brought their beliefs with them, whereas Java became Islamized. In Bali, Shiva still rules the festivals and ceremonies at which the priests preside, and prayers are offered before any dancing takes place.

The most impressive ceremony one may witness is the cremation of the dead. We were fortunate to be in Bali during one of these extraordinary events. Thirteen bodies had been prepared and wrapped in their shrouds and kept in the outer covered buildings of their various family compounds. As the cost of these cremations is very heavy the family waits sometimes many months, until all the relatives and friends combine in the mutual effort to construct a gigantic *papier-mâché* and wooden tower, painted with brilliant colors and covered with banners. This is lashed and supported on a huge bamboo raft. At the top of this tower, often fifty or sixty feet high, the body of the dead is lashed and is carried on the shoulders of a hundred men across country, up to the highest hill, where the funeral pyres are prepared and the colored wooden coffins placed in rows over the fagots. When the towers reach the hilltop, the shrouded body is carried down an inclined platform and placed in the open coffin. Relatives are given torches with which to ignite the fires. The quivering, scorching air is filled with the crackling of flames and clouds of smoke. After many hours the thousands of spectators gradually disperse, and the ashes are carefully sifted and bits of bones collected in jars and replaced in the gilded towers, which are again carried by the hundred men down the hillside to the seashore. There the men walk out into the water until the great bamboo raft on their shoulders is floated off on the surface of the sea and carried by the wind far away into oblivion and lost to sight forevermore.

These ceremonies are accompanied by gamelon orchestras and a procession of gift-bearers who place their rich offerings around the body as the fires begin to mount about the coffins. They are occasions of great rejoicing, for the Balinese believe that by these cremations the souls of their dead are liberated to eternal happiness.

While in Bali I modelled the head of a dancer named Ni Polog, in the village of Den Pasar, and made chalk portraits of our Balinese table-boy and of the Papuan room-boy who insisted on removing the long bone which pierced his nose, when he came to pose for me.

Crossing from Bali to Java may be a simple matter if the weather is good, but our experience was something of an adventure. For two days a storm had lashed the sea into a frenzy and had destroyed the fragile jetty from which the small boats carried passengers to the

Dutch steamers. A few hardy sailors tried their luck pushing off directly from the beach in their native canoes, but even these were soon overturned, and signals were sent to the steamer to proceed thirty miles down the coast, where a little bay might offer shelter from the heavy swell that made embarking impossible.

Our little group of travellers always included the twenty-seven boxes and trunks in which all photographic and modelling supplies were carried, so it was quite an undertaking to find immediate transportation to the promised shelter. However, by good fortune cars were procured, the haven reached, and from the pebbled beach we were carried aloft in chairs on the shoulders of good-natured natives who waded through the breakers, waist deep, until all of us were safely tumbled into the rowboats, which were kept beyond the waves and ultimately carried us to the waiting steamer.

Java

As an artist, one of the things which struck me as most interesting in Bali and Java was the native schools of silversmiths and wood and stone carvers, where boys from fourteen to twenty-four years of age are carefully trained, in the shade of palm-trees, to become expert craftsmen. They spend ten years of daily toil under their masters' guidance and constant surveillance, without pay except their midday meal of rice. When a temple falls into ruin or ancient sculpture disintegrates, they are copied and replaced by these young sculptors. The island of Bali is therefore rich in its ornate temples, and the growing generations feel a natural pride in keeping these temples in repair.

The art of dancing is considered as the chief delight and occupation of the young men and women from childhood until they come to marriageable age. Certain local variations in the gestures and rhythm are very noticeable. The Javanese school seems more formal and sophisticated than the Balinese, but in both one finds the tech-

THE IMPRESSIVE PYRAMIDAL TERRACES OF THE TEMPLE OF BOROBODOUR, JAVA

AN ARRAY OF THE FIGURES OF JAVANESE PUPPETS AND VARIOUS NATIVE MUSICAL
INSTRUMENTS OF THE GAMELON ORCHESTRA

265

TWO OF THE SCULPTURED PANELS ON THE WALLS OF PRAMBANAN TEMPLE, CENTRAL JAVA

Above is shown the Hindu influence and rugged technique. Below are types of Africans on the right, and great richness of design and decoration very evident in all of these

DOCTOR DE VINK AND M. H. STANDING BESIDE THE STATUE OF VISHNU AT 6:30 A.M.

The Temple of Prambanan, near Jokjo, Java. This great figure was buried during an earthquake

Left: THE CHIEF DANCER OF THE SULTAN'S COURT AT JOKJO, JAVA, AS SHE APPEARED
TO DANCE FOR THE MOVING–PICTURE TAKEN BY S. B. G.

The costume is made of Javanese batiks, blue and gold brocades. The three flat discs hung from the neck
are of perforated buffalo hide, gilded in an intricate design

Right: MALE DANCER OF THE SULTAN'S COURT, SOLO, JAVA, WEARING BLACK AND GOLD
BUFFALO HIDE HELMET

IN JAVA AND BALI THE YOUNG BOYS ARE EXPERT CARVERS AND METAL–WORKERS

This boy is making a design on a brass bowl in the streets of Java

nique of hand-gestures, or "mudras" as they are called, highly developed. In Solo and **Jokjo,** Sam was able to record the court dancers in moving-pictures, and they were also persuaded to pose for me to make a series of accurate casts of their hands, showing the fingers bent backwards in unbelievable positions, only possible after years of practice, beginning in early childhood.

The Wayang players, in picturesque costumes, gave exciting and dramatic performances in an out-of-door theatre, lasting throughout the night and the following day. The acting was accompanied by constant music. Some of the musicians fell asleep at odd moments during the long program, propped against the wall of their covered platform, resuming their parts as they awoke, without changing the position of their legs, folded tailor fashion under their slim bronze bodies. The most ferocious-looking masks, with lions' teeth, were worn, and pantomimes enacted to suggest dragons and demons.

The chief actor of these terrorizing characters fascinated me. With the aid of our interpreter I worked my way through the crowd to where he made his exit, and we arranged an interview for the following day. When I arrived at the stage entrance of the theatre at eleven o'clock the next morning I noticed the seated figure of a man swaying back and forth and crooning softly to a sleeping babe which he rocked gently to and fro in his arms in the shade of a palm-tree. As I drew nearer I recognized the figure and head of the demon actor of the previous evening. It was difficult to believe in such a metamorphosis, but it was a fact, and the gentle father quietly laid the sleeping baby on a pile of leaves and tiptoed into the hallway, beckoning me to follow. In the property room he opened the carved wooden chests and showed me his collections of costumes, masks, head-dresses, and gilded wings. These helmets and wings are made of buffalo hide, beautifully designed and pierced in intricate lacelike patterns and then gilded. We were able to acquire a few samples of this local work, and we were fortunate enough to have this actor-dancer give a complete performance of a Kriss dance in the garden of our hotel, which was photographed by Sam in moving-pictures.

Bats and flying foxes are nightly visitors; so it is well to examine your mosquito-netting cage and see that there are no holes in it.

Lizards, being harmless and attending strictly to their own business of catching flies and mosquitoes for you, should be left on the wall and ceiling and respected as moving decorations.

Beware of rest-houses where, in damp tropical climates, the bed and chair and table are enclosed in a wire metal cage instead of the white cotton mosquito-nets over the beds! These wire-netted rooms often act as a cage in a zoo, because the door seldom reaches to the floor and all the local animal life crawls in, explores, hides, and waits for the night occupant, who, innocently thinking he will shut out bats and rats with safety and security, locks his cage, undresses and, just before blowing out his candle, notices to his horror that spiders are casting shadows on his white sheet and that the floor is decorated with various forms of natural-history specimens. The hunt then starts, everything seems to be alive—slippers, clothing; everything has to be shaken, searched, and swept outside. The cracks between the panels of wire netting are now seen to be wide enough to admit any herculean mosquito or centipede, and the hoped-for night's rest often becomes a nightmare of apprehension. Fatigue from the day's activities, however, comes as a blessing, and the exhausted traveller falls asleep on his flat, hard bed, gasping for air and thanking his stars that there is at least a "Dutch wife" under his knees to share his nocturnal hours.

One day we met a young Dutchman with a good-looking wife, who said after being in New Guinea a fortnight, that he noticed a Papuan native leading a pig who seemed to be following them day after day. "What does that fellow want?" he asked as soon as he met some one who could speak both Dutch and Papuan.

"He wants to sell you his pig, sir."

"Ah, what does he want for it?"

"Your wife, sir." You see, it is an old local custom.

Although not officially tolerated, the national sport of cockfighting still persists, and splendid specimens of cocks are bred and trained and carried about in bell-shaped baskets often placed in rows along the highway, to accustom the birds to passers-by, and to the noise and confusion of crowds. In Bali the fighting cock wears only one spur, but this is five inches long and very sharp. At a recent combat one of the birds flew into the audience and drove his spur through the skull of an observer with fatal results.

One evening in Jokjokarta, central Java, we started off after dinner in a high-wheeled, open carriage to explore the night-life of the town. The festivities of the New Year's celebration were still trailing along, so we noticed many candles lighted in the Chinese quarter and the usual gay paper lanterns hanging over the doorways. We had asked our diminutive Javanese driver if he could not wangle us into some Chinese place where there was a puppet-show going on. He smiled knowingly, and after winding in and out of endless picturesque streets and alleyways, drove up to the curb and handed me the reins of the horse. He disappeared into a house and after some time came out beaming and chatting with a Chinese merchant in the inevitable blue cotton coat.

Apparently we were expected to enter his house. He spoke no word of English. The driver tied the horse to a fence and led us into the dimly lighted Chinese interior. We walked quietly from one room into another. Along the walls of the rooms were bamboo beds and on these were the sleeping inmates of the house. Some, on hearing our footsteps, opened an eye and looked us over and, quite undisturbed, turned over and resumed their sonorous and rhythmic breathing. Entering the fourth room, we found it filled with low, wooden benches. In the dark background were seated a few silent figures. These were watching the performance of a shadow play which was being enacted on a screen at the opposite end of the room. Our Chinese host motioned us to sit down in the front rows and, with much bowing and smiling, left us to enjoy the performance. On one side of the room was a great altar of gifts and offerings; candles and incense were burning amidst a galaxy of paper flowers, fruits, cakes, and all manner of gifts. The worship of their ancestors was still going on and we, without more introduction than some word from our *fiacre* driver, had been admitted and quite naturally invited to enjoy and share their oriental entertainment.

Some of the finest examples of architecture and bas-relief sculpture are found in the recently restored temple cf Prambanan, near Jokjo, in Java. An ardent Dutch archeologist, Doctor de Vink, has spent twenty-two years directing the excavating and replacing, stone by stone, of the half-buried ruins of the grandiose structure. In many ways the carvings exceed even those of the vast and renowned Borobodour Temple. The latter is, of course, far more monumental in scale and is in an amazingly good state of preservation. From its various terraces, which pile up upon one another from the foundation to the peak, growing smaller at each level, one has magnificent views of all the surrounding country of Java. This great temple might be the inspirational ancestor of all modern "set-backs" in architecture.

The schools of flying-fish darted about over the surface of the water like crystal spray glittering in the sharp sunlight.

After visiting Batavia, with its extraordinary museum, and modelling the Sundanese type of Javanese woman, we continued our journey to the Straits Settlements by steamer, stopping at Sumatra en route, and landing finally at Singapore.

Singapore and the Malay Jungles

Forewarned of our imminent arrival and of our program of work, Mr. Chasens of the Singapore Museum met us at the dock and agreed to assist us in our search for the three aboriginal tribes of the Malay Peninsula—the Jakuns, the Sakais, and the Semang pygmies, who live in the dense jungle between Johore and Penang.

The plan in Singapore to secure Malay, Borneo, and Sumatra types started off under the direction of Doctor Harrower, who lost no time in assembling in two days fifteen types for us to study and photograph.

At Raffle's Hotel, the outside sitting-room adjoining each bedroom provided a splendid studio, and by a little word to the management we were able to bring our collection of natives through a side-entrance directly into our own quarters, to be photographed and duly modelled by me. A huge electric fan hung from the ceiling and kept the air stirring, and frequent showers revived us from time to time. Tropical architecture builds its swinging doors between all the rooms, with

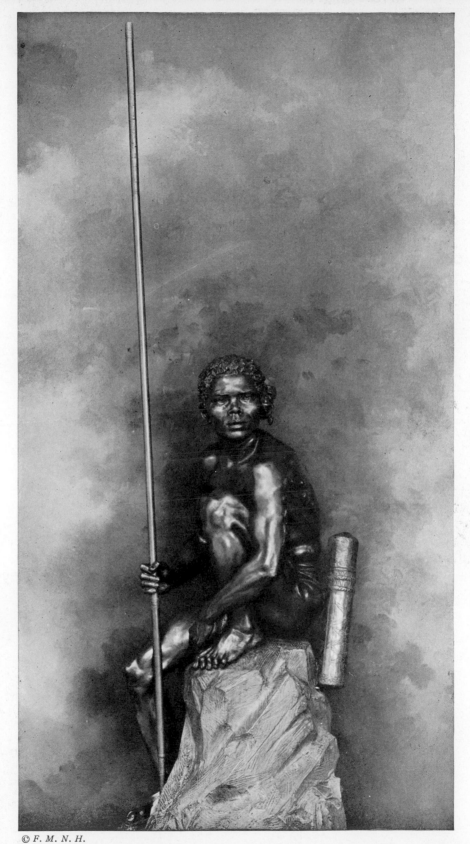

LIFE–SIZE BRONZE FIGURE OF SEMANG PIGMY OF THE MALAY JUNGLE TRIBES

Showing his blow-pipe and quiver of poisoned arrows. (Hall of Man)   273

THE JAKUN TRIBE
IN THE MALAY JUN-
GLE. FATHER 42,
MOTHER 15

Baby of one year strap-
ped on the father's
back. Portraits of both
are in the Hall of Man

M. H. STANDING WITH
TWO SAKAI WARRIORS

Showing relative size of
these little people. M. H.
is 5'7". Temperature average in the shade 108° at
midday

GROUP OF SEMANG PIGMIES

Many of them, seeing the bright blossoms on hibiscus bushes, plucked the flowers and stuck them over their ears

M. H. PREPARING A CLAY HEAD ON THE TRUNK-RACK OF A FORD CAR

The baby gazelle ran out of the jungle and played with us in a most friendly manner

A HANDSOME CHIEF OF THE SAKAI TRIBE

THE BOY I SELECTED AS MY MODEL FOR THE
SEMANG PIGMY TYPE IN THE HALL OF MAN

© F. M. N. H.

LIFE–SIZE BRONZE FIGURE OF SOLOMON ISLANDER CLIMBING A PALM–TREE, A RING IN
HIS NOSE AND A PLUG IN HIS EAR

(Hall of Man).

a clearance of two feet above the floor, and as they do not reach to the top of the door-frames what little air there is may circulate throughout the house. The beds are in the center of the rooms, covered with their canopy of mosquito-nets.

Evenings in Singapore were often spent in exploring the docks and watching the numberless vessels, yachts, and sailing craft lying at anchor and silhouetted in the moonlight—laden with all the treasures and aromatic products of the South Seas and extreme orient.

To enumerate the exotic dishes of which we were fortunate enough to partake would sound more like a poem than a menu. Consider, for instance, baskets heaped high with figs of Barbary, with golden bananas and pineapples, coconuts and pimentos; dishes containing mangoes, cumquats and ginger; bunches of dates and oranges, lemons and apricots piled upon trays of laurel leaves. Ships crowding the port were constantly being loaded with cargoes of thyme, saffron, yellow peppers of Nepal, kropeks, and cinnamon, all exuding their penetrating perfumes that filled the air with a staggering combination of aromas.

In the Singapore Botanical Garden we obtained a section of the palm-tree trunk indigenous to the Solomon Islands. On this we made a plaster-cast so that I could have it for reference in Paris when I finished the full-size model of my Solomon Islander climbing on a tree. I had forgotten to do this when I was modelling the native climber. His coal-black personality had so completely absorbed my attention that I had only sketched in the tree as a means of support to his body in the hand-and-foot-gripping pose.

The Jakuns were the first group of jungle folk to be captured by our scouts in the woods north of Johore. With the assistance of the police and some of the government officials we were able to entice a family of three—father, mother, and baby. They were wrapped in blankets and stealthily transported in the dawn hours to the back courtyard of the Singapore Museum, where Sam photographed them and where, by superhuman effort, I modelled the full-size bust of the father and the fifteen-year-old mother in one day.

All day long the half pygmy warrior, about four feet ten inches tall, carried his baby slung in a cloth over his shoulder. He held a large steel knife across his knees and never for a moment took his eyes off me. How could he guess what manner of black magic might be in action? He was watching an unexplained phenomenon, a duplication of his wife, created before his eyes by an interloping white woman. This was sufficient cause for him to be on guard. Only after many hours did the little family relax enough to drink coffee, smoke cigarettes, and munch various sweets and chocolates which we gladly provided. The baby of fifteen months was a confirmed smoker, and seemed content in its snug little bundle for hours at a time.

The climax of our understanding was reached after the heads were completed, when the father Jakun agreed to undergo the ordeal of having his foot cast in negocoll. During the afternoon we had cast the hand of a tame Borneo Dyak close to the spot where the Jakun was posing for me, so that he could watch the process. When our Jakun saw us reimburse the smiling and unharmed Dyak, whose hand had been painlessly reproduced in a half hour, his mind was already prepared. The offer of more cigarettes, beads, and salt was sufficient to entice him to submit his curious, bunchy, little foot, which had climbed so many trees, and trotted over so many jungle paths that the muscles on the soles were like pads under an animal's paw and none of his toes touched the ground when he stood upright on both feet. The plaster ran underneath and gave us a sharp cast of the underside of his ten toes as well as the complete upper foot.

A curious case of the interest taken in sculpture by savages was that of a young Borneo Dyak. He had lived his life in the traditional manner of his tribe and had three or four human heads to his credit. Before asking the young lady of his choice to marry, it was customary for the young lover to slay a few enemies and bring the heads as a proof of his courage, and lay them before his future wife. The young Dyak, two years later, worked for a visiting Englishman as an assistant hunter in a scientific exploration.

When the white visitor prepared to leave, the young native begged to accompany him to Malay Straits Settlements and to be permitted to continue working for the Englishman, who was attached to a museum of ethnography. He proved to be very clever with his hands and keen to learn all about stuffing animals.

When I arrived to model the local types, the Dyak had cut his hair like the other Malays and was wearing khaki trousers and shirt. After helping me a few days, he asked if I would give him lessons in measuring heads and teach him how to build an armature. The next day he took me to the end of the workroom, behind a pile of packing cases, where he showed me what he had done in secret since my arrival. He had dipped old newspapers into plaster and pressed them around sticks of wood, until by pushing and adding lumps of plaster he had constructed a full-length figure of a man. This, he said, did not satisfy him and he would work all night if I would only show him how to build up real earth on strong framework. It was gratifying and certainly astonishing to find such an apt pupil so recently graduated from the jungle school of real head-hunting.

In Hawaii, the same passionate desire to learn the first steps in modelling and plaster-casting had been expressed by a Japanese and a Maori, both of whom made most remarkable progress in a very short time.

In fact, in four or five museums we were able to train some member of the group of native assistants to use the tools and ingredients of the Negocoll casting method so competently that they were able to continue this work under supervision of the foreman of the workroom after we had left.

Carefully following instructions from the British officials, we proceeded northward by train to Tapah Road, where we were met by a cheery young Britisher in a Ford car. This was Mr. Noone, assistant anthropologist of the Taiping Museum, who was to act as our guide and interpreter. He had studied the dialects of the jungle people and was welcomed by them as a friendly visitor, "a bringer of gifts."

When I found it would be necessary to model these wild jungle people "on the hoof," so to speak, we rigged up a very serviceable model stand on the trunk-rack at the back of the Ford car, by strapping a packing-case securely to the metal frame. To the top of this, I fastened the baseboard of my plasteline head, with strong thumb screws. This placed the work on a level with my standing model's head.

In our first encounter with the Sakai tribes, we received proof of the tact and naturalness of manner with which he had won their confidence. *We* presented a new and stiff problem, however; a black picture-machine that made a noise and suggested a box of magic, and a white woman who smoked like their women, but who made soft lumps of clay into faces.

After lengthy explanations and the exhibition of all our materials and tools, they were assured that we carried no weapons and not only meant them no harm but would reward them if they played fair and did not run away. Bright beads and colored ribbons and cigarettes were shown to them as bait. A compromise was finally arranged. They would lead us along their trails to their camps; they would climb trees, shoot blowpipes, chase away tigers, kill snakes, and be our friends, provided that while I was making the mud faces the two men in our party would walk away out of sight with brother Sakais and leave me alone with my victim for two hours.

To this plan we all agreed. As soon as I was alone with my subject, I carefully demonstrated that my modelling tool was made of harmless wood, although it was shaped like a blade. I drew it across my arm to prove that it had a dull edge; then I pointed to the Sakai's sharp steel blade and in eye-and-sign language asked him to lend it to me. As I began to draw the handle of his blade over my arm, he sprang forward and gripped my wrist, frightened and wide-eyed as a child. He shook his head and chattered nervously, taking back his knife and pushing it into its sheath for the first time since we had met. I offered him my hand, but seeing that he did not understand, I took his in mine and shook it. After a friendly and eloquent exchange of glances, we set to work, both smiling. He observed all my preparations with keen interest. When I mentioned to him that I was ready to start, he straightened his little loin-cloth, smiled, made sure that his head-band was in place, and seemed at last to understand what was expected of him. Instinctive personal pride is common to all men. When I could find this Achilles tendon, it was like finding the key to an international language.

An occasional cigarette permitted him to move about a little and feel at ease, but he never stepped out of the circle of twigs which I had laid on the ground to keep him within bounds while posing.

Frequent interruptions were caused by a group of gibbons that climbed far out on the branches of neighboring trees, threw bananas at us, and laughed merrily at my efforts. After a while they grew too bold, and dropped heavy stems of jungle ferns four to six feet long. At a signal from me, my little savage dispersed the monkeys with his blow pipe, shooting well-aimed poisoned arrows into the trees

My little "wild man" kept a watchful eye on the animal kingdom and proved a swift and dependable guardian. Without warning he suddenly sprang forward and struck the head off an overcurious snake that I had not even noticed crawling near my feet. I tried not to look startled. Then he smiled and pointed to my sandals and shook his finger warningly. I could only answer by pointing to his own bare feet and body. This struck him as being so humorous that his hearty laughter brought out of the neighboring bushes two or three little Sakais that I had not seen or suspected. Their appearance speeded up my circulation a bit. Again I resorted to cigarettes as a calming influence and kept on working for an hour and fifty minutes, when I heard the voices and footsteps of our returning companions. At this moment there was a rustle in the leaves and a frail young fawn, on wobbly legs, ran out into the sunlight. Never having seen a human being, he was not afraid, and jumped lightly into my outstretched arms, just in time to be photographed by Sam, whose ever-ready camera never missed.

The Sakai incident was a thrilling experience and proved to our satisfaction that fair play and trust, though sometimes lacking in civilized countries, are constantly in use among so-called savage tribes. A reassuring look was a sufficient guarantee of safety. It is the paupers, sometimes, who live in palaces, and the princes who live in the jungles.

The head was completed and set back into its own case and screwed firmly by the baseboard to the lower end, so that it did not move when lifted by the metal carrying-handle on top. The ribbons and beads and packets of cigarettes were distributed to our model and the Sakai guides, and they were as pleased as children with new toys.

This open-air sculpture act took place between Taiping and Lenggong. The weather conditions were uncertain, for we were kept guessing when the heavens would open and pour a deluge of the

wettest rain in the world over us. During the year this Malay Peninsula has a heavier rainfall than any other country in the world.

We were told that only a few weeks before our arrival, an American
expedition under the leadership of Mr. Vernay had shot the last of
a rare species of rhinoceros in this territory. Some of the well-known
movies of "Bring 'em Back Alive," by Frank Buck, had been staged
in this region.

I couldn't help thinking what a good scene for a movie it would
make to bring a ribbon and glass-bead counter from Woolworth's,
a window-display of salt and chocolate, and a United Cigar store
supply of cigarettes and other tobacco "uplifters," with the magic
blue flame burning forever on the pagan altar of inveterate smokers.
To defend such a surprise caravan from a band of savages, one would
probably have to travel in an armored truck and wear a complete suit
of mediæval armor, but it might be worth the effort to see the fun.

From Tapah Road, where we had enjoyed the hospitality of the
District Officer, Colonel G. A. de C. Mowbray, and his wife, we continued northward by motor, following the narrow, winding roadway
cut by the British through the dense jungles.

Hunting aboriginal tribes in the Malay jungles was an experience
worth the entire trip. The magnificent scale of the stage-setting, the
elemental struggle of humans, animals, and plants for existence, made
life in one of our tram-line cities seem a very tame and artificial affair.

The trails cut by the British through these jungles are the only
means of communication when the railroad line is abandoned. The
various tribes have their own distinct localities, and they each have
their own dialects and traditions.

Mr. Noone of the Taiping Museum knew the probable location of
certain tribes, and guided us to a little government bungalow in their
vicinity, where we spent the night. We managed to track down another little band of Sakais. They seemed quite tame, but very shy. I
started the portrait of a young male, building up the life-size head in
plasteline. We made plans to return the following morning at seven
A.M. to the same place, where they had built their palm-leaved shelter.
Alas, when we kept our appointment we found no trace of our friends
of the previous day; the camp had been completely demolished and

no trace of any of our Sakais was left. No doubt they had suspected our motives or had been frightened away by some tribal taboo.

Not too encouraged by this experience, we continued our search northward and by good fortune found a trail leading to another Sakai shelter. This time a little hunter carrying his blow-pipe was persuaded to be our guide, but when we urged him to climb into the Ford car and direct us, his superstitions and religious principles reduced him to a state of trembling, and terrified gasping sounds came out of his quivering lips. For nothing on earth would he be seen touching our noisy "demon wagon" with fire in its body. He at last agreed to run along beside us, showing the way. This he did for a mile or two, when suddenly two more Sakais appeared in the bushes at the roadside.

One of these was so striking a type that we at once started work and tempted him and his fellow hunter to stay with us and pose for the mysterious purpose of "making another myself"—as he explained in his own language to his friends and to the interpreter.

This little fellow taught me the real value of a good American dollar bill in a Malay jungle. By chance, I found a "greenback" in my wallet, and just to divert his attention and interest him, I offered the bill to him. Our cigarettes had tempted him to submit to our demands, and now he examined this green paper with curiosity. Suddenly an idea struck his fancy and he tore the bill in half, rolling it in his hands like a cigarette and putting it in his mouth for a light. The other half was offered to his friend, who did likewise, and we had a good laugh at the originality of this use of Uncle Sam's fluctuating currency!

The great problem after modelling one of these heads in the midst of a jungle was to transport it safely to some place where we could make a plaster cast on the original and pack it in some receptacle that could be shipped to Paris. As there was never any cotton-wool or excelsior or tissue-paper available to protect these plasters, we resorted to collecting all the straw covers on mineral-water bottles and wrapping them in banana-leaves and ferns. The fact that forty-eight cases of plasters were shipped during our journey with only one finger broken in transit was a record for which we were very grateful and a little proud. All the portrait heads were made life-size from the various subjects. Sam was constantly taking accurate photographs (front, side, and back views) and measurements were taken to assist me to complete all details in Paris on my return.

The trail would occasionally pass through a marshy area of blasted gray tree trunks, denuded of all their foliage, endless regiments of these stark sentinels, whose roots had been killed in some ancient flood, and which remained standing like the echo of some primordial disaster, held in the grip of the oozing mud. The air was pervaded with a strange, dank stench of rotting vegetation, and we drove through these sections holding our noses, but staring with amazement and curiosity at these gigantic, implacable wooden arabesques glinting like metal in the sharp sunlight that comes after a soaking tropical shower.

The Sakais and Semang pygmies climb tall palm-trees without difficulty. Clasping the trunk between their arms and knees, they become so expert that for our moving-picture demonstrations they were able to stand almost erect on the trunks of these trees by the side pressure of their feet and hands only. Sometimes swarms of red ants on the trees would make them slide down from their high perches and run into the tall, soft ferns to brush these biting insects off their bodies.

The Semang pygmies, who dwell in the northern districts of the Malay Peninsula, resemble in many respects the pygmies of the Philippine Islands, the Andaman Islands, and Central Africa. They have short, crinkly hair and are stocky and strong in build, although less than five feet tall. When the little warriors are not aroused to fighting ardor, they are soft-voiced, smiling, and friendly, but they are often too shy to be conveniently approached. It was a most difficult task to collect a large enough number of these little people to form a comprehensive group of types.

The British officer in charge of this district was Anthony Churchill, a nephew of Winston Churchill. Wearing a green-lined pith helmet, immaculate white linen shorts and white woollen golf stockings, and carrying a swanky jungle stick, he welcomed us to his little wooden hut with true colonial hospitality.

With his assistance and the services of his jungle police, we were able to surround a goodly number of Semangs and persuade them to

MALE SAKAI TYPE

THE SHY AND RETIRING FEMININE REPRESEN-
TATIVE OF THE SAKAI FAMILY

OUR EARLY MORNING VISITORS WHO RETURNED TO SHOW US HOW THEY WHITTLE
THEIR BAMBOO ARROWS AND DIP THEM IN DEADLY POISON

LIFE–SIZE PORTRAIT IN BRONZE OF SAKAI WARRIOR

Made by M. H. in two hours, when left alone with the subject in the jungle
(Hall of Man)

come out of the shadowy jungle into a clearing where there was enough sunlight to permit us to take their photographs. They instinctively fell into single file as if following a narrow trail, until we succeeded in convincing them of our friendliness, and induced them to come out on an open roadway by offering them steaming rice served in banana leaves.

The motion pictures that Sam made describe far better than I can do the agile movements of these little people. Two I especially noted: the gesture of raising the arms and pushing the head back with the right hand as an expression of greeting, and the crouching position taken for blowing through the blow-pipes the poisoned darts which are so deadly and so sure in aim that they kill at fifty feet. By good luck that afternoon we obtained quivers of arrows and indigenous examples of weaving in exchange for chocolates, salt, and cigarettes.

We considered ourselves even more fortunate, however, when, looking out through our bungalow shelter at dawn the next morning, we saw two pygmies, fully armed, but approaching in what seemed to be a friendly mood. We stepped out on the veranda and, through our interpreter, were informed that the little men had returned of their own accord to ask us whether we should like to see them make a new supply of poisoned arrows. If so, they were willing to work on our grassy, sunlit lawn. They were not afraid of us. They had accepted our offer of friendship, and in return would give a demonstration of their local craft of weapon-making in front of the magic box. This enabled us to make a complete record, from the first step of cutting the length of wood to the final step of dipping the dart into the poison and attaching the pith ball at the heavy end. When the pygmies, squatting on their hams, had whittled the arrows to a fine point, they stuck them through their curly hair until their heads bristled like porcupines. We were delighted with the results of their visit. We felt, too, that socially we had been a success, considering that the two little warriors had walked from six to eight miles to offer us the opportunity of making a unique picture. Their co-operation was all the more remarkable in view of the fact that the pygmies have no idea of what a photograph really is. If you show them a picture of another tribe, they look at it upside down and sidewise and then smilingly give it back without any understanding of a two-dimensional impression.

The part of the jungle through which we were travelling is considered by wild-game hunters to have more examples of wild life "on the hoof" than any other part of the world. It abounds in leopards, black panthers, monkeys, gibbons, snakes, rhinoceroses, and herds of wandering elephants. We often noted the distant sounds of the splintering of trees which were being pushed aside by the leaders of the herds on the way to the various water-holes. As we penetrated into the depths of the forest we became increasingly aware of the pungent perfumes exuded by gigantic tropical flowers and, in crossing swampy land, of the suffocatingly heavy odor of decaying fruit. The ferns in these swamps grew straight out of the ground to a height of forty or fifty feet, the graceful line of their stems making incredibly beautiful patterns. Roots dangled from the branches of many jungle trees, and were often indistinguishable from the sleeping pythons which coiled part of their bodies around the branches and left their tails waving in the air. Toward night a feeling came over us that even the leaves and the mossy, spongy ground were alive; the air was full of sounds of myriad insects, droning, buzzing, fluttering.

Unseen noises that slide down into the night, the snapping of twigs near the bungalow entrance, and the sudden thud against the wall of some great bat that has miscalculated his distance, all these sensations add to the eery fascination of sleeping in the jungle.

Huge toads glittering in the streak of moonlight gave me a distinct shiver whenever I met one—and their name was legion; they were able to work their way between cracked walls and seemed to enjoy especially the damp, soggy earth that surrounded the water-barrels from which we drew our bath-water in pails, or from which we could ladle out our own shower-bath with a tin dipper and pour it over our shoulders. Snakes also seemed to feel a special attraction for our bathing-rooms, and used to coil up in corners or glide in and out of the cooling shadows. How potent must be the lure of the jungle in its ageless grandeur, that it should retain an everlasting glamor in one's memory, with all these drawbacks obliterated and forgotten!

At a certain water-hole known for the number of big-game specimens that came there for their refreshment, we stopped our car behind some big trees and waited. Opposite the water-hole was a high rock, and this was used as a lookout by the animals. Tigers, panthers, elephants, and rhinos are found in this area of the Malay jungle. True to tradition, we heard the elephants pushing down the trees as they crashed their way through the thick underbrush.

Only one black panther appeared on the scene, but he was a good specimen, and was almost run over by the little Ford car in which Miss Green and Mr. Bellamy Brown were riding just ahead of us. The animal was more frightened than they were, and leaped into the forest and disappeared. On reaching our ultimate destination of Penang, we were much interested to hear that another traveller arriving just after us had been startled, while driving his covered motor-car past this same water-hole, to have a tiger spring from a rocky ledge on to his canvas-covered top. Luckily, he was going at a good speed and the tiger fell off, tearing the top to shreds with his claws as he tried to hang on.

The two excellent English interpreters in our party, Mr. Noone, the anthropologist, and Mr. Bellamy Brown, were both fearless young adventurers. Their natural delight in the beauty and drama of the jungle added a great deal to our pleasure, and their utter indifference to danger was so contagious that we were never conscious of fear during the entire trip.

It was hard to leave this wilderness of adventure, but the trail brought us to Penang, where we met our man Jean, who had come up from Singapore by boat, with all our heavy luggage. From there we sailed on a coast steamer bound for Rangoon, Burma.

During this trip we were able to cast the clay heads into plaster on the forward deck of the coast steamer and dry them in the sun. We then packed them and shipped them back to Paris, care of Marshall Field & Co.

Burma

Our entrance into the harbor of Rangoon was prefaced by a notice to all passengers that they should take particular care not to ride in rickshaws or rub their hands on the motor-door handles, etc., as there was a scourge of the plague and smallpox, and infection was easily carried. As these reports are frequently met with, one grows accustomed to avoiding any unnecessary contacts that might convey evil microbes.

My first experience in the hotel was to ring for a boy to take our laundry-bag. To my surprise the bell was answered by a small native servant of the "sweeper class," who extended a long pole in my direction, on which I was told to hang my bundle. I wondered at this long-distance technique, and was informed that the boy was of the untouchable class and so could not take anything from my hand to his. Such class distinction came as something of a shock to me.

A most delightful afternoon was spent on the country estate of a wealthy Chinese who owned a racing-stable. Our host had permitted us to use his garden as the setting for a moving-picture of the Burmese Court dancing troupe. These amazing, diminutive performers delighted us with their quaint and agile steps. They wore pink brocade wrapped tightly around the hips, and short white muslin jackets ending in a wired flounce which curved out in most surprising points just below the waistline. The headdress was complicated and piled high with gay-colored paper flowers and gold and silver trinkets.

The heat was so intense and the glare so blinding that even the metal of the camera expanded too far and stopped the mechanism at odd intervals. Both the dancers and the musicians, and Sam as well, who had to remain in the full glare of the sun, were thankful when the event came to a close, and our host offered a display of pink and golden soft drinks to revive the entertainers. After these beverages, we were invited to explore the racing-stables; then tea was formally served in the drawing-room, and to top off the afternoon, champagne was brought in a great bowl, filled with squares of ice—a Frigidaire having been added recently to this luxurious household!

THE THREE PADAUNG LADIES OF UPPER BURMA
ON THEIR VOYAGE TO U. S. A.

© F. M. N. H.

PORTRAIT IN BRONZE OF LEFT-HAND GIRL IN GROUP
BY M. H. (Hall of Man)

Photo. S. B. G.

YOUNG BURMESE PRIEST AT THE BUDDHIST
MONASTERY, RANGOON

YOUNG ANDAMAN ISLANDER DRINKING FROM A
NAUTILUS SHELL KNOWN AS "ODA–DA"

THE LEADING LADIES OF THE COURT DANCERS IN RANGOON
Their graceful hands express an infinite variety of symbolic meaning

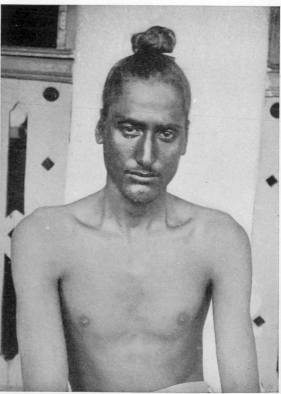

Photo. S. B. G.

U. AUNG THIN IN HIS NATIVE COSTUME
Burmese representative from Mandalay; legal advisor to the
Council of Princes, London

JEET SINGH, OUR SIKH CHAUFFEUR DURING OUR
VISIT TO SINGAPORE

Our models were selected by the eminent lawyer, Doctor Aung Thin, and by Doctor Lack of the Rangoon hospital. The local musical instruments of Burma were played during the performance of our dancers, and the star performer was a young lad of eleven years who came the following day to the hotel to pose for his portrait. Between the dancing numbers, the leading-lady ballet mistress lighted her whacking black cheroot and smoked it quite unconcernedly. This is a strong cigar, about nine inches long and one inch in diameter. Sam took a good movie of her, wreathed in the blue plumes of her cigar smoke.

The huge statue of a seated Buddha and the Shwe Dagon Pagoda of the sixth century are some of the great sights of Rangoon. This town of twenty-two square miles abounds in parks, lakes, gilded pagodas, and the noisiest tram-lines on earth.

The Burmese seem to be rather a composite type, combining certain Indian and Chinese characteristics in their anthropological make-up. We have to go back but a few years to find that in 1885 the whole of upper Burma was annexed to the British Empire, and their king, Thebaud, with his entire court, was captured and his power overthrown.

Kipling has given voice to the many charms of the country from Rangoon to Mandalay. A curious type of Burmese native comes from the northern hills. Three members of this remote Padaung tribe, in which the women wear on their necks and legs brass rings weighing a total of sixty pounds, and who were certainly most extraordinary-looking people, were imported to America by the Ringling circus company in 1933—two years after we had visited Burma. By arrangement with the management I was able to model the portrait of one of these "giraffe-necked" women in my own studio in New York, and carry out the difficult details of her brass collar, without the usual strain and fatigue of modelling while travelling. These curious and shy creatures came from their hotel with Gretchen Green quite willingly in a taxi, and they explored our house with as much excitement as we might experience in exploring one of their ornate temples. I found them as simple as children and very quick to understand hand-gestures and picture-puzzles. Their brass collars are seven or eight inches high, are never removed after the age of twelve or fifteen, and are worn into their graves; the neck becomes so fragile and drawn out that it would break if the metal coils were removed. All these local customs are adhered to by the girls cheerfully to enhance their beauty and add to their feminine charms.

I told them we would go to the circus on a certain night, and just where to look for us over one of the arena exits—and great was the amusement of our neighbors when suddenly three of these extraordinary brass-necked and brass-legged creatures turned in our direction, beaming with smiles and, reaching up their little hands, laughed like children at the pleasure of seeing our familiar and friendly faces in the vast ocean of unknown pale-faced strangers that filled the new Madison Square Garden. We had given them silk handkerchiefs and colored beads, which they wore around their brass collars when they went out walking.

One wintry Saturday I asked if they would come to see us the following morning at my studio. Their interpreter very solemnly replied, "Not possible, lady, we have all appointment go see Virgin Mary tomorrow, Sunday. We very catholics. See, we wear our little scapulas under brass collars!" So it was agreed that we would assist them to disguise themselves so as to avoid too much notoriety in visiting Saint Patrick's Cathedral. Never having worn shoes, they managed to get into some leather fleece-lined slippers; loose golf stockings were pulled over their "brass legs," and a second-hand fur coat with a high collar was provided by the circus management. We pinned this together, after tucking the silk handkerchief tightly into the highest brass ring. A towel from the hotel was twisted into rather a stylish turban, and the little group started off in a taxi for their appointment with Virgin Mary. The difficult part of the affair was to get them to leave the cathedral, for they were so enthralled by its size and the grandeur of its ritual that they wished to spend the entire day there. At their exit they found a group of newspaper photographers ready to shoot them for the following Sunday's illustrated papers!

It was in the port of Rangoon that I had the good fortune to study a few little Negritos from the Andaman Islands. They were on a sailing ship, and our local adviser assured me that they were

TRYING OUT HIS NEW BOW OF TYPICAL DESIGN

Life-size bronze figure of Andaman Islander. (Hall of Man)

Photo. Galloway.

PIGMY ANDAMAN ISLANDER WAITING TO HARPOON HIS NEXT TURTLE WHICH HE HAS
SHOT WITH BOW AND ARROW

Photo. Galloway.

THE "WEDDING WAIL"

Andaman Island ceremony in which friends and relatives huddle around the couple and cry over them for some time

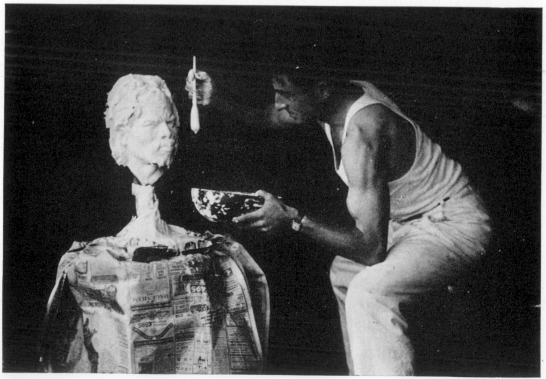

Photo. S. B. G.

JEAN DE MARCO, ON THE DECK OF A COAST STEAMER BETWEEN PENANG AND RANGOON

Making the plaster-cast on the head of the Sakai warrior modelled in the Malay jungle by M. H.

good representatives of their tribes. The figure I modelled of an Andaman Islander shows the little Negrito hunter seated on a rock, trying out the elasticity of his bow. This typical weapon is of a very special design, not found in any other part of the world. Very stiff and powerful, the wood is carefully selected and shaped with a primitive sort of adze, and finally smoothed off with the edge of a sharp shell. When drawn, the upper half of the bow bends towards the body, but the lower end, which when relaxed is slightly bent away from the body, becomes practically straight. The Andaman Islands are now kept as a penal colony by the British, and no accommodations are provided for tourists except at Port Blair. They are in the Bay of Bengal (Indian Ocean), just north of the Nicobar group of islands, southwest of Burma.

The name Andaman is Malay for "abode of monkey-people." In the year 1050 record has it that they were cannibals, living on an island known then as Tima Tittwar—or Isle of Impurity. The land is hilly and the forests are dense and very unhealthy. Cobras, vipers, and hamadryads enjoy the shelter of bamboo and satinwood jungles. There are also wild pigs, iguanas, and other delicacies. The natives have a blood-curdling habit of catching huge turtles, dragging them up on the shore, and cutting off their shells with sharp knives, apparently unconcerned as to the torture they inflict on the helpless victim. The tortoises serve as food and their shells are sold for a good profit.

There are many quaint customs among the tribes. One of them is the widow's practice of wearing the skull of her husband suspended on a cord around her neck, while her body is painted and striped in clay and ashes. A three days' separation of husband and wife is considered a long absence, and the return of the hunter is celebrated with rejoicing.

Their long racing canoes are decorated with flying banners on long, thin, bamboo rods, and make a shimmering and decorative display. Paddled by a crew of twenty or more of these polished black natives, they go at great speed.

India

The approach to Calcutta, that great seaport of India and central Asia, is a revelation. For five or six hours the little coast-steamer ploughs its way against the mighty currents of yellow, turbulent waters. Pouring down from the inland mountains and rivers, this sandy wash of India's shores has defied the annual efforts of "modern progress" to control and direct its treacherous and vacillating currents. It causes many an accident and long delays to shipping, and prepares the traveller for a series of mental bumps.

Early on the morning of our arrival, I was startled by the cry of "man overboard!" No one seemed to know what had happened. Passengers were dashing about in bathrobes or shorts, and cabin boys gesticulated and "no savvied" and "yes lady'd" exasperatingly. Sam, having gone on deck to have a walk before breakfast (something quite exceptional, I may add) made me all the more anxious. Seeing an empty cabin near ours, I ran in and looked out of the porthole. There, in the murky yellow current, I saw a man of dark skin waving his arms frantically and crying out for help, as the choppy waves broke over him and forced him to swallow quarts of this filthy silt. Watching the efforts of the Malay crew to lower a life-boat and manage the oars was a ludicrous as well as a pitiable sight. They tipped the boat and fell over one another pell-mell, grasping at the oars as if they had never known their use or meaning, the native officer shouting wild orders—and all the time the wretched "man overboard" was being carried screaming past the side of the ship and far away. Finally the captain changed our course and we circled round in the current and came nearer the man, whose cries had now been silenced by exhaustion. By superhuman endurance the drowning man kept coming to the surface and was finally dragged over the side of the life-boat and brought shivering and shaking on his knees to the level of our deck. Here he was ordered by the officers to help pull the ropes! At this he collapsed and was only restored to consciousness by the swift and efficient service of our Miss Green, who had the foresight to procure a glass of brandy and pour it down his throat before any

M. H. AND S. B. G. WITH TWO GYPSY DANCERS IN CALCUTTA

Photo. S. B. G.

Left: TYPE OF FEMININE BEAUTY IN BENGAL—MRS. KAMALA CHATTERJI, CALCUTTA

Right: TRAVELLING THROUGH INDIA, IT IS NOT A RARE EXPERIENCE TO FIND MEN
IN THIS EXTRAORDINARY POSITION DOING PENANCE ALONG THE ROADSIDE

They are known as religious mendicants, and live on the charity of the passer-by who may drop an
encouraging coin in the cup which is set beside him on the ground

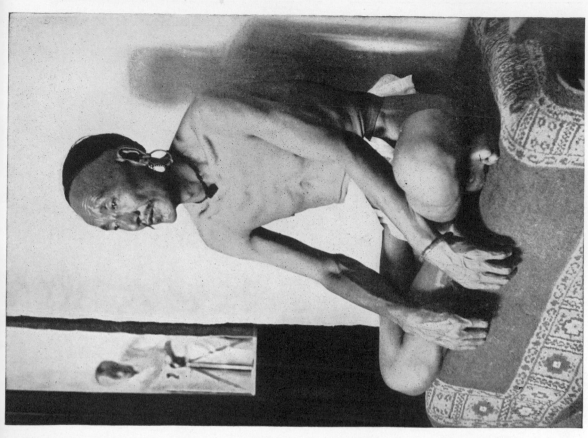

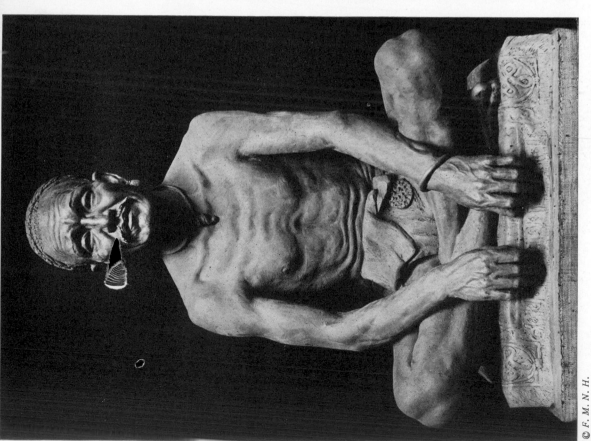

Left: LIFE-SIZE BRONZE TIBETAN FIGURE BY M. H. (HALL OF MAN)

On the right is the Tibetan jewel merchant of Lhasa, the subject of the bronze opposite, posing on a

Photo. S. B. G.

STREET BEGGAR IN CALCUTTA

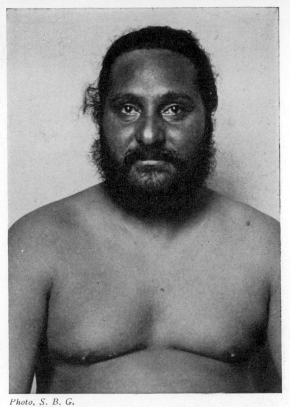

Photo. S. B. G.

MONEY–LENDER OF AFGHANISTAN, WHOSE POR-
TRAIT IN BRONZE IS IN THE HALL OF MAN

© *Anthropological Institute, Munich.*

HINDU WOMAN OF RAJPUTANA

Photo. S. B. G.

MERCHANT TYPE OF KASHMIR

THE ORIENTAL BEAUTY, SITA DEVI
Indian singer and musician

COLONEL NAWAB MALIK, SiR UMAR HYAT KHAN
He assisted and advised me concerning my work in India
The King's herald at the Durbar Festival, and renowned for
his brilliant military career

SNAKE–CHARMERS AT AGRA, INDIA

one could object to the alcoholic treatment, which was of course taboo to a Mohammedan but just the thing that saved his life. The fact that the wretched victim went mad during the afternoon seemed to concern no one except ourselves.

This incident gave a poignant quality to our entrance, two hours later, to the straits of "William and Mary," which must be passed before entering the port channel. Here is the shallow and shifting sand bottom, which cannot be controlled by dredging. India may have submitted to British rule on the surface, but she still maintains her submarine resistance.

The order of "all hands on deck in their life-belts" was anything but reassuring—atoned for, however, by the comic appearance of the passengers, looking like models for "Pneus Michelin" in all stages of nervous tension. The life-boats were lowered to just above water-level, and soundings were taken every two minutes as we slowly and cautiously threaded our winding course in and out of the invisible sand ridges. Looking over the wilderness of the shores, I casually asked an officer where we would be landed in case we did run amok on a sand ledge, and he said, "That is the awkward part of this business, because those Sundeban woods are full of tigers; we always hope to avoid landing our passengers before reaching Calcutta."

As we walked in slow, single file down the gangplank, the blade-like heat of midday sun struck us like a blow on the back of our necks. In the midst of swarming, brown bodies in white dhotis, the smiling, cheerful face of our bearer, Mariados, seemed to recognize his new master and *memsahib,* and he at once took charge. I was staggered at the thought of having to select a handful of distinct types that could represent this multitude of chattering and steaming humanity and millions more.

When we reached Calcutta my first inquiry at the consulate was for news of the Haardt Expedition. At the very moment the Consul put down the telephone and said: "Your answer has just come. Mr. Haardt has died of 'pestuous pneumonia' in Hong Kong."

Sic transit. . . .

Before leaving Paris in 1931 I had many conferences with George

Marie Haardt, the leader of the Citroën Expedition across Africa and central Asia. We had planned to meet in Peiping in December, if we both could keep approximately to our proposed schedule of travel. Monsieur Haardt and my gifted friend, Alexander Iacovleff, the painter, had both been most helpful to me throughout all the preparations for our journey. As experienced and fearless explorers, they could give me valuable suggestions that only seasoned travellers in tropical climes know about.

The amazing amount of material gathered by Haardt, and the vast collection of paintings and chalk portraits made by Iacovleff during the journey from North Africa to Madagascar, had proved the high aims and ability of these two devoted friends. When they set forth on their Asiatic "crusade," we attended the farewell celebration at the Citroën factory in Paris—and no one could follow the endless dotted lines across the great map of the world, indicating their proposed journey, without feeling that this courageous band of explorers, scientists, and artists were challenging the elements themselves and risking everything in their great adventure.

While I was making the portrait of an eminent Chinese authority in Peiping the following December I had been informed that all wireless communications with the Citroën Expedition, then in northwestern China, had been cut off, that their progress had been blocked, and that their lives were threatened by bandits and rebels.

My anxiety was aroused, for I knew what severe weather conditions existed in that region and how exhausted my friends must be by the responsibility and fatigue of such a prolonged test of endurance. I was finally able to obtain direct news through my sitter that my two friends were alive and well, but that there was little use of my delaying our departure in the hope of seeing them, as the expedition would probably not be able to reach Peiping for six or eight weeks, if then. Their expedition of sixty camels and eighty ponies had joined their four cars at Aksu. It was twenty-three hundred miles from Urumchi to Peiping—a hard road for them yet to travel.

This was a great disappointment to me, but we left our itinerary with the French Embassy and hoped with good luck to meet Monsieur Haardt in India, where we knew we might be staying several months.

On Christmas day they had reached Kanchow, and on January 7 we left for Nanking and Shanghai.

The long months of strain and exposure had worn out the resistance needed to combat such a microbe as Chinese pneumonia, or whatever it may have been that finally overcame this intrepid leader. It was a calamitous tragedy for all the members of his staff and for the ultimate success of the enterprise. The return journey that brought his body home to France must have weighed heavily upon their broken hopes. The thought of it certainly threw a dark cloud over those of us who had enjoyed his stimulating and sympathetic friendship.

Once established in our hotel, we were able, through the kindness of Doctor Guha of the Indian Museum and other officials, to study many local types. When they had been carefully measured and photographed they were brought to my room, where after lengthy explanations through our tactful interpreter, they were at last persuaded to pose quietly while I modelled their portraits.

The lift-boys and hall-porters in the hotel all had to be included in our plan of action. To induce many of these out-of-door creatures to brave the unknown dangers of marble halls and electric elevators was not as simple as it might appear. Everything had to be done with friendly smiles, for at the least suggestion of insistence our models escaped and never appeared again.

In the Calcutta Museum there is a splendid collection of ancient sculpture. Doctor Guha offered to place a workroom at our disposition where the more elusive models would pose when they refused to go to our hotel. It was also through Doctor Guha's helpful co-operation that we collected hundreds of valuable anthropological photographs of the various castes and tribes located in India. He also managed to induce two Tibetans, who were about to return to their home in Lhassa with their camel caravan, to postpone their departure so that I might model a full-length figure of one and a portrait head of the other.

The Indian attendants at the museum took a very personal interest in our activities, and seemed anxious to watch every process of my modelling or Jean's casting of the plaster heads. One of these men stayed very late one evening to help us do our final packing; so we offered to give him a lift to his home in our taxi. He was as excited as a child at the experience of riding through the hot streets, and smiled proudly at the passers-by. After driving a long distance, he spoke to the chauffeur and said we had reached his home. I stepped out, rather curious to see what kind of a house he lived in, for he had been a most active and helpful companion throughout our stay at the museum. There were several men lying motionless on the street with their dhotis wrapped around their bodies like shrouds. Our friend stepped between two of these and, pointing to some Hindustani scribbled on the white wall, quite cheerfully said, "This is my address, lady. I sleep here—not so hot like in hotel. . . ." And pressing the palms of his hands together and bowing his head, he politely bid us *Namascar*—adieu "until the morrow."

Often after some evening engagement we would come home to our hotel to find endless rows of these shrouded sleepers lying on their sides and backs and stretching out their arms on the stone sidewalks, trying to find some cool spot to ease the burning of the fever-heated atmosphere.

India brought back one of my vivid memories of childhood, an exciting evening spent with a relative of my father's who lived in a modest boarding-house in West Thirty-eighth Street. In the midst of this group of old-fashioned city boarders was introduced suddenly a newcomer—the oriental philosopher and teacher, Swami Vivekananda. When he entered the dining-room there was a hush. His dark, bronzed countenance and hands were in sharp contrast to the voluminous, light folds of his turban and robes. .

His dark eyes hardly glanced up to notice his neighbors, but there was a sense of tranquillity and power about him that made an imperishable impression upon me. He seemed to personify the mystery and religious "aloofness" of all true teachers of Brahma, and combined with this a kindly and gentle attitude of simplicity towards his fellow men.

It was many years later, in 1931, that we visited outside of Calcutta, at Belur, the marble temple which was dedicated to this same man by the thousands of his devoted followers. When I offered the garland of jasmin to be laid on the altar, I recalled, with emotion, that the only time I had seen this holy man, he had revealed to me more of the true spirit of India, without even uttering a word, than I had ever sensed in the many lectures *on* India, or *by* Indians, which I had attended since.

When the poet Rabindranath Tagore was in New York, my friend, Miss Green, took me to his apartment, and he very graciously gave me letters of introduction for India and also one to a nephew who was then living in Berlin and who represented a very definite type of Bengali modern youth. We saw the latter during our visit to Germany, dressed in Russian blouse and bareheaded. His shock of heavy, black hair framed a handsome, well-defined face. We dined with him in a forlorn Hindu restaurant the evening of the great "red parade," which had filled the streets of Berlin with scarlet shirts and flying banners. The crowds were amazingly controlled by the city police.

The advanced and violent opinions on politics and life often expressed by "young India" give one, by the way, a very different impression of the Orient from what has been the accepted traditional attitude. The swarming millions seem to preserve an endless supply of mental energy and saliva when it comes to expressing rather inconsistent programs of reform and freedom of thought. It was, therefore, quite a relief when we visited the older generations of this extraordinary Tagore family in Calcutta, to find the "old homestead" filled with quiet, white-robed youths and venerable scholars, who extended to us a most gracious hospitality amidst clouds of incense and collections of ancient paintings and sculpture.

Abinandranath Tagore, the painter, was most interested in our project. He has for many years directed the School of Art in Calcutta, and when we spoke of our methods of casting in Negocoll, directly from living models or from stone or wood carvings, he agreed to pose for me to make a cast of his very beautiful right hand, holding the delicate brush with which he painted his well-known miniatures. The day was set and his pupils and relatives were invited to come to the house to witness the performance.

His venerable brother, who was an invalid in a wheel chair, was present for the casting, looking like a Biblical prophet. Great was the curiosity of the audience when we started laying out our tools and boiling the pot of Negocoll over his charcoal brazier. The scene took place on the verandah, back of his great living-room. The heat was, of course, overpowering to us, but was taken as a matter of daily routine by the Indians present.

I placed a board on the knees of the painter and asked him to start painting as if he really had color on his brush and were going to start a miniature. Every one leaned forward eagerly; the pot of steaming thick liquid was being stirred by my assistant, Jean. At the moment when all was ready, I asked Tagore to stop moving his fingers and hold the brush exactly in correct pose—*and not to move again*. Having tested the liquid myself to be sure it was not too hot, Jean and I quickly spooned it out, pouring it gently but thoroughly over and under and around the hand and brush, until it piled up into a thick mass all over his hand and wrist. When the surface felt hard I started to make a slit along the side of the wrist joint, just to the widest point of the hand, using a thin wooden blade which would not injure the skin. Then, carefully pulling apart the wrist portion of the mould, I asked Tagore to *think* of the tips of his fingers, to let go his hold on the brush inside, and to start ever so gently to move his fingers inside the mould—always with great care not to make a violent effort—but to gradually work his hand out of the warm, thick, slightly flexible mould, as I drew it away with a steady, slow pull from his arm. Everything went smoothly, to the delight of ourselves as well as our audience.

When the mould was cooled off and the seam held closed, Jean mixed his plaster in a bowl and poured it into the mould, which I held in full view so that each step of the process could be followed by the art-students and the twenty-six grandchildren who surrounded us. When the plaster in turn had cooled and hardened, we carefully divided the Negocoll mould, which broke apart cleanly—and there was a perfect reproduction of Tagore's aristocratic hand, with just the space left between thumb and forefinger which had been filled by the wooden stem of the brush. We then removed the brush from the Negocoll covering and replaced it in its identical position between the plaster fingers. There are no seams in the cast when made in this manner.

There was a clamor of applause and enthusiastic babel of voices. Tagore himself was as eager and excited as any of the art-students. The entire performance had taken about fifty minutes.

A bronze cast of this hand was sent by the Field Museum to Tagore a year later, as an appreciation of his helpful co-operation in our work, and a plaster replica is shown in the Scientific department adjoining the Hall of Man in the Field Museum.

In Santiniketan, one hundred miles west of Calcutta, the poet Tagore had founded an International University, Visva Bharati. Having felt the need of more mutual understanding between the East and the Western methods of education and progress, he has established there an active center of schools; a rural institute (Sriniketan) and hospital; and a library of 36,000 volumes in Sanskrit, Indian, Chinese, Tibetan, and other languages. There is a school of music and dancing, where researches are made to develop the ceremonial and seasonal dances of old India.

The Indian women are instructed in domestic science and home nursing. There is also a sanitarium for tubercular patients and a clinic set apart for lepers.

To pay the expenses of this great project, the poet Tagore has donated over £50,000 of his own fortune—obtained by the Nobel Prize and the sale of his Bengali works.

The rajahs of India have contributed about the same amount, American and English friends give generous annual support, and local membership adds its share yearly. This outstanding enterprise has certainly done a great work in improving the conditions of the poor and in widening the scope of mutual understanding.

The scenes enacted in our hotel bedroom-studio during our three weeks' stay in Calcutta would often have provided good copy for moving-picture scenarios. One group of three Sikkims, with their cone-shaped felt hats and long pig-tails, were ushered in before we had completed a difficult *séance* with a swarthy Kabuli, a money-lender from a northwestern border province, who is a terror to thousands of Indians who borrow his money and are often unable to repay on the day he makes his demand. To cajole a real Kabuli to disrobe and sit quietly on a steamer trunk for hours in a hotel bedroom was considered something of a triumph, and had it not been for the clever tact of our ever helpful bearer, Mariados, the portrait of this 300-pound, curly-bearded border type would never have been in the Chicago collection. Street-beggars, priests, ladies of high rank, and gypsy dancers came in endless procession, until the concièrge finally gave up his struggle to find out what might be the limits of our social circle.

From Calcutta we moved northwest to Benares—the Holy City of Death. To this river town on the Ganges we made our pilgrimage in company with the ever moving stream of sick and dying pilgrims. Most wonderful, indeed, is this city of living faith. To die, bathed in the healing waters of this sacred river, is the utmost ecstasy. If one cannot live to reach the purifying water, one can at least be assured of being carried down the great stone steps of the burning ghats after death. And then, at the edge of this miraculous river, relatives will adorn their dead in beautiful jewels and quietly wrap the body in shrouds of white or yellow or red material, as the case may be—for each color denotes the character and status of the dead. The shrouded corpse is then dipped into the water and carried to the waiting pyre, on which it is reverently laid. The flaming torch is handed to the nearest of kin to ignite the fire. The silent groups stand about the flaming fagots until only ashes are left smouldering on the stone terrace. These ashes are swept into the river and another pyre is laid for the next cremation.

Never-ending crowds of young and old, of sick and healthy and maimed humanity come to this age-old city of miracles and bathe themselves in the same waters that have received generations of ashes —and bones. The gutters of the steep streets leading to the ghats are running with mud, but the believers bow down and fill their hands in these gutters and drink this dank filth with a look of wild ecstasy in their great, dark eyes, knowing in their hearts that no harm can

Photo. S. B. G.

PAHALWAN NATS

They came originally from Gwalior, but live now a nomadic life in the Jaipur district. The old man at the right is Wazir Khan, drummer now, but in his day a famous tumbler and acrobat. These people are illiterate Mohammedans of the Lodi Pathan race; there are about 400 of them. Another criminal tribe of this area is called Saunsis. They live like savages, wearing no clothes. (See page 315)

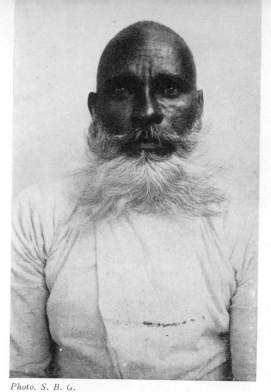

DHUL SINGH OF RAJPUTANA

PAHALWAN NATS IN ONE OF THEIR ACROBATIC STUNTS, WHICH SAM RECORDED IN A MOVING-PICTURE

THE FIGHTING ORDER OF PRIESTS, KNOWN AS BHATS, JAIPUR, INDIA

Very young children are initiated into this order and are trained in the art of swordsmanship. Celibacy is rigidly observed by each member. As fighters this order has won many honors and is highly esteemed throughout the country

M. H. DRAWING THE PORTRAIT OF HAMMAN PERSHAD VAISH, DIRECTOR OF THE
MUSEUM OF JAIPUR

The tower of this building is lined with carved pink marble and overlooks the gardens

THE WOMAN OF JAIPUR WHOM WE SPOTTED WALKING ON THE ROAD, AND AFTER GREAT
PERSUASION MANAGED TO ENTICE TO POSE FOR THE PORTRAIT, WHICH IS NOW IN
STONE (SHOWN AT THE RIGHT) IN THE HALL OF MAN

ROYAL COURTESAN DANCERS SURROUNDED BY THEIR MUSICIANS, JAIPUR. (SEE PAGE 318)

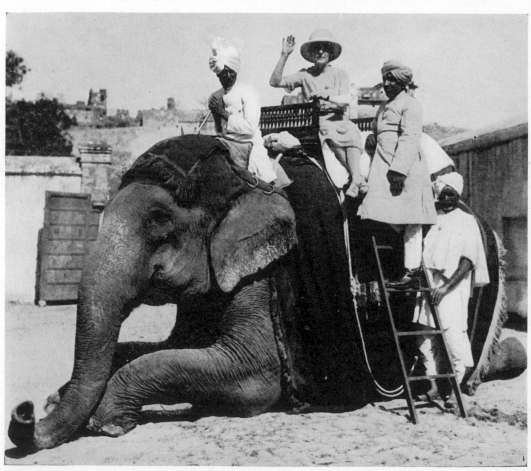

M. H. ON THE ROYAL ELEPHANT THAT CARRIED US TO THE PALACE OF AMBER

Mr. Vaish, Director of Jaipur Museum, is on the ladder

come to them in Benares. And when they bathe they pray, and then drink the water that has laved their bodies of earthly disease.

To the dismay of scientists the world over, this Ganges water has never been found to contain a harmful microbe. Each day adds its record to the centuries, the procession continues, and any one may go to Benares and witness this spectacle of macabre religious power working its miracle of healing and liberation.

The general plan for our activities in India was all worked out in 1931 in London under the kind auspices of Lord Reading and of Colonel Haksar, the latter at that time being one of the most important figures in the Council of Indian Princes. Through their helpfulness, important letters of introduction were given us to be used in the different localities where typical Indian subjects might be persuaded to pose for portraits. A year later, when we had reached New Delhi and had half completed our work on Indian territory, we were fortunate in meeting Colonel Haksar again, and with his cooperation obtained photographs of numberless examples of the Kashmir, Gwalior, and northwest Indian types. After spending a few weeks studying various racial characteristics we became aware of the very definite changes in type, marked both in the shape of the skull structure, the lines of the profiles, and the color of the skin.

One day while we were lunching at the Viceroy's palace at New Delhi, His Excellency inquired as to the progress of our expedition throughout India. I had the temerity to ask if it would be possible to see any of the nomad criminal tribes on our way south to Bombay. We explained how valuable photographs and movies of these extraordinary types would be, and as if by magic the Viceroy's wand was waved, and messages were sent to the various police officers in the vicinity of Jaipur in preparation for our arrival. These travelling groups of criminals were soon located, and we were notified when they would be visible. They are the finest examples of physical strength and agility. Thin and tall, they keep their long, sinewy muscles in such a state of flexibility and training that they are able to perform feats of unbelievable strength and courage. Their deep-set, dark eyes blaze like those of wild animals, their oily black hair hangs to their shoulders, and to see one of them whirl a naked sword blade under his feet and over his head while turning hand-springs makes one realize the wisdom of keeping friendly at all costs. The general custom of innkeepers is to engage one of these criminals as a night watchman. He sleeps on the terrace or lawn near the hotel, and any vagrant quickly changes his plans if he encounters a representative of this tribe. They are known as "Nats," and have to notify the local police officers of their plans each week as to where they are wandering.

One of the stunts performed by a star member of their tribe was a dance on long stilts which had no notches or foot-rests, but which were gripped between the big toe and second toe about five feet from the ground so tightly that the agile dancer could kick sideways or backward with one leg while hopping about on the other one. He would even take one stilt in his free hand and wave it about over his head in rhythm with the accompanying drummer.

Another *tour de force* was the lifting of a great tree-trunk, twenty feet long, from the ground. A rope was slung around the center of the tree. The Nat straddled the trunk in a bowed position and the two loose ends of the rope were fastened to his twisted locks of hair, which he parted and wove into the rope so that it could not possibly slip. Then he gradually straightened his thin, sinuous, dark body to its full height, and walked slowly along, carrying the tree between his legs.

Not satisfied with this effort, he called to his men to pile a great square rock on the tree. This rock we found weighed eighty pounds. A third Nat jumped into the ring and, seizing the rock, lashed a rope around it on four sides, leaving a loop about a foot long at the top. Then he crouched before it, spreading his knees wide apart and bracing his hands on his legs. Bending his head far forward, he grasped the rope loop between his strong, white teeth and gave a violent upward and backward fling to his head, which lifted the eighty-pound rock off the ground, over his head, and flung it across a space of fifteen feet!

During all this unexpected performance Sam was darting about, taking moving-pictures of every event. As soon as one man completed his act, another would rush out from the group, leap into the air, slap his left shoulder a loud whack with his right hand, and hop high into the air on one foot. Then a thin young boy was tossed onto the ground, lying on his back. A strip of palm-leaf was pushed under the string of his snugly wrapped loin-cloth, so that the leaf lay flat on his stomach. One of the wild men grabbed a long, waving sword and sprang about the boy, shouting and slapping his shoulder, throwing his long, glistening hair back and forth over his face, a look of fanatical ecstasy shooting from his big, black eyes. He stopped suddenly and laid the naked blade on the boy's body just over the leaf, then in a flash jumped backward and took aim, holding the heavy sword now in both hands. With a tiger-like spring his body shot forward and the sword-blade severed the palm-leaf in two pieces without scratching the quivering body of the unfortunate boy, who had to submit several times to this dangerous sport without flinching.

Our nerves were by this time standing on end with excitement. Sam's face was streaming with perspiration, his pith helmet driven back over his neck, and all of us were in a state of amazement. The elderly drummer pounded more and more violently to accelerate the rhythm of the performers, and whenever there was a lull, pairs of the Nats would clutch each other, one standing up and the other upside down, and folding up into a bunch of arms and legs, these human bundles would roll about the ground, crashing into bushes and rolling so fast that they were lost in a cloud of dust.

Another experience of unusual interest was the excursion, mounted on a royal elephant, to the Palace of Amber. This resplendent female elephant was fifty years old and had three personal servants, one to ride on her head and two to brush the flies off her flanks and feed her. We mounted by a ladder which was carried slung on her side, and the houdah was draped in red velvet trappings and much heavy gold lace to denote her royal status. This court elephant was loaned to us by the Maharaja of Jaipur and we were escorted through the Palace of Amber by Mr. Vaish, the director of the fine museum at Jaipur, who offered us every hospitality and courtesy.

Through the British officials connected with the court of His Highness the Maharaja of Jaipur we were notified to be in readiness at eight A.M. for the arrival of the court dancers. Although appointments in India always seem to be misunderstood, it was still something of a shock to be awakened at seven A.M. by the arrival of the courtesans of the local court with their assistants and property-trunks. These languid beauties had seldom faced the sun's rays in the morning brilliance, and it was a disarming and strange experience for them to go through their paces without the shadowy glamour of red lamps and deep divans half hidden in the smoke, to say nothing of their usual responsive male audience. However, the moving-pictures were taken to the accompaniment of constant shouts from Sam to the interpreter: "Tell them to step on the gas! Don't be shy, sister, we're not missionaries!" and so on. The caskets containing their jewels and rich gold-and-silver costumes were repacked and loaded into the little two-wheeled covered cart which had brought them from the Maharaja's court to the gardens of our delightful hotel.

After a hearty breakfast they bade us adieu and drove away in a cloud of dust, still rubbing their heavy-lidded dark eyes, which seemed to resent their exposure to so much out-of-door light!

To my amazement, that same afternoon about six o'clock I was lying on my bed resting after an exhausting day of work and tropical heat, when suddenly there appeared in my room the two dancing favorites of our morning event. They seemed far more at ease and without hesitation draped themselves over the foot of my bed and offered me signed photographs of themselves, encased in most alarming metal repoussé frames. They made known through their interpreter that they would like to know all about "court life in America," and whether dances like theirs would be in demand. I was as non-committal as possible about court life in America, but gleaned a good deal of local news and information from them about their own occupations, which had begun to bore them with their monotony.

They wore most beautiful red-and-silver saris and their jewels were of finely wrought gold, studded with precious stones. Their heavy eyelashes made natural shadows where European ladies have to resort to cosmetics, and their seductive smiles, combined with the graceful gestures of their jewelled hands, were eloquent substitutes for their incomprehensible conversation, which lasted over an hour. When they left, my room was redolent with exotic perfume.

During our visit to Bombay we were advised not to venture into certain districts, owing to the local difference of opinion concerning Mr. Gandhi's campaign. His chief ally at that time (for he was temporarily in residence at the prison of Poona) was Madame Naidu, the Indian poet, a most charming and cultivated personality whom I had had the pleasure of meeting two years previously at my own studio in New York when she had come with Ruth Draper to a fancy-dress dance. Both were dressed in exquisite scarlet-and-gold saris. It was a great surprise and pleasure to find that this distinguished poet had an apartment adjoining ours at the hotel in Bombay and to learn that she was most interested to secure for us a number of types of the locality. Upon our departure she hung a garland of jasmin blossoms over my shoulders, and wrapped me in a diaphanous magenta chiffon scarf made by Indian artists and having a peculiar, cloudlike delicacy of texture and design.

The art of making scarfs, saris, and turbans is highly developed in India, because of the national costumes of the men and women. Millions of turbans are made by the "tie and dye" process. The material is tied into numberless little knots with tightly woven thread, so that when it is dipped in the color vat, the portion inside the knots remains white. These turbans are sold in coils of tightly twisted and tied gauze, many meters in length, and dyed with the most brilliant and fantastic colors. One has to pull and almost tear them apart to unroll their hidden secrets of design before winding them deftly around the head into the various local types of head-dress.

Walking along the streets of Jaipur (the façades of nearly all the buildings are colored salmon pink) we were enchanted by the constant number of Indian boys running along each side of the street holding, stretched out between them, the strips of colored gauze still dripping from the dying vats. Like resplendent banners waving in the hot sun, these strips are quickly dried. From an upper window, or riding on an elephant, we had a long-distance view of such an unbelievable riot of color that the effect was like rainbows floating down from the sky. We swayed along through this pageant on a slow-moving colossus, from whose neck hung a great bell, the ringing of which was a traffic signal and cleared the way for our progress.

One of the strangest places we visited outside of Bombay is known as "The Towers of Silence." Within the high walls of this gruesome precinct the Parsees bring their dead and lay them on the stone terraces which form a great amphitheatre around a central pit. Perched on the walls, uttering their guttural and morbid cries, hundreds of gaunt, black vultures keep watch, awaiting their next victim to be devoured. The trees around the walled arena are worn bare by the crowds of these scavengers of death that collect on the branches.

When the funeral procession arrives at the little entrance gate, the dead body is carried into the arena by two men. These men have been carrying corpses for generations. As soon as they lay the body on the stone and start towards the gate the air is filled with the cries of the birds who rise in clouds and swoop down out of sight to start their feasting.

The Parsees or Parsis are a religious sect who follow the teachings of Zoroaster, and are descended from the Persians who moved to India in the eighth century, having been driven out of Persia by the Arabs. They have very marked physical characteristics—aquiline noses, heavy eyebrows, soft moustaches, black eyes, and rather heavy lips. The men wear a curious, stiff hat of black or maroon patent leather, rising up from the forehead in a backward slant about six inches high without a brim. On their New Year's day the Parsees worship at the fire temples, the sacred fire which burns forever on the altar. This ceremony is the bridge across which their souls must pass to reach heaven.

Besides the teaching of human charity and brotherly love, the Parsees are renowned for their commercial and banking activities and for their worldly wisdom. Even the women of this sect have become famous for their extraordinary intelligence in business affairs. The appropriateness of names would seem exceptionally fine in the case of Sir Kavasji Jehangir Readymoney, a well-known banker, the history of whose life is a series of successes, profits, and generous distributions of his huge fortune.

I quote the following statements from a paper written by Doctor J. J. Modi of Bombay, who very kindly explained to us the principles of his religion and enabled us to visit the Towers of the Dead:

Preserving all possible respect for the dead, the body, after its separation from the immortal soul, should be disposed of in a way the least harmful and the least injurious to the living.

Death levels everybody, whether he dies as a king on the throne or as a poor man without a bed on the ground.

Three days after death the body is removed to the Tower of Silence any time during the day. As it is essential that the body should be exposed to the sun it is strictly forbidden to carry it at night.

The body must be so exposed and left without clothes as to draw towards it the eye of the flesh-devouring birds and may fall an easy prey to them, so that, the sooner it is devoured the lesser the chance of further decomposition and the greater the sanitary good and safety.

A deep central well in the tower, one hundred and fifty feet in circumference (the sides and bottom of which are also paved with stone slabs) is used for depositing the dry bones. The corpse is completely stripped of its flesh by vultures within an hour or two, and the bones of the denuded skeleton, when perfectly dried up by atmospheric influences and the powerful heat of the tropical sun, are thrown into this well, where they gradually crumble to dust, chiefly consisting of lime and phosphorus—thus the rich and the poor meet together on one level of equality after death.

On the damn after the third night after death, the soul goes to the other world. The soul passes over a bridge called Chinvat.

According to the Zoroastrian belief, the relation between a pious deceased and his surviving relations does not altogether cease after death. His holy spirit continues to take some interest in his living dear ones. If the surviving relatives cherish his memory, remember him with gratefulness, try to please him with pious thoughts, pious words and pious deeds, it is likely that these invisible departed spirits will take an interest in their welfare, and assist them with an invisible hand.

Going southward toward Ceylon we were struck by the gradual darkening of the skin of all these people until we reached the seacoast, where Tamils, with their long, black hair and their dark brown skins, were in striking contrast to the Kashmir Aryan type of the north.

The south of India in April was an endurance test for us all. Under such conditions, to have to work all day and never feel a cool breeze even at night was almost more than we could stand. I felt exhausted and weak all the time and kept marvelling at Sam's energy and will-power, which drove him out into the blazing sun with his camera from early morning until noon, and again after three o'clock until dinner-time. "Mad dogs and Englishmen go out in the midday sun." Every time my strength collapsed he seemed to be able to carry more and more of the load of responsibility which often threatened to over-whelm me.

Clouds of dry, thin dust would blow about, and the emaciated, burnt-out bodies of the road-workers made one ache, for these Indian laborers look like living skeletons that have been charred in a fire.

Before we could move on to Ceylon we had to cast the clay heads into plaster and find boxes and materials with which to pack them securely. Jean was sent to collect any straw covers from mineral water bottles that might be found in the hotel storerooms and kitchens. Palm leaves and some old straw and local newspapers were carefully wrapped into pads and wedged between the plaster casts. Sweat streamed from our bodies as we strained and bent over the cases. I felt as if my bones had turned to water. The heat was staggering, but we kept on.

One afternoon we drove out of Madras with our faithful bearer, Mariados, to where we could find some Toddy wine collectors. These agile tree-climbers performed their feats going up the tall palm-trees with their heels held together by a raffia loop about fifteen inches long, and a great rope of raffia lashed around their bodies and around the trees. Their movements lurching upward were like those of a toy monkey on a stick. The heat grew more suffocating, and as I walked across a sandy field hoping to reach the shade beyond I suddenly felt faint and collapsed. My companion, a half naked Tamil carrier, bent over me and, recognizing my plight, said: "All right, lady, just lie flat, I go get coconut quick, make you quick alive—wait!"

Through a haze I saw him run to a tree, sling his rope around the trunk, and start climbing at mad speed until he was far up, fifty feet or more. There he whipped out his knife, lopped off the "coco,"

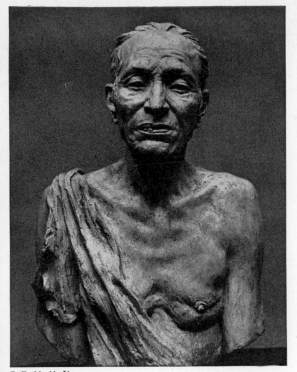

A WOMAN OF HIEEDLEY CASTE, OF JAIPUR

Hunger and heat have wasted her body, but not her pride
and courage. Portrait in bronze, Hall of Man

Photo. S. B. G.

KHURSHEDJI NASARWANJE WADYA, OF BOMBAY

A learned Parsee, and a follower of Zoroaster

Photo. S. B. G.

MADAME SAROJINI NAIDU, SCHOLAR AND
POETESS OF INDIA

Wearing a brooch of two lion-teeth set in gold

JANOO SINGH, OF THE BHAT TRIBE, JODHPUR

THE GREAT TEMPLE AT MADURA, SOUTHERN INDIA, A MARVEL OF SCULPTURE AND
ARCHITECTURE

A TYPICAL PALM GROVE, SOUTH INDIA

EMACIATED ROAD MENDER OF MADRAS

his workman is no exceptional type, as most of the South India laboring class
look like famine victims

LIFE–SIZE BRONZE FIGURE OF A TAMIL CLIMBING A PALM–TREE
TO COLLECT TODDY FOR WINE

(Hall of Man)

TEA–PICKER IN THE GARDENS OF CEYLON. TAMIL
OF SOUTH INDIA

UNTOUCHABLE TAMIL WOMAN OF SALEM, SOUTH
INDIA

Portrait in pastel by M. H.   (Courtesy of Anne Archbold)

GROUP OF DEVIL–DANCERS IN SILVER COSTUMES AT KANDY, CEYLON.
S. B. G. CENTER FOREGROUND

and came down. Running over to me he crouched in the dust beside me, and with a clean, sure blow of his knife cut the top neatly off the coconut as one lifts the shell top off a hard-boiled egg. With both hands he held the precious cup of liquid to my lips. I drank and drank, feeling that this was indeed a life-saver. He poured some of the cold liquid over my head, and at last I was able to speak. "Thanks, my boy, now go and tell Sahib to come back. I cannot go on today—too hot." The moving-pictures taken of these men came out splendidly, and in spite of my collapse the effort of this Toddy palm afternoon was well worth while. This was our last experience in India, and we all realized that we had reached the end of our tether.

Ceylon

We started the journey to Ceylon by train. I find a note in my diary—"Gross heat; hard, black leather benches; narrow gauge railway compartment all day, all night. Sam and I try every soft drink offered for sale. In desperation I try the shower bath—result? More like a mud bath. Hotter than ever. Sam prefers to stew in his own juice . . . clever boy that! We are called at four thirty A.M.! 'Change trains, all out!' "

Oh, the mockery of advertised "luxury travel"—and of the gay, attractive covers on all the pamphlets that lure us from the comforts of Beauty Rest mattresses, to explore the world on an economic budget.

Good old world—we must not undervalue its charms and compensations! We were simply over-tired and had completely forgotten that there *were* ways and means of travelling luxuriously even in India.

An amusing incident at Bombay comes to my mind in which this problem of travel "had the laugh on us." We had met at our hotel quite unexpectedly the party of Mr. James Simpson of Chicago, one of the trustees of the Field Museum, who, with his son and Mr.

Armour, had flown over Africa at high speed and had collected wild fauna for the Field Museum zoological department.

Mr. Simpson was planning to move up to Kashmir, and when he came to see us off on our train, which was like an oven, having baked in the sunlight for hours, his opinion of Indian railroad comforts seemed to suffer a severe shock. We felt quite sorry for him, and thinking it over on our journey we framed up a telegram to him which we sent back from the first station-stop. "Suggest your consulting American Express, Bombay. Hire your own bed linen and pillows, take pails of ice, plenty bottled water, soft drinks, fruit. Good luck."

When we reached Kandy we found the answer to our wire. "Thanks thoughtful suggestions. Have hired private car. Cheerio."

Sam and I looked at each other rather sheepishly. Yes, the joke was on us, for we had forgotten the American magnate's genius for "getting what he wants"—and producing a Frigidaire in a desert if need be.

Transferring ourselves and our luggage from the train to a ferry steamer, we crossed the little strip of water which divides India from Ceylon. Behind two panting engines we started to climb up over the mountains of Ceylon—fresh air at last! What a blessed feeling to be able to breathe deeply again! Succulent, wet, paddy fields spread out under our parched and weary gaze. The life-giving phenomenon of a sudden rain-storm restored our wilted spirits. There appeared the miracle of green grass, thick forests carpeted with damp moss and echoing with songs of exotic birds!

The hillsides were aglow with blossoms. Ravines, flanked with palm groves, startled us by their precipitous depths. The breezes of evening revived the weary travellers, and at last Kandy, the fairyland on the heights, welcomed us to a comfortable, cool hotel! The place seemed like an oasis of fragrant, flowerlike beauty. We explored the surrounding country under the delightful guidance of Doctor Nell, a great student of Ceylon's history.

Slim young Singalese youths trotting between their rickshaw shafts, their thighs wrapped in long cotton skirts, offered to pull us up the steep hillsides. The town was crowded with jewel merchants, who displayed their varied collections of local gems to tempt the eye and lighten the weight of many purses. Kings and emperors have studded their crowns and offered rich gifts to their queens and favorites from the brilliant galaxy of gems found on this exotic isle.

We selected the lift-boy at our hotel as the most representative type of Singalese and persuaded him to pose for his portrait. The local custom of these men is to wear the hair in a coil at the nape of the neck, holding in place the upper strands on the top of the head with a tortoise-shell comb in the shape of a horseshoe.

One finds many Tamils from the south coast of India working as tea-pickers in the world-famous tea plantations of Ceylon. The hillsides are covered with millions of compact little bushes, the leaves of which are carefully picked, dried, and selected to furnish this universal stimulant to a thirsty world.

The great event in Kandy is the procession and festival of the Temple of the Tooth. Legend has it that the sacred tooth of Buddha is here enshrined. Pilgrims and worshippers crowd daily into this ancient edifice to pay homage to Buddha. The stone floors are strewn with myriads of flowers; scarlet and white blossoms are crushed by the bare feet of endless crowds into a thick slime of heavy-scented mud. During the festival, elephants are caparisoned in gorgeous velvet-and-gold fringe, tusks are gilded, and the shrine containing the tooth is carried around the countryside at the head of the procession. Buddhist priests, draped in their voluminous saffron robes, lend constantly startling color groups to the thickly wooded landscape. The horticultural gardens are a triumph of exotic beauty.

Driving into the country to the edge of the jungle, we had the pleasure of seeing a troupe of working elephants put through their various occupations and tricks by their agile "mahouts." These beasts of the jungle can be trained to do man's will and labor industriously, pushing down trees and carrying them in their trunks, hauling great loads and behaving in a most orderly and submissive manner as long as a boy rider holds a short steel spike over the elephant's head. In the early afternoon, however, there seems to be a tacit understanding among the elephants that they stop work and march down to the river where their daily bath and scrubbing takes place. The harsh brushes that are used to rub down their leathery hides are made of the inside of palm bark, the bristles being very much like short wires. These are rubbed for hours over the sides and flanks of the elephants as they roll first on one side and then on the other on the shallow river bed, trumpeting with joy or spurting great geysers of water into the air. There is something primordial about these great monsters oozing out of the mud and tearing the air with their cries. This bathing scene was one of the best films that Sam made during the trip, and forms part of the collection in the Field Museum.

After their bath these elephants pick up one or two bales of hay in their trunks and carry them home along the roads for their evening meal. If you happen to meet one of these swaying gray hulks in the jungle road while motoring, the elephant quite calmly steps aside, pushing over two or three tall trees that may be in his way, and waits for you to pass by.

One day we went to tea at our friend Doctor Andreas Nell's apartment and found many pictures of Anna Pavlowa on the wall; before these there were bowls of fragrant flowers. She had danced in Ceylon once and had never been forgotten; the memory of her visit was kept vivid.

One of the most exciting dances we witnessed was arranged for us at eight o'clock in the morning. The light then was sharp and good for moving-pictures, and it was not too hot for the performers.

A troupe of devil-dancers and native musicians gave us a varied and splendid performance. The jangle and glitter of their silver ornaments and costumes added much barbaric glamor to the picture. Their movements were violent and quite different from those of any other country—their white skirts flew out about their dark bodies, and their hands and feet moved in strange barbaric rhythms. As a finale, a huge elephant was ridden into their midst, raising his trunk in the air and opening his cavernous jaws over their silver headdresses.

Descending from the mountains to Colombo, the visitor finds a city of Arabs, Indians, and Singalese; there are waving palms, seashore hotels, and thousands of rickshaws threading their way between motorcars and native oxcarts. The art treasures stored in the Colombo Museum are worth many hours of study. Doctor Hill, an ardent anthro-pologist and anatomist, and Doctor Spittel were very helpful in giving us direct information concerning the aboriginal races of Ceylon, known as the Veddas. The few remaining descendants of this race live in the southeastern jungles. They are small of stature, very dark-skinned, and wear their hair long about the neck and shoulders. They have rather a slim, graceful build; their eyes have a wild look and are very deep-set under heavy brows. Their typical weapon is a bow about six feet long. They often use their feet as well as their hands to string and pull their bows, lying on their backs to do so.

These people are rather a delicate edition of the Australian Bush-man type. We were told that they were monogamous, and that hus-band and wife generally remained faithful to one another until death. When not hunting, they collect honey, which forms their chief food-product. The Bambara or wild Indian bee makes her hive in rocky caves, and to collect this honey is a dangerous occupation.

Doctor Hill, whom we visited at the Laboratory of Anatomy and Anthropology, has procured very rare skeletons of these almost extinct tribes, and has spent much time in extensive study of the subject. He and his wife spend their spare hours caring for his menagerie of mon-keys, parrots, snakes, and other wild pets. There are several places in tropical countries where the domestic snake is generally kept in the cellar to catch rats and other house pests. Do not be alarmed if it crawls into your bedroom by mistake—just ring for the "boy" and, showing him the snake, say, like the Frenchman visiting Ceylon, *"Garçon, desservez-moi ce serpent,"* and he will pick him up by the tail and take him away, probably depositing him in the next room until another tourist arrives and repeats the operation!

The Return to Paris

We came from Ceylon by way of the Red Sea, the Suez Canal, and the Mediterranean, to our ultimate destination of Marseilles.

This last voyage of the trip, made in a fortnight on the good ship *Dempo,* permitted us to review in peace and comfort the memories of the Orient. The ship glided between the two great continents of Africa and Asia. At the northern end of the Red Sea the Suez Canal cleaves them asunder. Lying on the cool, linen deck-chairs we watched the shores recede into oblivion on either side; the hazy mists and trackless desert plains of Arabia and Egypt evoked the past history of Biblical days, and it was rather a shock after twelve hours of deck-dreaming in the canal to come into the dusty, squalid town of Port Saïd, swarming with flies, beggars, and unscrupulous merchants.

And so adieu to palm-groves and dark-skinned natives; adieu to pith helmets, shorts, punkas and quinine. . . . Europe, with her orchards and spring blossoms, loomed high on the horizon. The smiling Sicilians waved at us as we passed. The luxurious ease of living in such climate! Here the lucky inhabitants had no eternal struggle against the cruel elements, against famines and floods. Here was peace and fertility, balanced temperature and modern plumbing. Humanity relieved of its daily struggle for sheer existence has had time and strength to spread its wings. . . . No wonder France and Italy are the homes of art and beauty, of poetry and epicures.

On a spring morning in 1932 Marseilles welcomed our little band of sunburned travellers, thankful and happy to have had the opportunity of sailing beyond the sunsets and the seven seas, and to have shared life and adventures with so many friendly members of our great human family.

The panorama of our long journey, so crowded with facts, surprises, and revelations, seemed to stretch into the infinite distance. How could one condense and select from all these countries a few incidents that might be administered in capsule form to the interested friends awaiting our return? Would any one *be* interested? The world was an odd place, I thought, as I separated the double layers of my tropical mascot, the wide-brimmed felt hat, and removed the shrivelled remains of banana leaves which, dipped in water and laid between the felt crowns, had so often protected and cooled my head under the burning sun. We might prepare our spicy little tales to answer whatever questions came up, but we felt reasonably certain that in America the subject of conversation would be changed before we had finished the second sentence. We had led such an uncalendared existence for many months, that the idea of having to refit our life into weeks and "weekends" loomed ominously on the horizon as we noticed the silhouette of Europe's southern coast line. Such a thing as "society" in its musclebound sophistication and convention suddenly struck me in all its *naïf* artificiality. I drove away the inevitable need of facing these facts, and decided to let them slide into their gear on their own momentum as the situations might arise.

A cable from Field Museum, Chicago, was forwarded to us from Paris. Somehow this was the final link in the encircling chain of events. The news it contained was none too good, for it notified us to return at once and dismiss the members of our little company. When we had visited Chicago before starting our westward journey around the world, the first threatening symptoms of the financial crash were beginning to be felt, but the extent of such a universal business collapse could hardly have been predicted by the most exaggerated pessimist. We had been notified, before starting, to keep our expenses down, and the services of a professional photographer had been dispensed with at the last moment. At this point Sam had offered to take on the job of photographer, to add to his list of responsibilities in directing the expedition. This saved serious loss both to the Museum and to me, as I was forced of necessity to depend on photographic records for many details and accuracies such as weapons, ornaments, etc., which, under the fantastic circumstances in which I was obliged to work, were often impossible for me to finish at the time of modelling my subject.

Reviewing our trip, on this homeward stretch of the blue Mediterranean, it was more than evident to us that we could never have accomplished what we did if we had taken along the professional photographer. The necessities listed for his apparatus and supplies, the inevitable difficulties of transportation and extra living accommodations, would have added insurmountable obstacles and expense. As it turned out, Sam, with his Zeiss Ikon and folding tripod slung over his shoulder, was able to adjust himself to all the exigencies of the varied occasions. Whether he disguised himself as a visiting surgeon in cap and gown and goggles, or as "old Doctor Grimson," the anthropologist, with a long beard and gray cotton coat, the results were always successful, and the collection of 2000 still photos and many movie reels were a vital and indispensable part of the whole enterprise.

The fact that the officials in the different cities were all forewarned and interested to assist us, made our work a friendly and generally amusing episode. For do not think, dear reader, that humor is a commodity that can be dispensed with or left out of such an experience. It is the stuff that makes an otherwise hopeless task seem often so ludicrous that one manages to laugh it off and begin again.

For we had constantly to "begin again." As soon as one chapter was closed we were faced with the next problem. This restful homeward voyage enabled us to collect enough energy to tackle the summer of hard work in Paris. For hard work it most certainly was to sort out and list and file away the mass of information, photographs, and data collected in the year of travelling.

Arriving in Paris the end of May, 1932, our first problem was to extricate from the French custom house the forty-eight boxes of materials and plaster casts which we had shipped from the various oriental ports. Good fortune had blessed us again, for nothing had been lost or stolen in transit, and only one plaster finger had broken. To complete the life-size studies made on the trip entailed many months of work, and an extra studio near our house was equipped. When the time came to finish the full-length figure of my Sicilian fisherman, I was left in an awkward situation, for my subject suddenly decided he had posed enough and simply evaporated with his fishing-net and could not be found anywhere.

As there were certain details of the net still left to be completed, I asked at the Trocadéro Museum if they knew of some one who could lend me such a net in Paris. I was given a card of introduction to Henri de Monfreid, and proceeded in my car to hunt him down in his lair near Boulogne. When I explained the reason of my visit, I was taken upstairs and shown various collections of photographs,

SYMBOLIC GROUP IN BRONZE REPRESENTING THE THREE RACES OF MAN: WHITE, YELLOW, BLACK. EACH FIGURE HOLDS THE WEAPON BY WHICH THE RACE HAS DEFENDED ITS OWN BOUNDARIES

Total height fifteen feet, including the globe. The Americas are above the white man, Asia over the yellow, Africa over the black

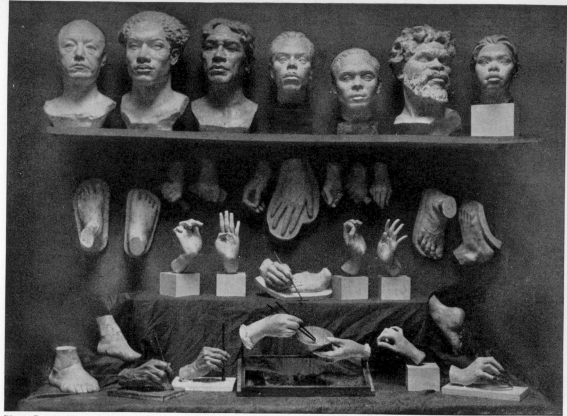

Photo. Bernès Maroteau.

HEADS FROM CHINA, SAMOA, HAWAII, JAVA, BORNEO, AUSTRALIA, AND MALAY JUNGLES

Casts made from hands and feet to show the racial differences in form, and gestures of the hand in dancing, sewing, writing, eating, etc.

Photo. M. H.

HENRI DE MONFREID ON HIS SAILBOAT IN THE RED SEA

OUR MASCOT, KIKI OF SIAM, BESIDE HIMSELF AS MODELLED BY M. H.

weapons, nets, and extraordinary paintings and South Sea carvings by Gauguin—exceeding in actual native character any other carvings I had ever seen from Tahiti or nearby islands, made by the natives themselves.

Not having known of Monsieur de Monfreid's prowess as an artist and adventurer, as pearl and hashish trader and author of breathless tales of the Red Sea, my visit was rather an adventure for me. We sat on the floor and looked through endless boxes of drawings and photographs. I was intrigued by the alert and vivid countenance of my host; his piercing, deep-set eyes peered out from a network of finely etched wind- and sun-made wrinkles—the face of a sailor who searches the horizon and sees beyond, who has known the scorching blades of tropical sun and the searing blasts of sand-storms in the desert.

When we parted he had agreed to come to my studio and give me a word of final criticism about my fisherman's net. *"Je viendrai de bonne heure, je suis un marin, même à Paris—à jeudi prochain."*

When Thursday came along, I arose much earlier than usual. I had a feeling the *marin* would be arriving long before we had started our busy day, which got into its stride before nine A.M.

At eight o'clock, the roar of a motor sounded in the Villa driveway, and I looked down to see de Monfreid jumping from his car—a red muffler, a beret Basque and odd bits of homespun clothes rather slung about him. White tennis sneakers—and such a smile!

We went to the studio and in a flash he caught just what was the matter with the twist of my fisherman's net. De Monfreid caught up the net, jumped up on the model-stand, fell into the pose, and started casting the net over the studio floor, as if he were going to scoop up a big catch in deadly earnest. Possibly two or three plaster heads, I thought, as I realized the crowded space at his disposal.

I saw what to do at once and asked him to keep on fishing while I gave the few final corrections. His sharp, searching gaze kept roving over the surface of the imaginary sea, hunting his prey. In a short time I had "snapped up" certain details which gave a livelier and more natural effect. Then we jumped into his car and went off to see the films of his recent journey in Ethiopia.

337

I asked him where we were going. He said he did not know the address but could find the place. Two or three times on the way to his laboratory he would stop the car, step out on the running-board and scan the heavens; returning to the wheel, he would casually remark, "I take all my bearings by the sun, even in Paris, and then I never get lost. We must go eastward now and then north. This will bring us to the laboratory." And strange as it may seem, it did.

The film was run off and showed an exciting chase by de Monfreid of a band of Arab robbers, who had stolen some of his camp firewood. The Arabs were fleeing in their sailboat, being followed by de Monfreid and his men in another sailboat. The robbers were gaining in the race; their sail was bigger and the wind was strong.

Suddenly de Monfreid was seen climbing out to the bow of his boat with a gun. He braced himself, took aim and fired. His shot severed the halyard on the lee side of the Arab's mast, and the great sail pulled over the mast and fell flapping into the sea; de Monfreid's boat gained on the unlucky robbers and when it came alongside all hands dove into the water—robbers and de Monfreid's sailors. There was a desperate struggle between the men, but finally with ropes and wrestling, the robbers were captured and bound. The movie was excellently taken by another member of de Monfreid's party, who very conveniently happened to be in another boat at the same time, and was an eye-witness to the battle.

Most of the figures for the Hall of Man were cast into bronze in Paris, and before many weeks had passed there were sixty men busy on my bronzes at the foundry. In patining these bronzes, the tones were slightly varied to suggest the degrees of skin colors of the different races. This avoided any monotony of effect in the final arrangement of the collection. It was at this time that we made the scale model of the proposed hall—mentioned in an earlier chapter—modelling the statues in wax to the same scale as their complete setting. This model, about 60 inches long, was wired electrically and gave an exact effect in miniature of just how each figure and head would be placed and lighted. The color scheme of walls, shadow-boxes, stands, pedestals, and flooring was all studied and suggested.

When it was decided that the central symbolic group of the Hall of Man should represent the three great races of mankind surmounted by a globe, on an architectural column, the problem was to find the correct scale and relation of these elements: the globe, the column, the figures, and the base.

After the column and the figures were made, we began casting various sizes of globes in plaster. As these never seemed to be just right and were difficult to make, I finally resorted to the idea of blowing up a thin rubber balloon to the size of one meter in diameter. After three or four of these had burst, I went to the aviation supply company and asked if they could not make me a strong balloon which could expand evenly to four feet if necessary, and remain at this size by some valve attachment. They were interested, and came over with the balloon and a bicycle pump, to inflate it and place it for me on the column.

The figures were six feet, eight inches high, and the column about eight feet. My models and a group of plaster-casters and neighbors came to see the experiment. Having heard the numerous tales of explosions, and having seen us going between the two studios holding balloons over our heads, every one's curiosity was aroused.

The photographer was ready to take his shots of the ensemble, for it is often easier to judge relative sizes in a photograph than to judge the scale of a large group in a small studio. The pump was attached and the balloon began to swell. Great was the tensity of anticipation. To play safe, we expanded the balloon to four inches beyond the size we thought would be necessary, so we could let out the air easily by the valve without taking down the globe, and photograph it in four or five dimensions.

The photographer turned his spot-light on the transparent globe and ducked his head under his black camera-cloth. Just as he said "Ready," the heat from the strong lamp decided to expand the globe and a report like a rifle tore the precious balloon to ribbons. The men from the aviation company looked deflated—we all felt deflated. What next?

Another globe of stronger material was ordered. Finally the balloon was made that could withstand the expansion and the photographs were taken. We even decorated this one in colors and hung it from the studio rafters as a mascot. The size determined was 3 feet, 7 inches in diameter. The next move was to cast a sphere of this size in plaster, transfer to its smooth surface an accurate map of the world continents, and cut away the oceans to an even depth of half an inch. This may all sound very simple but it was not.

Map-makers, moulders, carvers, and founders all spent many hours of perplexity and study. When the bronze globe was cast and the time came to set it in place on the column, we had to hang it on a strong chain, on a travelling crane, and tilt the globe on its axis until, at a certain point, America came over the white man, Asia over the yellow, and Africa over the black. The position of the earth which we adopted actually exists at a certain season of the year.

Every one breathed a sigh of relief and we celebrated with an informal party at the foundry, which was attended by the directors of French museums, art-critics, writers, and visitors from America. At this time we had assembled quite a bronze gallery of twenty life-size figures and thirty or more heads. Shortly afterwards these were crated and shipped to Chicago. The central group weighed nearly two tons when boxed. The packing of these bronzes demanded much care, and luckily there was no damage during transit throughout the entire enterprise, either to the bronzes or to the plaster models.

Taking the scale model with me, I sailed for America, where the officers of the Field Museum and I spent many weeks in collaboration, studying the problem of installation, indirect lighting, and proper background for the Hall of Man.

Sam's chief concern was to cut and splice and edit the miles of moving-picture films, write and photograph their correct captions, and compile the albums of 2000 still pictures with their corresponding negatives and anthropological histories. When these were completed we had three or four informal exhibits for the officials of the museums and friends in Paris.

Later on in America we gave a lecture at the Colony Club in New York. We showed seventy-five lantern slides, many of them colored, and ended the evening by showing the films of jungle tribes and the temple dancers of Bali, with musical accompaniment of their gamelon orchestra.

To speak before an audience was a far more terrifying experience than any of our adventures in the jungles!

V

THE END OF IT ALL

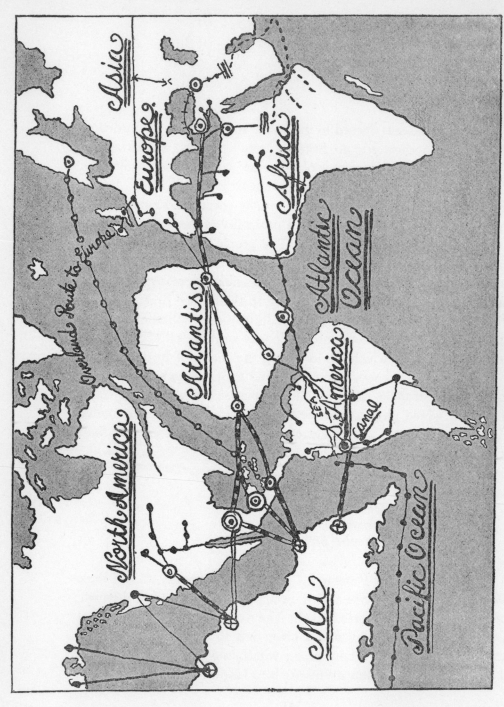

IF ATLANTIS, WHY NOT MU?

Map showing the supposed location of the submerged continents and the paths along which are traced the evolution of similar cultures. *Adapted from Churchward's "The Lost Continent of Mu."* (See page 352)

THE END OF IT ALL

Finistère

After the Hall was opened to the public in June 1933, I returned to France, and a short trip to Brittany completed our wanderings in Europe and added the portrait of a Breton woman to the collection. This type I modelled in St. Guénolé, Finistère "Land's End." Land's end indeed, and well named, is this remote corner of France which, by reason of its isolated location and proximity to the ocean, has kept its original and rugged character. The people of recent years, alas, have had too many contacts with tourists; the constantly growing omnibus facilities have made travelling possible for many who, until the present time, were satisfied to stay in their stone houses and let the rest of the world wear itself out with futile complications. These and other factors have combined to destroy a great deal of the beauty and remote quality which has long been the charm of Brittany.

Only at the far corners, where rocks and tempestuous seas still wage their eternal struggle, can we find the splendid, silent type of sailor-fisherman whose physiognomy reflects the strain of constant combat against the elements and that strength of character which one finds so clearly marked in those men who go down to the sea in ships.

> *"A deux pas de la mer*
> *Qu'on entend bourdonner*
> *Je sais un coin perdu*
> *De la terre Bretonne. . . ."*

In the peninsula of Penmarch I have for many years studied these Bretons. The farmer type differs in appearance from the fisherman, but there is an archaic force in both. The women in their black bodices and spotless white coiffes add a great deal to the picturesque landscape. The land is swept by strong winds, and the few valiant trees that withstand the winter storms are bent landwards, with their crests forever bowed by the long strain of the ocean storms. An occasional wooden windmill breaks the outline of the horizon, as one crosses the country leading to Finistère. When one reaches the coast at night the great revolving shafts of light from the *phares* give warning of the jagged perils that lie beneath the surface of the sea. It is indeed no wonder that the sailors still pray for the protection of their fragile boats as they thread their course between the Ile de Sein and the Pointe du Raz. Even on the clearest and bluest of summer days, there frequently occurs the phenomenal event of a *lame du fond,* or a gathering together of the waves in a united mass, which, without a cloud or warning of any kind, suddenly rises near the shore and sweeps over the cliffs and beaches, taking its toll of any living creature who may have ventured too near the water's treacherous grasp.

As one travels inland, the faces of the people appear less rugged and the eyes less watchful and less deeply shadowed by the furrowed brows. The coiffes change in their design in each successive village. The "Bigoudens" of St. Guénolé wear the stiff white peak of embroidery on their heads, tied tightly under the chin. Dainty white lace bonnets denote Audierne, and the stiffly pleated ruffs worn on the shoulders as a wide collar tell the world that the wearer comes from Fouesnant, near Beg-Meil.

Threading our way along the south coast, we find at Carnac the ruins of Druidic times—the great alignments of granitic menhirs, set in endless rows, all leading, according to scientific conjecture, to the rising sun. In Morbihan and other places one finds the stone dolmens and sacrificial rocks, all evocative of the ancient race that once inhabited this area. If we study the symbolism of their designs, we find in the embroidery on the coiffes made at Pont-l'Abbé and worn by every Breton woman of that district, which includes Penmarch and St. Guénolé, the triangular pattern of the bonnet filled with circles and sprays of laurel, a crescent moon, and the horns of a ram.

In the symbolic language of the ancients, these designs may be interpreted as the eternal sacred triangle—the generation of life; the central circle with radiating rays represents the sun, surrounded by eight smaller discs; the rays indicate movement of the stars. The ram's horns represent conductive energy of fecundity. The branches suggest new life and growth. This sacred language is accurately carried on from generation to generation—even in 1934 in Brittany. It may be traced back to the era of the pyramids of Egypt, and by many is believed even to antedate hieroglyphics.

The Bretons are a quiet, self-assured people, who make friends slowly and carefully. When once assured of the sincerity of the new-comer, they are content to wait patiently before allowing any familiarity, and only after a thorough period of examination and trial may one hope to be admitted as a friend to their rigid laws of hospitality. Once a friend, however, there is no race more loyal, devoted, or trusting than these people are, when their minds have been convinced and their hearts touched. In the extreme southwestern part of Brittany one still finds the definite type of the primitive race—short, dark hair, dark eyes, sharp features, serious and independent in character. Many speak only Breton and no French, but can understand the sailor-folk of Western Ireland and Cornwall and are known as "Bigauds" or "Bigoudens," very likely the direct descendants of the dolmen builders.

Pierre Loti, Chateaubriand, Le Goffic, Le Braz, and Edward Schuré have, with many other writers, felt the lure and magnetic inspiration of these Breton lands, legends, and people. The radiant colors of the sky and sea, landscapes, and festivals have been interpreted by many painters, but most vividly by Jean-Julien Lemordant, of St. Malo, who, just after decorating the great ceiling of the opera house at Rennes, volunteered in the French army in 1914 and by tragic fate was blinded in the Great War; his masterly art has recorded for all time the picturesque life of St. Guénolé and Finistère.

Really to understand the Breton man of the sea, it is well to go out in his boat at four A.M. and feel the sharp edge of the wind blowing through a foggy dawn over the rocks and seaweed. As you approach the end of the stone jetty, your sailorman cups his mouth with his rough, red hands and calls his *"mousse"*—a lad of fourteen, who is the watchdog of the fishing-boat and sleeps in the little cabin, rolled up in a coarse blanket. Each boat has its *mousse,* and as the captains collect on the pier and call their names, the little chaps climb out on deck, jump into the dingy and row in to the jetty. There the crew has assembled, and all hands climb into the rowboat and row out to the fishing smack. In certain seasons it is, of course, quite dark when these departures take place. The men stay out until three or six o'clock in the afternoon, returning with their heavy cargo of sardines, which is sold under the watchful eye of the port douanier to the factories, to be soaked in oil and canned for the world's market.

The only rations of food taken out by the fishermen at dawn are loaves of bread, slabs of cheese, and jugs of fresh water; they take tubs of bait for their nets, and barrels of gasoline for their motors. If, on reaching the port, the boats find that the day's supply of fish has been bought up by the factories, they are obliged to throw their entire cargo back into the sea and lose all their profits and the cost of their bait.

The first time that Sam and I had visited St. Guénolé we had been both rather appalled by the dour aspect of this storm-swept land, but I felt a deep and fundamental stirring of my blood as I walked along the miles of flat sand beaches under the June stars. Here I seemed to feel that the roots of my being had found their home. Some strange kinship of other days bound me to these rocks and primitive children of the sea.

After we had visited St. Guénolé for three seasons we made many good friends among the fishermen and their families. One group in particular became our Breton hosts. They were collecting funds to build a fine new boat, stronger and able to carry more sail. When the boat was nearing completion, the captain wrote me to ask if they might name their new boat *La Malvina*. I was very touched and proud to have my name on the sides of this sturdy Breton boat, for I knew the fine character of the captain and the gallant loyalty of his crew.

I went over to the drydocks where the carpenters of Pont-l'Abbé were nailing up the last planks over the wooden hull of "our boat." The captain handed me a brush and asked me to draw my name in large, white letters on the black boards. All work was stopped; workmen, sailors, and their families stood about, and I felt a pounding in my veins as I drew out the letters of my name.

After the boat was launched into the harbor at Pont-l'Abbé, the

Upper left: THE FISHING–BOAT *MALVINA* IN THE PORT OF ST. GUÉNOLÉ, BRITTANY

Upper right: GUILLAUME TANNEAU

Type of Breton sailor

ROCKS AND SURF AT ST. GUÉNOLÉ, AND THE STUDIO OF JEAN JULIEN LEMORDANT 349

TYPE OF OLD BRETON FISHERMAN,
PENMARC'H

LA FILLE DE ROLAND

Lace maker of St. Guénolé, knitting the traditional
stitches that are similar to Irish lace

DRAWING OF THE CHAPEL
ON THE EDGE OF THE SEA,
"NOTRE DAME DE LA JOIE,"
BY M. H.

The sixteenth-century Calvary in
stone has an archaic piéta at the
foot of the Cross. It is here that
the sailors and fisher folk hold a
beautiful Pardon each September,
with procession and religious ceremony

christening with prayers and religious service took place at St. Guénolé. This was directed by the local priest in purple and lace vest-
ments.

As certain of the more educated members of the little colony had
known of the fact that "Malvina" was the name of their legendary
"Queen of the Fairies," they thought the boat was named for her.
When they found that my name was actually identical with their
legend's heroine, we all had a celebration at the jetty *bistro;* with
many bottles of red wine and cherry brandy we drank to *la pêche
miraculeuse.*

Soon after the launching there was a great storm on the coast of
Brittany, and some of the crews of the fishing-boats were missing and
apparently could not bring their boats into port—so great were the
waves and so wild the tempest. Volunteers were called for by the life-
saving squad to brave the perils of the rocky entrance to the port and
to go out into the teeth of the storm to hunt for the two missing boats.
Every member of the *Malvina's* crew stepped forward and offered to
act as a life-saving crew, and they offered their boat as well, for it
was stronger than some others and they had great confidence in her.
"Il faut vouloir vivre et savoir mourir," Napoleon said well.

So the wives and children of these brave men gathered in groups,
bracing themselves against the stone walls of the port houses, and
shivering in their heavy, black shawls. Not a word was said—there
was no weeping or evident fear. The rain and wind howled, and the
men in their great oil-skins and helmets shook hands with the mayor
of the port, pulled up their rubber boots, and marched off to their fate.

The *Malvina* set sail with many reefs and lurched about furiously
as she buffeted the cross-currents of the narrows between the high,
jagged rocks. She disappeared in the haze and swish of the rain.
After two hours of agonized, silent waiting she returned, having on
board the rescued crews of the two abandoned boats, which had
foundered and had been swallowed by the storm.

To spend a few weeks of summer holiday in St. Guénolé has been
a frequent life-saver for me after the long months of continuous work.
The air has a quality of bubbling champagne, and after a few hours

of deep breathing our lungs feel stretched and cleansed of smoke and city dust. White clouds in sculptured masses float across the inverted bowl of blue. Further than the eye can see, the flat beach stretches along the wind-swept coast. What vigils have these great dunes been keeping through the ages! Slowly, as the sea changes, do these billowing breasts of sand rise and fall and shift their silhouettes so silently, so slowly, that man cannot discern or date their heavings or their hollows. It is enough to lie between them under the sun, within their warm, ineffable embrace, and feel the streak of golden sunlight draw its blade ever so slowly across your burning body.

During the winter the ageless depths of sea-drenched sand, ground fine and tempered by the wind and sun, are suddenly torn up and whirled away by cyclone power; an endless conflict rages over this primitive coast: sea, wind, sun, each triumphant in its appointed time.

It is in these primitive surroundings that we may become almost unconsciously attuned to the phenomena of natural forces—our inner mind hears the choir of invisible voices; all the noise and distraction of daily life is blotted out and one has a sense of renewal and courage. It is perhaps because of our desperate need of such renascence that we seek the extremes of solitude and silence from which we may learn to "tap in on the Infinite" and gain a true perspective on our finite values, so often distorted by habit and convention.

If Atlantis, Why Not Mu?

In the folklore of Brittany and Cornwall we find the picturesque legends of the lost islands off the coast—and it is not difficult to believe these tales if we visit these storm-swept edges of the continent of Europe. The Atlantic rises without warning in its mighty omnipotence and occasionally sweeps over the rocks and fields, wiping out villages and taking years to recede to its former boundaries—sometimes never reaching them.

The dramatic legend of Le Roi d'Ys and King Gradlon, how St. Guénolé gave his timely warning of the storm to save the people— all these tales live on in the minds of the Bretons as vividly today as they did hundreds of years ago. In the summer evenings, if you join the groups of Breton sailor-folk sitting on the rocks at the edge of the sea, you may ask why they are so silent, and they will answer very solemnly: *"Nous écoutons les cloches de la cathédrale engloutie."*

As recently as 1929 there was an earthquake reported in the ocean-bed of the Atlantic. The effects of this were felt on the coast of Brittany and as far west as the coast of New Jersey; the surface of the ocean was in a violent state of upheaval. The idea that continents could have been swallowed up and submerged is not an unreasonable supposition, and these legends add rather a fairy glamor to the volumes which have been written on this subject.

The story of Atlantis has intrigued minds since Plato to the present day. This mythical, lost continent was first described as being the home of a flourishing and ideal civilization, located beyond the Pillars of Hercules, or westward of the continent of Africa. The intrepid Ulysses is supposed to have been the first to venture west of this gateway to the uncharted seas, but alas, his reports were not registered either in newspapers or on the radio. Hamilcar, the powerful ruler of Carthage in the fifth century B.C. was also credited with a voyage into the unknown Atlantis.

To many scientists, there is convincing evidence that there was another submerged continent known as Mu, which was almost completely destroyed and covered by what is now known as the Pacific Ocean. The South Sea Islands, Easter Islands, the Marquesas, Hawaii, Samoa, and others are by many believed to be the remaining fragments of this great continent.

The discovery of many similar patterns and symbols in widely separated areas has given added credence to the possible existence of these lost continents. An instinctive sense of design and color is found in nearly all primitive races. They decorate every weapon or household utensil with intricate and beautifully balanced patterns. Their art can teach great lessons, without the need of words, to many a modern sculptor.

Migrations of peoples carry their symbolism with them and account for the frequent reappearance of the various national or religious patterns; these in turn form a sort of endless chain of civilization, new links of which are constantly being discovered through archeological researches in all parts of the world.

> If what we say and what we do
> Can give historians a clue,
> If old ways do beget the new,
> (Tho' many won't believe this true)
> I'd like to speculate with you
> On . . . If ATLANTIS, why not MU?

My Trocadéro Exhibition

At last all of the bronzes made in Paris had been shipped to Chicago, and the autumn months I spent preparing an exhibition of the small-size originals and reductions in bronze at the Trocadéro Museum in Paris. It was very gratifying to me as an artist to be invited to exhibit 100 pieces of my work under such cordial and distinguished patronage as Les Musées Nationaux, and to feel that the French scientists and museum directors were interested enough to place such a seal of approval on my racial types. It was my first exhibition since 1911, when I had shown the first two portraits that I had ever modelled, one of my father and one of Sam.

It was something of a task, however, to supervise the finishing and patining of such a collection. The installation was made possible by the wholehearted co-operation of the museum staff, including Doctor Rivet, Monsieur George Henri Rivière, Monsieur Marcel Griaule and Monsieur Eric Lutten of the Mission Dakar Djibouti. The week preceding the formal opening was a test of endurance and good humor. As it was not yet November first, there was no central heating allowed, and the weather was freezing and damp. The Parisian population

MONSIEUR RUDIER AND M. H. INSPECTING THE FIRST ASSEMBLING OF THE BRONZES
FOR THE HALL OF MAN, IN THE PARIS FOUNDRY

THE ARRANGEMENT OF THE FULL–SIZE MODELS AND SMALL BRONZES OF ONE HUNDRED
AND TWO RACIAL TYPES IN THE TROCADÉRO MUSEUM, PARIS

Lieutenant Jean Julien Lemordant with his dog Romeo, as he appeared when he came to America to receive the Howland Prize at Yale, after being blinded in battle and imprisoned in Germany

Lieutenant Lemordant being escorted by his Breton friends during the local Pardon, which he had organized according to the old traditions. In 1936, after twenty years of total blindness, his sight has been partially restored. His story confirms one's faith in miracles

Over-life-size bronze of t[...] right hand of Jean Julien L[...] mordant by M. H.

seems to submit, year after year, to this national test of their physical powers of resistance, in spite of the fact that each autumn the entire city has the "flu" and coughs steadily until the first of November. It is simply *not done* to turn on "chauffage centrale" before this date.

Our breath rose in vaporous clouds and our hands turned blue as we lifted, pushed, and arranged the icy bronzes on the glass shelves. Sweaters and sealskin underwear were not sufficient to keep out the penetrating draughts that whistled up and down the circular gallery from which there radiated the glorious view over the Seine to the Eiffel Tower and Champ de Mars.

Many were the amusing incidents that helped to make this experience one of good fellowship and laughter. Our friends at the museum and my pupil "La Gazelle," otherwise known as Frances Rich, worked with me until late at night, arranging the infinite details that always precede an exhibition. It was well that we were amused, for on the opening day 5000 distinguished *"rubans rouges"* and the *élite* of Paris society crowded into the museum to inaugurate Pre-historic Africa, Salle de la Mission Dakar Djibouti and the Races of Man—and when four o'clock ticked off the daylight and each one of us had been given the signal to switch on all the electric lights in our various exhibitions, there was a sudden flash and then complete darkness throughout the entire building! A blow-out of the main line was the cause, and it took *an hour* to repair the fuses and get the lights going.

The crowds were a bit staggered by the situation, but soon decided to stay on and patiently wait for the electricity; no panic or hysteria. The ministers, whose crowded schedules of *"inaugurations"* allowed them their *"bon quart d'heure"* for each hall, were desperate. They could not escape, and time ticked on with its tongue in its cheek. Restive and humiliated, they had to submit to an accident like all the rest of the mere humans.

My valiant friend, Jean Julien Lemordant (the painter who had been blinded in the war), was surrounded by a group of admiring friends when the lights went out. I hurriedly explained to him what had occurred and asked him to hold the interest of the crowd for me and keep them under control until I could investigate matters. My friend Irene Wyle offered to send her motor post-haste to collect the best electricians in Paris. When the car returned with eleven men, the situation was saved and the damage repaired. A rising shout of pleasure and relief rang through the halls and stairways as floor after floor was re-illuminated.

Even if the exhibits failed to make an indelible impression on the visitors, I doubt if any one who attended this inauguration will ever forget the experience.

When these 100 bronzes were finally packed and shipped to America, an overwhelming sense of finality settled over me. The ever receding horizons of the past five years were actually coming too close, and the fact that there was no longer any need to drive either with or against the tide was the cause of an inevitable cessation of nervous energy and the realization of great fatigue. There was an accounting to be made in which we were not able to foresee, or defend ourselves from, the red pencil which Mother Nature so deftly wields when she balances her books. The law of mechanics applies to our own over-driven machines, but we seldom have the common sense to have our machines overhauled and tuned up unless some vital force becomes suddenly incapable of responding to our demands.

Climbing up the long mountain trail and cutting notches in the trees has exhilaration and enticement. The peaks lure us beyond our capacity and then we find out—many things, worlds of wisdom and a new perspective and the revelation that comes of infinite fatigue. Does not the dreamer who follows the mirage know in his heart that he is lost before he starts his quest? And yet—is it not just this passionate faith in life's illusions that makes the fight glamorous and tempers the sword in golden flames?

Our Aboriginal Americans

To understand Indian life, one must be aware of Nature—her moods and seasons—the element of sky and sunlight—the mystic evolution of seed, fructification, growth, harvest—death—lightning and clouds, in ourselves as well as in the heavens—seasons in our own lives: birth, youth, maturity, old age, and death, synchronizing with the cosmic cycle.

The ceremonial festivals recognize and celebrate these seasons. Pollen is shaken into the air, the seed being the symbol of life. The continuance of race, the rich harvest, the earth reaching out to the sun, the heavens pouring the rain in benediction; each needs the other to bring forth the sacred corn or the wheat by which they may live. The storms are answers to prayer, and the rainbow encircling the whole stands as the symbol of hope and promise.

In the heart of the Indian country of our Southwest is Santa Fe, New Mexico, one of the oldest cities in the United States. The Museum of New Mexico and the Rockefeller Laboratory of Anthropology (both in Santa Fe) have collected the relics of ancient days and specimens of arts and crafts of all the tribes in that vicinity, and these are of inestimable value as a record of ancient and contemporary history.

It might be well to recall that it is less than one hundred years since the United States, in 1846, took possession of New Mexico and recognized the rights of the Southwest Indians living there in their pueblos. The Indian governors who were responsible for this village were presented with silver-headed canes by Abraham Lincoln, as a sign of authority and of his friendliness—a symbol which was cherished until the Indians found themselves slowly but surely being herded together and fenced in by government authority, forced to limit their wanderings, to relinquish their age-old rights to land and to water-supplies, and to become a captive race.

Both Catholic and Protestant missions have been diligently establishing their churches in the reservations, and their influence is felt in every village. Today the Indians politely attend Christian services, at the same time believing in their ancestral religion and turning to their own gods for any spiritual help of vital importance. Their own ceremonies are carried out underground in their "kiwas," unseen and unattended by any white man. Crucifixes hang on the adobe walls with highly colored lithographs of Biblical scenes, surrounded by feather war-bonnets and the ever-present tom-toms and necklaces of bear's teeth. In some of the houses the Indians have fallen to the ignominious level of making and selling "knick-knacks" for the tourist trade.

Having completed all the racial tribes needed for the Hall of Man except our own Indians—I saved for my last choice morsel this trip to the Southwest to "see America last"—I found, as in many other places, that I would have to overcome the serious handicap of primitive repulsion to sculpture. Any resemblance to a human face made in clay is almost always "taboo." An ancient superstition lives on in the primitive tribes of many countries. The image of a man is believed to steal away his strength, and in some places this resistance is developed to such a point that the younger men of a tribe are threatened by their elders with slow but sure death if they continue to pose for a sculptor. Here in our own country, less than fifty miles from the trans-continental railroad, I found taboos as strong as in Africa.

A fine type of Indian was selected to pose for me. He seemed more amused than anything else, while I took his measurements and watched him in his various poses. After the first long day, however, I sensed that he was growing suspicious and unhappy. I had made good progress with my portrait and had worked from memory late into the night. The following morning he arrived with his head hanging, and no sign of cheerfulness. After questioning him I was forced to accept his explanation:

"Last night two men come my hogan tell me I surely die soon. All night they tell me, if I come again to give my head to your hands my heart dry up, fall out. No, I no come . . . want more to live . . . sorry, but I go now," and he evaporated, awed and trembling with fright.

I watched his powerful, lithe body swinging across the fields; then I slowly tore down the modelled head, realizing that I would have to start a new search for another type.

This sort of experience in various shades of intensity was met with in Africa, Asia, and the Pacific Islands, but I was surprised to find it so general among our own Indians. Such superstition caused me many bitter disappointments and many hours of wasted effort. In one of the tribes in New Mexico, the feeling is so strong that no member of the tribe is permitted by the governor even to be photographed. This last winter one of their young men who had been in contact with the city and had a friend in the artist colony, finally agreed to pose for his portrait. After a week of sittings he was summoned before the Indian Council in their *kiwa*. They put him "on the spot" for twelve hours. His legs began to swell and his breathing grew short and heavy. He listened to his doom being prophesied—"Before one year you will surely die"—and he knew that his time was set. With this conviction, and when the elders felt sure that their threats had sunk fatally into his heart, he was liberated. Within ten months the young man failed, grew thin, developed tuberculosis and died—fully aware that no force was left in him to combat anything. His mind was under the spell of their condemnation.

While modelling, I usually asked my sitters to tell me about their tribal customs. I was interested to learn that the Pueblo woman is not a wife of slave-like submission. The matriarchal tradition of woman ruling at home and having the upper hand in bringing up the children is still very apparent in many instances. One finds the mother constructing the adobe walls of her house, moulding her chimneys and smoothing the wet earth floors with the palms of her hands, to make the compact surface more easily cleaned. If her husband's behavior fails to meet with her approval, she calmly sets his saddle and blankets, etc., outside the door, and on his return, if he is wise, he accepts the situation, carries off his belongings, and faces the fact that he is no longer wanted and his job is to find a new wife and a new home.

One of the most interesting discoveries of recent years has been the instinctive talent and ability of the Indian youths to paint in water-colors. About 1917 they were given supplies of paper, brushes, and colors and told to paint their impressions of the various ceremonial dances and costumes. Collections of these paintings have been made by certain far-sighted Indian traders and connoisseurs of art. They show an extraordinary sense of formal design and clean, vital coloring. A few years ago the walls of the United States Indian School at Santa

Fe were decorated by the older pupils, and these murals have been the subject of many enthusiastic articles by art critics. The better known artists come from San Ildefonso, Cochiti, Kiowa, and Hopiland.

The Indian seems to have a remarkable memory for color and line. The fact that the parents have, for generations, taught the children all they know of their own history and geography by word-of-mouth, has developed an accurate mechanism of memory pictures and a sense of proportion and direction which is rare. This training enables an Indian to find his way easily across the miles of uncharted desert lands and to recognize at a glance the formation of mesas or clumps of bushes, which serve to guide him better than the very occasional sign-post which so often has blown down and is found pointing in the wrong direction.

Many of the tribes have contributed pictures to the local art exhibitions, and there is a steadily increasing number of artists whose work has become recognized. The usual peril of exploitation by dealers is to be guarded against, for the Indian artist, like all the others, is quickly demoralized by a too easy market, and the inevitable result of this is more production of less artistic value. The same may be said of the Pueblo pottery-makers, who in certain instances have grown careless in their technique through the demand for more work than they can conscientiously produce.

It is amazing to watch the finest pottery-makers build up their jars and bowls without the aid of modern tools or even a potter's wheel. The Pueblo Indians use only their deft fingers to mould the forms of the bowls with prodigious craftsmanship. The clay is glazed and baked and in many instances smoked until it is a luminous black color. On this the designers draw or etch the intricate designs handed down from one generation to the other, using no compass or measuring instruments and always adhering to the local tradition of their tribe, both in form and color.

At the time of the mound-builders, they seem to have worked skillfully in repoussé silver and native copper; certain ceremonial tablets and cooking utensils show a sense of sculptural form and decoration, but these examples date back before the advent of the white man.

The plumed or bearded serpent which appears in the Toltec, Aztec,

362

and Maya civilizations is used frequently in the ceremonial rites of the Pueblo Indians. The recent excavations and discoveries in the field of archeology have added many treasures and authentic links by which the story of our Pueblo Indians may be traced back to the age of cliff-dwellers and mastodons over 12,000 years ago. Rock pictures in the Hava Supai Canyon of Arizona show huge reptiles and prehistoric dinosaurs. Fragments of the Pueblo language and sacred symbols connect their origin with that of the Quiche Maya civilization. It has been established that four branches of the Maya language were in use in the rock pictures of the Southwest cliff dwellers.

In America the swastika symbol is found on pottery of the mound builders, and in Yucatan. It also appears on the rattles of gourds used in ceremonial dances by Pueblo Indians and most frequently in the designs for Navajo sand-paintings, where two human figures often form the part of the swastika that is turned back. Among our Indians there are special sand-paintings for curing each disease. When the mind is troubled and the patient is melancholy the chant of "Terrestrial Beauty" is the one which restores the sick man to equilibrium and heals his spirit.

The mother-earth and the father-sky figure in many of the designs, and the constellations, the sun, and the moon are frequently shown, and with great accuracy. The gourd held by the medicine man who posed for me was pierced in the pattern of the Great Dipper and North Star and other constellations.

In San Felipe we witnessed the corn and rain dance. Crowds of Indians from other pueblos made a colorful audience. The grouping of the Indians in costume, chanting and dancing to the rhythmic pounding of the tom-tom, was a most brilliant affair. The blazing sun added a certain splendor to the swaying lines of glistening, brown bodies and waving pine boughs, and the breeze blew their long, black hair about their shoulders. Two groups from the opposite sides of the village kept up a continual rhythmic intonation and invocation for rain, hour after hour, until sunset. A leader carried a long pole, ending in a bunch of corn leaves. This he waved over the heads of the other dancers, shaking out the sacred pollen and calling the rain to shed its benediction on the seeded earth. On our way home the heavens darkened and a thunderstorm came as a response to their prayers.

These dances are carried out in the most reverential manner. They are closely interwoven with symbolic significance and are the expression of a living religious conviction. Each generation learns from the preceding one every step and formation of the dance. The chants are learned by heart from early childhood, the dance becomes a part of life, and the Indian feels a deep and powerful association between his own life-current and the life of the earth about him.

From Santa Fe I telephoned ahead to a well-known Indian trading-post at Coolidge, New Mexico. I persuaded the owner, one Mr. B. I. Staples, to motor as far as Thoreau, a small settlement that could boast of a postoffice and a railway station, a trading-post, and a few scattered wooden houses, to meet me on my arrival.

As the train was not even scheduled to stop at this place except on signals, I took the conductor into my confidence and told him the object of my journey, first presenting a letter from the Harvey Hotel System's director. This Harvey System is one of the great American institutions for the assistance of travellers. It was agreed, as we approached the designated place, that the train would be slowed down and I would be able to decide whether the mysterious person to whom I had telephoned was of the type that I would be ready to be left alone with in the midst of the Arizona desert! Naturally the conductor and porters took a personal interest in such a situation, and the platform was soon crowded with smiling observers. My bags, boxes, and portfolios were all on the steps, ready for my signal to cast off. We saw the little Ford car, a solitary black dot against the walls of pink mesas, these gaunt mountains whose summits had been levelled off by some primordial super-sculptor. Standing by his motor and waving a handkerchief was our unknown hero, unsuspecting and quite unconcerned about his impending fate.

"That's my man," I called, "he would seem to be a perfect 'uncle' in the wilderness," and the signal to stop was pulled.

With bag and baggage I was deposited in the friendly care of Mr. Staples, whose cheerful New England countenance made me feel quite

THE MASKED DANCE OF THE APACHE INDIANS OF AMERICA

Photo, M. H.

BAS–RELIEF PANEL BY M. H. DEPICTING THE MASKED DEATH CEREMONY OF THE DOGGON
TRIBE, NORTH OF NIGERIA, AFRICA

The wooden masks are black and white, the skirts and fly swats are of raffia dyed red. The warriors
climb to the top of the house of the dead man, touch it bowing their heads, while his wife wails for
hours in the courtyard below. (See page 382)

THE ANCIENT HOPI PUEBLO OF WALPI, PERCHED ON A PRECIPITOUS CLIFF
FIFTEEN HUNDRED FEET HIGH

THREE GENERATIONS OF A FAMILY OF
HOPI INDIANS

THE VIRGINAL HEAD–DRESS, KNOWN AS THE
"SQUASH BLOSSOM," WORN BY THE GIRLS OF
THE HOPI TRIBE

SANTA CLARA PUEBLO CHIEF IN
CEREMONIAL COSTUME

PUYE PUEBLO. WALL OF THE KIVA

GOVERNOR OF ZUNI PUEBLO

DESIDERIA, POTTERY–MAKER OF SAN ILDEFONSO

ORIGINAL MURAL PAINTING OF RUNNING DEER, BY MA–PE–WE, PUEBLO OF ZIA,
NEW MEXICO

NAVAJO WOMAN, WEARING HER TRIBAL
BLANKET, VELVET COSTUME, AND SILVER
AND TURQUOISE JEWELS

NAVAJO MEDICINE–MAN OF COOLIDGE,
NEW MEXICO

at home and eager to undertake the difficult task of hunting and modelling Navajo Indians "on the spot." We motored along, waving adieus to the disappearing train, and after a short drive into a blazing sunset came to the "Crafts del Navajo" Trading Post at Coolidge. I decided upon arrival to keep this transplanted fragment of New England as my headquarters, and from this point our various trips radiated to north, south, and west. It took only a few hours for Mr. and Mrs. Staples and myself to become the best of companions. They told me many tales about the Indians and covered wagons and their rugged experiences as pioneers driving from Vermont across the plains in the early days before railroads.

To gain the attention and interest of my Indian models I occasionally would spread out the photographs of the most varied racial types that I had modelled in Africa, Asia, and the Pacific Islands. When asked to select those which the Indians thought most like their own race, they would invariably choose Tibetans, Mongols, Eskimos, and, in some cases, the northwest East Indian types of Kashmiris. The Navajos seemed to agree to the supposition that their ancestors came from the Far East, travelling westward and coming to North America via Alaska and then southward, whereas the Pueblo Indians of the Southwest seemed quite certain that their forefathers had migrated from the south northward, coming from South or Central America.

For about 1200 years the Navajo tribes have inhabited the regions of Arizona and those states northward through which they are, by many authorities, supposed to have come down from Alaska, and possibly originally from Asia. Their high cheek-bones and mongoloid features would suggest this heritage to a marked degree.

The country is renowned for turquoise mines and archeological ruins. Four hundred unexplored sites of prehistoric dwellings were situated within two or three miles of where I found some of my most typical models, buried relics of the days when Indians roved over the land they loved, and died as free of white man's dominion as the wolves and coyotes of the prairie.

It was often necessary to travel from eighty to one hundred miles a day to find three or four Indians who were willing to submit to being photographed in anything but their "store clothes," especially when I needed full-length figures for dance poses or authentic gestures of the medicine-men when they hold the gourd over the sick man and perform their extraordinary ceremony of healing by prayer and by the application of their secret medicaments and herbs. They use many small fetishes, carved in stone and buried in bags of sacred pollen selected from certain flowers. We questioned many of the patients who had been cured of serious illnesses by these men. All reports seemed to agree that the concerted will-power of the medicine-men was felt keenly by the patient. Hour after hour the healing chants, prayers, and mysterious sand-paintings worked the miracle. The design on the flat, hard floor grows more colorful and complex as the tiny streams of sand sift through the dark fingers of the Indian painters who work under the direction of the medicine-man. The sacred symbols are drawn with exquisite precision, and when the complete pattern has been finished the patient is seated naked on the painting, the colored sand is rubbed over his body, and the picture on the floor is destroyed. No trace of it is left; the embers of the fire smoulder into a thread of gray smoke, which finds its outlet in the roof-opening, and rises like a wraith into the outer air.

Navajo ceremonial dances may take from one to nine days to perform, and there are sand-paintings for each day's celebration. The medicine-men who have kept up a constant intensity of prayer and concentration, sometimes for fifty or sixty hours, withdraw to the edges of the hogan and fall exhausted on the sheep skins. They collect what is left of the sacred colors, and after resting they mount their ponies and ride off across the red mesas, returning to their various homes, sometimes fifty miles away. In some distant place, so isolated that he can hear his own echo, the medicine-man buries his offerings with turquoise gifts and shells, and then returns to his hogan and to his daily life of shepherding his flocks. What luxury of lonely communion must be his!

To be a medicine-man necessitates sometimes twenty years of study and apprenticeship, a good singing voice, an extraordinary memory, and a deep understanding of the spiritual beliefs of his tribe, as well as training in the art of healing by herbs and incantations, bone-setting, and the interpretation of dreams and the power of mental suggestion and hypnotism. His duty is to train and direct other sand-painters, for when the case demands a very complex design, it is necessary that three or four men work together, so that the pattern may be completed between sunrise and sunset of the same day.

During one of the Indian races one of the boys was laid out on the sidelines with a severe pain in his chest. It was soon found to be two ribs that had become cramped together, and the medicine-man could very quickly manipulate the diaphragm back into place. Cases of head injury from the kick of a horse were treated in a most curious manner. A lighted candle was stuck on a fifty-cent piece, and this was set on the part of the skull which had been pushed in by the blow. Over the candle the medicine-man held an inverted glass, which, forming a vacuum, was pulled up until the bone surface was drawn back into place again, and the patient recovered. These men combine the arts of the family doctor, the psychoanalyst, the osteopath, and the surgeon. They travel from one group to another to assist each other and study the methods of other medicine-men. If a patient is too poor to pay for the medicine-man's services he is treated free of charge. There is no stipulated fee, but when circumstances permit, the patient pays up to fifty dollars for the healing ceremonies and often adds gifts of skins and blankets.

The Navajo silversmiths and turquoise cutters are renowned for their fine work; their women for their colorful blanket-weaving. The silversmith squats in his little adobe hut before a small glowing fire with a short section of a railroad rail riveted to a log for an anvil. He uses the most primitive and often clumsy-looking home-made tools, hammers, dies, etc. But by patience and skill he can transform a silver dollar into a delicate teaspoon or the medallion of a belt or the setting of a turquoise ring in less time than one would think it possible to obtain the same result by machinery.

Hour after hour, and week after week, the Navajo women weave their intricate patterns into their world-renowned blankets, diligently remembering the instructions of their ancestors and letting their imaginations invent endless variations on the traditional theme.

These Navajos are shepherd folk, wandering forever over the track-less mountains in search of pasture for their flocks. Nomadic by nature, they build their temporary hogans from heavy logs in an octagonal shape, covering the roof and walls with adobe mud, and leaving a small opening in the center of the roof for ventilation and to carry out the smoke of their ever-burning fire of pinion pine logs, with their exotic pungency.

The Navajo children may marry into the same tribe as their parents, but not into the same clan. This law prevents inbreeding too closely. The children automatically belong to their mother's clan.

The chief difficulty at present for these nomadic Indians to overcome is the poor quality of their pasture-land. As a result the sheep give a very cheap grade of wool, which in turn brings a very low market price. The natural erosion of the land has caused serious concern to both the Indians and the United States Government, which has recently established a test station near Gallup to find out just how this erosion problem may be combated to best advantage.

This enduring tribe of Navajos has more than doubled its population during the past twenty years. There are no villages, for their wandering flocks have obliged them to travel great distances over the reservation, seeking a water supply and enough pasture, which is at best inadequate and generally parched to a brittle dryness by the many months of blistering heat and lack of irrigation.

After many hours of persuasion and hard labor I finally completed the studies of my Navajo type and motored to Gallup, where I left the cases containing the plasteline models at the Harvey Hotel to be kept until my return. I then motored with Mr. Staples through the region of the new government station in Arizona, climbing up the mountain trails to the plateau of the timber forests. We struggled up the steep, damp sides of Kit Carson's cave, and at the dizzy top heard the trickle of water oozing mysteriously from nowhere through the rocky roof of the mesa.

We stopped one day for luncheon at Oraibi, enjoying the hearty hospitality of Don Lorenzo Hubbell, renowned as a trader—a historic character, worthy descendant of his Spanish father, whose dramatic career made one of the great histories of our pioneer West. Oraibi is probably the oldest town in the United States of America and was founded about 1200 A.D. It is in the Hopi reservation, and as archaic in aspect as a village might be in another planet.

Groups of Indians were tying their horses to posts about the house: swarthy, dark-skinned horsemen, bringing their silver and blankets to be traded in for bridles, grain, and foodstuffs. Lorenzo, our host, was stirring a great pot of beans on his kitchen stove. A cheery welcome from other guests! Grace Fairfax had joined me on this trip, and we all set the table, cut the bread, boiled the coffee, and prepared the ever-ready meal that is offered to the dusty, hungry traveller who has crossed many miles of desert land before he could reach this oasis in the great open spaces.

At this trading-post I was able to obtain many photographs of the Hopis and Navajos. Any favor asked of the Indians by Lorenzo Hubbell seemed to be immediately granted. This, of course, facilitated my task and temporarily removed the stigma of suspicion with which a camera is looked upon by the Indians who live a long distance from the railroad centers. Men that looked like eagles would stare at me from the dark corners; their women, in velvet jackets, did as their men told them, moving about as directed but never uttering a word or relaxing their expression of enforced submission; no smiles or child-like gaiety, like the little jungle folk in tropical countries.

Proceeding westward we motored over the arid plateaus to Keams Canyon, where the government agent invited us to stay with him in a perfectly equipped, modern house, adjoining the Indian school-building. Hundreds of little Indian children were playing about and trying to enjoy the mechanical see-saws, swings, and basketball equipment which the United States Government has put at their disposal. It was a startling effect, after driving all day across perfectly uncultivated desert wastes, to come suddenly upon this up-to-date settlement of stone and brick buildings, grouped under the shelter of an immense rocky mesa and facing the vast valley beyond the canyon. Mechanical toys seemed rather farcical as a means of distraction to these children of lightning and rainbows.

The real event in Hopiland was our visit to the ancient ruins of Walpi, the famous village perched perilously on the rocky prow of the precipitous mesa, commanding a limitless view over the surrounding territory. To reach this group of dwellings, however, one must wind up hairpin curves and miles of narrow, steep roads, finally reaching a height of some 9000 feet. The extreme point of the mesa has been almost entirely severed from the rest of the mountain—only a strip of rock, wide enough for a single wagon or car, is left by which one can reach the old village, and in the surface of this rock are worn the ruts of cart-wheels almost ten inches deep. A sheer drop of 1500 feet or more on each side makes this approach seem almost too dramatic to be enjoyed as a daily homecoming, especially after dark.

By good fortune I found a family of Hopis living at Walpi who were willing to pose for me. The young girl of fifteen was very beautiful, and her mother and grandmother finally agreed to arrange her long hair in the authentic virginal "squash blossom" coiffure, so that I could make her portrait in the style so long identified with the Hopi Indians and which greatly enhances the beauty of the wearer but which, alas, is now considered old-fashioned and out-of-date by the young girls, who prefer to look like all the other "city" girls and draw their hair straight back with a knot at the back of the neck. Or, worse yet, they indulge in permanent waves, easily obtained at the town beauty shop, when by some lucky chance the girls can find their way to the railroad stations.

The United States Government has divided the Apache tribe into four different reservations: in New Mexico, the Mescalero and the Jicarillas; two others are in the White Mountains of Arizona. Previous to 1885 this tribe of Indians was the most savage and elusive enemy of the white man. After frequent uprisings and warfare, the last chieftain who defied the white soldiers was Geronimo, and the punishment meted out to him and his fellow warriors was severe enough to break down any further attempts at rebellion. Now the Apache wears the clothes and goes to the church of his enemy, the white man, for he is a captive Indian. In spite of their enforced submission, one is struck by the defiant and savage look in the faces of these men. It is easy to imagine them with their long, black, braided hair, and naked, painted bodies, leading their stealthy followers along the trail of the enemies. There is a keen, far-searching look in their eyes that still persists, and in spite of cropped hair and United States school uniforms and discipline, one recognizes the fearless character of these aboriginal Americans and the submerged passion of an old enmity.

While driving through the desert land near Nastidi, Arizona, we noticed a group of Indians lounging outside a trader's shop. Their shaggy ponies were tied up to the posts, and some of the riders had flung themselves on the ground, while others were leaning against the wall of the building in a state of exhaustion. One of the Indians had a fine bridle slung over his arm, decorated with old Spanish silver rosettes and a cruel curb of finely etched steel. Throughout the afternoon a violent dust-storm had made both white man and Indian feel like fellow survivors of some elemental struggle. We offered them oranges and cigarettes, and they in turn thanked us and told us why a great bear's hide was hanging on the wall over their heads. It seemed that they had joined forces to hunt down a "killer" bear that had been prowling too near the chicken coops of the trader's camp. The bear was one of the bold, black, savage type and his reputation was a bad one. It was decided that he was a menace and must be sacrificed. So a hunting party was formed and the big bear was tracked up into the timber forest and shot.

The Indians then had a ceremony to punish the bear and help his spirit to reach its happy-hunting-ground. They spread him out on the ground, his head pointing west; then they scattered pollen from little buckskin bags over his four legs and along the backbone and over his head up the trunk of the tree against which his head was leaned. A chant was sung and the Indians offered him as a sacrifice, a lesson and a warning to his brother bears that they should stay up in their mountain forests and not sneak down to destroy or molest the herds and flocks of the valley.

So the hide had been bought by the trader and kept on the entrance wall and the bridle of Spanish silver coins and spades, diamonds, clubs, and hearts in repoussé silver was bought by me. After a brief rest we shook a friendly hand all round and continued our journey across the endless desert wastes, a land which seemed unpossessed by any living man, so gaunt and choked was it with its own dry dust. When we reached Winslow my escort and guide, Mr. Staples, deposited me and my friend, Miss Fairfax, at the Harvey Hotel and the next day went home to Coolidge to continue his daily tasks of sorting the mail and trading grain and groceries for silver and blankets.

The next problem which faced me was how to collect and transport the various boxes containing the plaster and clay heads that I had modelled on the reservations. With the attentive care of railroad officials and Harvey bus drivers I managed to reach Santa Fe with my "spoils" undamaged, but it was rather a nerve-racking experience watching three porters at once and warning them to "keep the boxes upright, there's the head of an Indian inside!" Many were the jokes along the platform as one man would pass on his load to the next carrier.

In Santa Fe, through the hospitality of Mrs. William Field, who loaned me her adobe studio, I was able to work under better conditions and under a top-light. This was real luxury after the casual shelters which had served me as studios on the journey.

Through the United States Indian school director I was enabled to photograph many types of younger Indians, especially the Apaches, from their three reservations. One of these men was so interested in sculpture that after I had finished his portrait he asked to assist me in casting the heads into plaster. He assured me that he would do some stone and wood carving when he went back to Jicarilla for the summer.

As we parted he very modestly said, "Maybe you go Mexican Museum some day and see Indian paintings. I make one there—a forest with boys running through it. My first picture not so good, but I make many more now!" I went to the exhibit the following day and was delighted to find the forest with painted bodies of Indians darting about behind the tree trunks. A most dreamlike and subtly colored fantasy, which seemed a curiously delicate conception to emerge from the brain of the "white man's most dreaded enemy."

There were many fine murals and decorative water-colors at this exhibit, all of them the work of the elder students of the United States Indian School. Certainly the unquestionable talent of these

SYMBOLIC INDIAN PAINTING ON DEERSKIN

Showing Swastika design with Mother Earth and Father Sky bound together by the rainbow

RELIGIOUS INDIAN SAND-PAINTING ON A FLOOR

Handicrafts of the Indian tribes in the background

TYPICAL NAVAJO HOGAN OR NOMADIC HOUSE, SO SIMILAR IN FORM TO THE *YURT* FOUND IN MONGOLIA

THE *YURT* OF MONGOLIA

NAVAJO RUG–WEAVER, WITH HER PA-POOSE BESIDE HER

Photo. M. H.

A VENERABLE AND LEARNED MEDICINE–MAN OF THE NAVAJO INDIANS AT NEWCOMB, ARIZONA

PORTRAIT OF APACHE BRAVE BY M. H.

(Hall of Man)

PORTRAIT OF SIOUX INDIAN CHIEF

(Hall of Man)

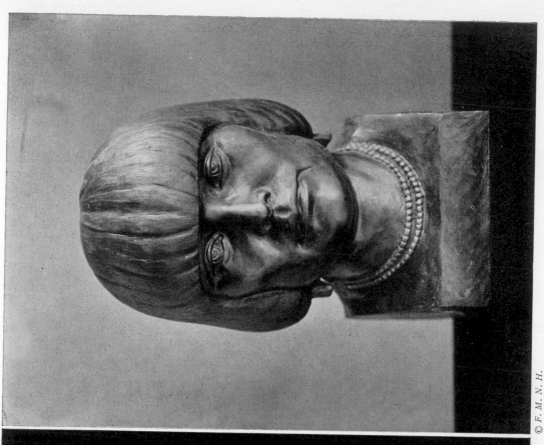

HEAD OF PUEBLO INDIAN WOMAN, BY M. H

HEAD OF APSAROKE INDIAN, BY M. H.

artists should be recognized and encouraged. There is a great fund of natural instinctive ability and an unerring sense of design and movement.

When I examined the collection of masks used in Indian ceremonies I found the decorative motifs almost infinite in variety. Throughout the ages in all countries there seems to have been a fascination in coloring and disguising the human face. Primitive dances and festivals called for effective disguises, and even in our modern times the shrewd business man practises certain facial expressions which he finds useful as a defense, sometimes completely disguising his personality behind a "poker face," which he wears as a mask. The girls of Hollywood have become experts in the art of "make-up" and false faces, plucking eyebrows, adding false eyelashes, painting the finger nails, and wearing red and green traffic signals on the toe-nails—simply modern variations on the old theme. Judging from the enormous profits made in beauty-parlors by the sale of cosmetics, we can but be convinced that man's primitive instincts are being cleverly commercialized by modern business. In less than an hour one can obtain a new set of eyelashes and plucked eyebrows, guaranteed to disguise any wife so that her own husband could not recognize her. The expert modern coiffeur can upset any anthropological calculations concerning the appearance of a type, and transform the character as well. No wonder that his profession above all others flourishes in spite of national depression.

We can trace this desire to change human appearances to the American Indian ceremonies, where there are as many as sixteen different masks used to disguise the wearer during a single chant. Our physiognomy not only affects ourselves but all those who observe us—to what extent, however, is still a matter of conjecture.

If we compare the tattooed faces of the Maori chiefs with the carved masks of the Miska Indians of British Columbia, we find great similarity of design. The world is full of surprises!

The Iroquois Indians in New York and Ontario have what is known as "False Face" society, the members of which wear their masks bordered with streamers of long, black hair; these men officiate at healing ceremonies. The carving of wooden masks is still carried on by these Indians with great skill. Grotesque birds are often used to make effective headdresses, such as the cannibal bird of the Quakiutl Indians of British Columbia. Certain Hopi masks are very reminiscent of the black-and-white wooden headgear worn over masks by the Doggon Negro tribes of Africa. These are made of strips of black-and-white wood resembling the Cross of Lorraine, or the primitive pattern of a lizard. They are worn on days of ceremonies in honor of some dead member of the tribe. The "mother mask" is often ten feet long and is held in place by the teeth of the wearer, who, by bracing his legs apart on the ground and waving his head in a circular motion, may wave the great wooden headpiece in rotating gyrations.

In the Hopi tribes the dancers are called Kachinas, and small wooden replicas of these fantastic figures are carved and painted by the Indian artists. Their coloring is brilliant and most effective. A Kachina is supposed to be the reincarnation of the spirit of some of the departed members of the tribe; spirits are believed to have supernatural powers.

The Zuni Indians introduce two huge giants with over-life-size head masks in their Shalako dance. Among the Zuni Pueblos the art of mask-making is carried further than in almost any other American Indian tribe. The infinite range of their imagination for grotesque and unnatural head disguise is world-renowned. One of the most primitive masks is known as "mud head," a spherical hollow of hard earth with two round knobs at the sides for ears, a top-knot, and three openings for the eyes and mouth. I found I could always make my Indian models laugh when they asked me what I was doing with clay and tools and strange-looking armatures. "I am making mud heads," I would answer, and as my initials were M. H., I adopted "mud head" as my Indian nickname.

During this last journey to the Indian reservations, I had hoped to find plaster-casters at the big towns to do that part of my job. Alas, in New Mexico and Arizona I found no such luxury and so had to resort to making my own casts. It was difficult to find irons which would bind the moulds and yet be pliable enough for me to bend into the necessary shapes. One day, after struggling to find a way to hold the iron firmly, I suddenly noticed an Indian pony hitched to a nearby post. I was ready to try anything once; so I raised the left hind hoof, slipped the strip of iron under his shoe, and then asked the Indian boy to raise the pony's left foreleg as if he were going to shoe him. Before the horse could shift his weight or suspect that I was using him as a vise, the other Indian and I pulled up the free end of the iron rod held under his hind hoof and succeeded in bending the metal at the desired angle. It was a long chance to take, but necessity is the mother of invention.

My models in many corners of the world were all most curious and interested in the process of casting. They all wanted to stir the plaster or taste it, and would ask for a present to take to their fellow tribesmen, thinking it looked like a cool and refreshing drink. We had to explain to them that if they drank it, it would quickly harden and they would die. As a matter of fact, I have only heard of one case where a man actually committed suicide by drinking a great quantity of plaster which he had mixed with salt; this latter material causes the plaster to harden much more quickly.

Taos

When I had completed my sculptural task with the Pueblos, Navajos, and other tribes, I decided to leave Santa Fe and have a real holiday visit with my friend, Mabel Dodge, in Taos. Steep, rocky canyons walled in the road from Santa Fe to Taos, and we passed through a series of phenomenal landscapes. At first the dust swirled over the flat desert land near the Pueblos of San Ildefonso; then we visited the erstwhile "dude ranches" of Alcalda, hidden behind the long adobe walls, where we pushed open a carved wooden door and found ourselves in a magical oasis of luscious green lawns, running streams, weeping willows, and brilliant flowering borders. One courtyard led into another, and the adobe buildings seemed to go on indefinitely around the various enclosed gardens.

From here we followed the river bed and wound along the precipitously rising walls, higher and higher, until the narrow road seemed to hang over abysmal depths. The air grew clearer and cooler, the crystalline atmosphere stretched our lungs. Finally we reached the high plateau country and away in the distance discerned the faint wisps of smoke and jagged outline of the village. Taos is a Mexican town built around a square, where we stopped at a little Mexican bar for rest and refreshment, with eighty miles of legendary scenery behind us since leaving the luxurious, modern installations of Santa Fe's hospitable hotel and picturesque settlement of villas, museums, Spanish and Indian shops—"the port of missing men and women" who have escaped the Eastern city life and gone native in New Mexico—an endless panorama of misfits, would-be cowboys, artists, writers, tourists, and hospitable residents.

As I had not seen my friend, Mabel Dodge Luhan of Taos, for twenty-four years, I had been more than surprised and pleased, soon after my arrival in Santa Fe, to receive a cordial telegram from her inviting me to visit her, and I had accepted with enthusiasm. This was the appointed day, and from the Mexican bar I telephoned to her to make sure that I was really expected.

"Hello, is that you, Mabel?"

"Who is speaking?" came the guarded answer. (Safety first in these great open spaces.)

"This is Malvina, and I wondered if you were at home and expecting me."

"Where are you? I have been waiting for you all the afternoon. Have you broken down on the way?"

"No, I am at the village bar, but being a wary traveller I stopped here first to make sure of a bed for the night, in case you had forgotten or possibly changed plans. We have not met for twenty-four years, you know."

"How absurd! What did you do that for? Come over right away and don't bring any one else along either. Ask the way from any one."

So that was settled, and I turned my little room over to a fellow traveller and motored up to Mabel's little cluster of pink-and-tan buildings on the hills a mile beyond the village. My friends left me at the gate.

"No Admittance. Tourists Unwelcome." This sign at the gate prepares one. The courtyard is surrounded with one-story buildings, and saffron canvas curtains hanging from a pergola, which divided the main house from a smaller one, were flapping in the evening breeze. Huge weeping-willow trees followed the line of the brook; hundreds of pigeons were cooing and gurgling on their white cotes. On each pillar of adobe from which the gate swung were skulls of buffaloes; blue-and-pink decorations covered the heavy gateway. One of the panels was swung open and my friend, "Mabel of long ago," came out to meet me, smiling and brisk as always.

"Our last meeting was in Florence in 1910, wasn't it?" I said, feeling my way. "Do you remember the good old days in the villa there when Paul and Muriel Draper and Janet Scudder and Mrs. Stanford White and Mother and I were all enjoying your hospitality? Do you remember the avenue of purple iris leading up the hill and the view over Florence at sunset?" It was exciting, this sudden contact after twenty-four years. We had both lived many lives in the meantime and had died many deaths.

"Well," said Mabel, in her staccato manner, "we can show you sunsets here too, and as for iris, come into the house!"

We went over the flat stone courtyard where hollyhocks shot up between the stones, laden with gorgeous bloom.

"This is Tony's room; he's away tonight for some Indian ceremony." (Tony is Mabel's husband; a full-blooded Indian chief of the Taos tribe.) Pointing to a glass case: "Those are Tony's guns, he's a fine shot, and this is your room. Have a look out of your window!"

The fields outside were lavender and gold; a sea of iris seemed to surround the house, lapping up against the frames of the windows, for the ground rose nearly to the sill level on the south side of the house. I was entranced. Here was pristine beauty on such a scale that it made one inarticulate.

We had tea in a pink-and-lavender corner of her sitting room; soft cushions, deep and unbelievably wide divans; a pinion pine log was simmering in the glowing adobe fireplace, spreading its fragrance throughout the house. There is always this pungent aroma hovering about in New Mexico. The very air is ecstatic, and one feels exhilarated, courageous, clean, lifted up out of reality.

"There is the two-story house where Lorenzo and Frieda [D. H. Lawrence and his wife] lived,"—pointing out to me a tan silhouette fading into the evening mist—"and there is Maurice Stern's studio, where he found out he was a sculptor! (I always knew he was.) And beyond is Tony's house and studio. Why don't you stay here and work, Malvina, and rest?"

I felt quite dazed by it all, and only smiled.

"We are expecting Robinson Jeffers, the poet, to come this summer with his family, in the two-story house, and Myron Brinig and Kady Wells will have my little house across the court where the saffron curtains are blowing. Myron wrote *Singermann* and *Out of Life* and he is writing a new book now. . . . Kady?—he is a painter. . . . Very modern? Oh, yes, modern *enough*. He's a dear boy. How about driving with me in the Ford over to the Pueblo to see the Indians before it grows dark? We won't get out; we will just look about and let it sift into your mind. Come on, let's go."

I was breathless, but willing. I shall never forget that drive—the fragrance of lilacs and honeysuckle, birds flying about, their wings dipped in the lambent sunset. We did not speak—no need—life was a matter of breathing and vibrating.

"Hello, Mabel!"—this from a sleek young Indian on the roadside, wrapped in a white shroud—"Comin' to races tomorr' morn'?"

"Of course, what time do they start?"

"Oh, early; ask Tony, he knows."

"Yes," said Mabel, "Tony always does know, but today he is miles away and we will have to start at dawn tomorrow, or else we will miss the best of the whole day. When Tony is here he senses what time the Indians do things and where. We never miss anything and never have to wait for things to start when he is at home. Do you see that tiny patch of green way up on the mountain over there? That is the ranch I gave to Lorenzo, or rather I gave it to Frieda. I had given it to my son, John Evans, some years before. Tony keeps our horses up there for grazing. Well, I traded it back from John for a buffalo-hide coat and some cash, and then I gave it to Frieda. It's about 10,000 feet altitude up there. We'll drive over if you like one day and call on her."

The gallant little Ford leaped over the dusty roads, responding in bounds to Mabel's erratic foot technique.

One must be fearless in this uncharted Indian country really to enjoy it, and save all one's alertness for the ever-changing panoramic scenery. We drove slowly about the Pueblo plaza, crossing little, creaking log bridges over the stream which constituted the "Main Street" of the village. Friendly greetings were exchanged, and then we returned across the darkening valley and watched the evening melt the world into a deep lavender silence. The aroma of pinion pines filled the air. One's senses seemed to expand and drink new depths of delight.

A few days later Mabel decided to drive me up the mountain to see Lorenzo's ranch, where Frieda was in "Residence." This place had been called "The Flying Heart."

Just as we had bounded over the last climbing road into the thickly forested area the plucky little Ford gave a few sharp coughs and stopped on a steep incline—exhausted.

"Well," Mabel said, "we seem to have run out of gas."

"Or else the altitude has knocked poor Fordy in the wind," I suggested, for my own feelings were rather strange and palpitating at 10,000 feet above sea level.

"We'll just let it rest and then try again," Mabel decided, "for if we can just make the next grade we will be at Frieda's, and when we come back we can coast down fast enough to carry us to the farm down in the valley, where we can get gas."

The mental picture of our descent at full speed around the hairpin curves was enough to counteract any other sensations. We lighted cigarettes, and when the car had rested we found it willing to make its last effort, in spite of the dial registering minus nothing for the tank. As we drew up in front of the little wooden ranch-house Mabel shot me one of her vivid looks; pointing to a field she said gaily, "There's the game—Tony's three horses graze up there . . . and there's a wild bull painted on that little wooden house by

Lawrence; did you ever read *St. Mawr* or *Lady Chatterley's Lover?"*

By this time we had climbed the short flight of steps leading into the house. "Wait outside," said Mabel, "I'll look over the situation and call you if Frieda will see you."

My ears were alternatingly shutting and opening from the high altitude. A gust of wind blew into the house as the door opened. A vigorous, squarely built Italian in riding togs greeted us. "Frieda is sick," he said.

Mabel went in, while I chatted with the signore. Shades of Lorenzo floated past in my imagination and I felt how this primeval wilderness above the world must have entranced him, body and soul. "The Woman Who Rode Away" . . . "Fantasia of the Unconscious" . . . "The Man Who Died" . . . and lived. . . .

"Come in, Malvina, Frieda will see you!" We pushed open the door; pictures and manuscripts blew about in the wind. We gathered up the loose pages. . . . Frieda's memoirs of Lawrence, *Not I, But the Wind,* her version of Lorenzo, since published.

There on a wooden sofa-bed, lying on her side with her head enveloped in a vague shawl or towel, was Frieda. One eagle eye flashed out from the confused drapery on the pillow and then a hearty stream of words emerged, with a rich middle European accent.

So this was Frieda, the much-heralded eternal Eve, the influence hovering over so many literary plots. Pointing to her head, she said "Abscess in my ear—such a bother, you see we are so far from doctors here. . . . I just use hot water and clean cloths. Such a thing to have in this wonderful clear air!"

I ventured to ask if she had bathed in the swimming pool on the steamer on her recent voyage from Europe. "Na, ya, of course," she answered.

"Well, that's probably where you picked up a microbe."

She smiled, seemed quite satisfied, and totally unconcerned about her recovery.

As I leaned over the wooden back of her sofa-bed, I realized the latent, healthy life-force that was temporarily subdued by the abscess. I felt the attraction and when she pushed up her bandage to get a final look at me with both her keen eyes, I suddenly saw a resem-

THE PUEBLO OF TAOS, NEW MEXICO (SOUTH HOUSE)
The race track to the right leads out from the central open square

INSIDE THE GATES
Mabel Dodge Luhan's courtyard echoes to the cooing of hundreds of pigeons

OUTSIDE STAIRWAY IN ONE OF MABEL'S HOUSES
First blossoms

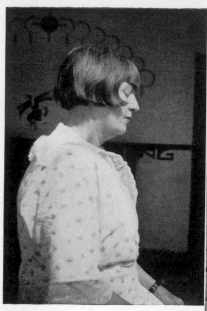

MABEL DODGE LUHAN IN THE
LOGGIA OF HER HOUSE, WHERE
THE OUTER WALLS ARE DECO-
RATED BY LOCAL INDIAN
PAINTERS

A YOUNG TAOS INDIAN, WITH
WHITE BLANKET THROWN O
HIS HEAD AND SHOULDER
TYPICAL FASHION

ALBERT LOOKING ELK, PAINTING
A LANDSCAPE

THE MAIN HOUSE OF MABEL'S COLONY, BUILT OF ADOBE AND TOPPED WITH A GLASS
SUN–ROOM ON THE THIRD FLOOR

From this one can see in every direction the magical, ever-changing panorama of mountains, valleys,
and seasons

blance to a photo of Lawrence's mother. This gave me another clue of understanding.

Frieda's eyes have a child-like expression. I doubt if this will ever change. It was this same look that she had detected behind the mask of D. H. Lawrence—this wistful loneliness of those who never grow old—the ever-seeking. She will believe in what she *sees* until the end of her days. The rest of her is an untrammelled, free individual who, having lived her life intensely and having paid for it at every step, seems to have made up her mind to return to the stark reality of the ranch and draw whatever she may need from its primitive eternal strength.

Meanwhile Mabel was wandering about, collecting books under her arm. I tried a little of my German on Frieda to make her laugh, and succeeded. At least for purposes of humor or lightening the conversation, my twists of the Teutonic tongue seem to inspire inevitable gaiety.

We took our leave with many *auf wiedersehens,* and then pushed the Ford along to the edge of the decline for a good start on our coasting descent! Between the trunks of pine trees we caught glimpses of a flamboyant sunset. Rounding the curves on two wheels, in a cloud of dust, we finally reached the farm where we could buy gas. After this we could take our time to enjoy the majestic beauty of the distant mountains which walled out the rest of the world and the opalescent colors of the desert that spread out into eternity below us. The ineffable tenderness of spring filled the evening air, and one listened to the silence as if some new-born loveliness had cast a spell over life.

If only one could utterly evaporate and become a part of this first fragrance of spring! Fragrance that sheathes the sharp sword, the thrust of which can sever life without a drop of blood—A pound of flesh?—or more? Oh, limitless, intangible aloneness, that sweeps over the heart at this, the great new-born moment of spring!

The Day After

It happened halfway between the house and the little studio hidden behind a wall of plum-bushes. Walking along a narrow board-walk across a wide, deeply plowed field, I saw that the tender new shoots of oats had started to force their way up through the heavy clods of earth. Pushing against stones and rough roots, the delicate new life sprang forth against the blade-like fire of the sun. Yesterday I only felt their buried potentiality; today the miracle had been achieved—the heaviness of earth had been cloven asunder—the spring had overcome the winter and life was glowing again in streams—glittering crystal streams, green, waving streams, pulsing tender life. One felt it in the whole universe—at night under the stars, vibrations at evening when the sky went suddenly soft after the harsh daylight and the mountains cupped their cool caverns in purple shadows to keep their dark secrets for the new life that stirred in their depths. Fecundity of nature giving forth new visions to man, new hope, new beauty born of pain; sorrow and even bitterness turned under the sod to enrich the next cycle of experience.

"Give them back into my womb," cries the earth, "all of your cravings and possessions, your puny achievements and your unworthy ambitions; turn them under the sod and from their roots and my sunlight I shall distill freshness and new beauty. Begin again and let the new-born vibrations of spring seep into your veins. Transform the agonies of your yesterdays into unvanquished strength. Give up the fragments of your personal life and draw from the oneness of my earth and my sky. Possess this current, nothing else counts. When my rhythm carries you, you are saved. The desperate cries in the wilderness sing in your cries, the wild animals hunt and tear their prey, as you hunt. The clash of thunder against lightning becomes the crash of your vitals when they meet defeat, and the rainbow will encircle your bleeding body, and rain will fall and cool the shaken soul and give back peace and wonderment, and you will be detached from little things and the barren land of desolation. Soar like the eagle until your wings break from your body and the precipice will gather you into the silent depths and the dawn will not be riven by the echoes of your agony."

And then—one evening we joined the Indians in a Bacchic dance in Mabel's house. Tony had arranged the party and we were holding our breath in anticipation.

The sleek Indian youths came into the great room in a single file, decorated with their barbaric eagle-feather wheels—one on each upper arm, one on the center of the back. Their splendid, naked, orange-brown bodies glistened in the firelight, the rhythmic padding of their moccasined feet shaking the bells on long, loose straps that hung from their belts and followed the outer line of their legs down to the ankle. The young warriors wore a beautiful headdress made of the stiff bristles of deer tails, dipped in scarlet and yellow dyes. The form of this head-gear was like the shape of a Roman helmet, following the center line of the head from the brow down to the back of the neck. Around their ankles were wrapped fringes of skunk bristles which sprayed out over the richly beaded moccasins. When the shield dance began they removed the feather wheels and carried on their left forearms a round shield of buffalo hide, in their right hands long eagle feathers.

Two by two they danced about, feigning stealthy attacks and sudden recoiling defenses. The group of four elders, wrapped in their white blankets, sat near the kindling fire; two ancient tom-toms were beaten incessantly by the leader and his aide. From the depths of their chests came chanting sounds of utter strangeness to the white man's ear. With downcast eyes and stern, dark faces these four chiefs gave the rhythm to the dancers, and their song continued hour after hour with only an occasional pause for rest.

Gradually, as the late evening drew on, the group of twelve dancers accelerated their tempo and cried out in sharp, wild *"Ayis,"* like coyotes barking. The air was charged with the shaking a hundred bells, the pounding of the strong, sure feet, and the current of electric energy seemed to include the few white onlookers who were catching the inevitable fire of this wild dancing.

One by one, the Indians widened their circle and started winding between us. Gradually we rose and joined the serpentine line of dancers—our feet pounding in unison with theirs, our shoulders pressing against their bronze shoulders, our faces transformed by the elemental thrill of this rhythmic orgy. Shouts and cries punctuated the thunder of the drums, and behind it all was the inevitable, deep, pulsing throb that has no words or meaning but which binds the elements to the emotions and the minds to the bodies of these children of the desert and the wilderness. . . .

The swaying line of dancers led us in strange, serpentine directions, finally coiling itself into a solid mass in the center of the room. Suddenly the chant and the pounding of the drums ceased and the deafening jangle of bells subsided. The dance was over, and the Indians, without a word, formed into a single file, slipped out of the room, and disappeared into the starry night, followed by the four chiefs carrying the drums and shrouded in their white blankets.

It was only after I had been initiated, so to speak, into these intimate phases of Indian life, that I began the task of visiting the families at the Pueblo, and with the tactful assistance of my Indian host, Tony Luhan, I was able to meet his friends and relatives and learn something of their tribal ways.

On the day following the dance, as we visited the various fields under cultivation on the way back to Taos village, I was amazed to recognize some of the splendid dancing warriors of the previous evening plowing the land with a Fordson machine, and looking like all the other tawny farmers in their overalls and heavy boots. Only by their black, braided hair, twisted and bound with colored tapes, was I able to distinguish them from the young men who had been to the Reservation School and as a result had cut off their beautiful, long hair.

Hic Incipit Vita Nova

One morning in the chill silence of dawn, when the first shell-like pink of the sun touched the peaks of snow-capped mountains, Mabel Luhan and I drove across the valley between walls of wild plum-bushes. The lavender mountains, wrapped in mist, slid down from the sky as the light flowed over their flanks, almost to the edge of the pyramidal adobe pueblo. There was no sign of life anywhere—not a human sound. The call of a thrush and the swish of the plum-blossoms against the car; one would think the whole place deserted by man. And yet we knew this was the first day of May, the day of dedication to Mother Earth.

Dotted about on the different roof-levels of the pueblo, the Indian women, wrapped in their colorful blankets, stood motionless and silent, like colored jars. We awaited the signal from the mound of the *kiwa*, the secret council-chamber of the tribe. Deep down under the earth, all the male youths of the tribe had been painted in barbaric colors from their heads to their feet. Tufts of white eagle down were stuck to the sides of their naked bodies, making a white silhouette, and the tops of their heads were covered with the same fluffy down.

Suddenly a sign was given by the elders and the crowd of seventy or eighty youths rushed up from the darkness into the light of day. They darted up the ladder and stopped, quivering, for an instant, as they raised their right hands to the rising sun and blew a handful of the downy feathers into the air. Each one in turn performed this age-old rite, and then they rushed, like disembodied spirits, to the opposite ends of the race-track leading along the plaza of the pueblo.

These painted specters were released by the older Indians, who gathered in groups at the ends of the track. Along the sidelines women and children collected, and the "coach" cried out "Oompawa, oompawa!" (Hurry on, hurry on!) as he waved the pine wands over the heads of the contestants. The flashing bodies of the runners seemed scarcely to touch the ground—heads thrown back, white teeth shining, and faces set in a sort of agony of effort. Ribbons and feathers streamed out stiffly horizontal from their heads, so swiftly did they fly through space until they reached the limits of the course. Their feet were bruised and cut by the sharp stones but they did not notice the pain. Fresh runners were released like arrows from a bow, and each one carried on the living stream of energy, like an electric current driving them beyond their own strength and will.

Hour after hour this race of dedication went on. As they walked back to re-enter the race, they clasped their heaving bodies with their arms; never glancing to right or left, they seemed in a state of trance. No idea of "winning" entered their minds—no prizes won, no applause given to any individual. Each gave the maximum effort of speed and endurance, feeling that the swifter he ran the more earth current was drawn into his body, the greater the ecstasy of dedication.

At a given signal the ceremony ended. An unseen drum was heard pounding its inevitable pulse. The boys wrapped themselves in white blankets and formed in line with the elders of the tribe, crowding closer and closer together into a long, waving column of strength, male against male, body against body, their feet pounding the dust as they wound along—a great serpent of strength and manhood—in and out of all the paths and buildings of the pueblo. The women on the roofs now unwrapped their blankets and threw offerings, trinkets, and cakes down to the men who passed below them. A strange chant rose from these men, like the gathered sound of the deep earth—not a song from their throats but rather a single, mammoth voice rising from the center of all their bodies.

Finally the writhing serpent wound its way back to the *kiwa* in a cloud of dust and disappeared into the secret depths, where no white man may enter or ever understand the meaning of their ageless traditions.

The life of the tribe goes on, peacefully withdrawn from outside curiosity. The united current is strong, and the young men reinforce the old; the women gladly belong to them and give naturally of their gentle patience. The children in wonderment wave their little pine wands and stamp their tiny feet in unison with the tribal stream of life, giving their strength to the earth and drawing new life from the sun.

This submerging of the individual for the united strength of the tribe is something from which the white man may well learn an important lesson; personal ambition has so frequently brought disaster in its train. All our competitions and prizes are an encouragement to this tendency of personal importance. "Self-expression"—how thin the pale-face record has been worn!

To be sure, the Indians of today are not as strong as the white man who controls them by law and military force, but they manage to survive in spite of the barren hardships they have been forced to accept and despite the battle against disease introduced by the white man, and they can still stir us by the primitive art of contacting their life currents with those of the elements about them and by their profound understanding of earth's eternal miracles.

"Know Thyself and Thou Shalt Know the Universe"

The cosmic influence of the air and sun, the subtle effects of the moon and stars are well understood and drawn upon by our aboriginal brothers. They form the basis of most Chinese philosophy as well; the idea of Confucianism considers man as a miniature cosmos existing merely in relation to the greater cosmos to which, through nature, he must be connected, and by which he is controlled both inwardly and outwardly. The basic thought of our American Indians is closely allied to the Oriental point of view and would serve as a bridge across the abyss which so often exists between the Oriental and Occidental understanding. Carrying the idea still further, we find the Hindu Yoga philosophy, as well as the ideals of Buddhism and Christianity in their essential essence, all leading the human race to certain similar ideals.

To release oneself from material appetites and values, to rise above external desires, the body must be controlled by the higher mind. Buddhism believes that the ego must be completely destroyed before Nirvana, or a state of bliss, may be obtained. Taoism leads to the transfigured being whose mental victories and experiences are preserved in the final identity of a personality.

The Chinese, the Indian Yoga philosophers, and all others, including the wiser scholars of Christianity, recognize the fact that to attain spiritual perfection one must achieve perfect serenity and calm, and only then can one concentrate with one's entire capacity. Without this power a person becomes simply a fragment broken off from the cosmic whole, unable to reinforce his life by the contact with earth's life-giving currents.

He who cultivates and attains this secret power may become the master of multitudes, but first he must become master of himself.

Oh wanderers, strangers all, looking for places to go and things to do! Are we not woefully unaware of ourselves? We drive along, never stopping to search our own natures, much less another's, living sometimes easily and often violently, but insensitive to the vibrations that direct our thoughts. Avoiding solitude, for it might reveal the ghost of ourselves, we play games with fate and refuse to make friends with our destiny.

Can we explain what it is that makes us all hide from ourselves and from each other? Certainly the artist has to overcome these walls of dual and triple personality and go after the truth that lies hidden at the core of all human beings.

After years of observation and contradictory discoveries, I have come to believe that the primitive instinct, that motive power of our real selves, is the one most strongly embedded in all of us—black, white, yellow, and red—brothers and sisters under the skin.

This primitive instinct is thwarted and covered over by layers of education and controls. These are imposed, first by our parents, secondly by our own wills that have acquired habits and customs through an endless series of criticisms, and thirdly by an inherited subconscious mind, which seems to grow along in spite of what we may think or do until it becomes a definite self of its own. When some crisis arises in which we are challenged by the collapse of some social standard or emotional cataclysm, we become acutely aware of this inherited self, and shock upon shock is felt in new depths of sensitivity. At such moments our whole mechanism of discipline appears to be held in suspense and there comes into being the deeper blood-and-bone reality unseen in the depths and rising like a tidal wave, gathering power invisibly without disturbing the surface until without warning this under-force sweeps over us, destroying every habit or former mental concept of life. The gentlest creature may, in such a crisis, turn into a savage, for the call of the blood is hot and omnipotent.

Our primitive or instinctive subconscious suddenly holds sway over our destiny and makes us aware of the barriers which have piled up year after year, binding us in, forming inhibitions, damming up instincts that gather together the power of dark forces, terrible and merciless. . . . When these fall over us we are impotent, lost atoms. At such moments we may see civilization turn into savagery and culture into barbarism.

Four-wheel brakes are none too many to keep a man from skidding over the precipice in such a crisis and throwing his better self and all his ideals to the four winds of heaven. Some of those who manage to make the dangerous curve find their slow way back, but others give up the fight. When life closes in about us with hard, rigid walls, we hardly dare to strike out lest we break our bones on the reality of life's nightmares. The survival of the fittest, however, continues the race, and the pageant of the world rolls on with its eternal struggle of destructions and survival, with grandeur and poetry, cruelty and revulsion; the inevitable forces of renewal move along beyond our knowledge or control.

It is the eternal cosmic consciousness which binds all the races of man together. Savages, scholars, saints, and heroes of all creeds and colors could understand one another, were they to be sounded in the depths of their being.

The beauty of individual effort and the separation of types by national boundaries have given the world its vast richness of local color and talent. Variety of thought, limitless imagination developed under opposite environments and national traditions, all go towards the general treasure-store.

In his evolution, man would do well to study the most ancient cults and cultures before growing too convinced that modern progress is based on modern invention. Contemporary science has certainly opened vistas beyond the ken of past or present civilizations, but in many cases the roots of our so-called discoveries are buried deeply in the long-forgotten past.

> *"La main touche la main,*
> *Et nous nous souvenons que nous marchions ensemble*
> *Que l'âme est immortelle*
> *Et qu'hier c'est demain."*

APPENDIX OF TRANSLATIONS

APPENDIX OF TRANSLATIONS

PAGE 14

Plus ça change. . . . The more it changes, the more is it the same thing.

PAGE 33

Vivre c'est rien. . . . "To live is nothing, but to sacrifice his life for an ideal is the one thing which gives man his highest quality."

PAGE 35

J'ai perdu ma force. . . .

> I have lost my strength and my life,
> My friends and my gaiety;
> I have almost lost the pride
> That made me believe in my genius.
>
> When I knew Truth
> I believed her to be a friend;
> When I understood her and sensed her
> I was already disgusted with her.
>
> And nevertheless, she is eternal
> And those who have evaded her
> Here below have missed everything.
>
> God speaks, it is necessary to answer him.
> The only thing that is left to me on earth
> Is to have sometimes wept.
>
> (*Tristesse,* by Alfred de Musset)

PAGE 36

Allons. . . . "Come, let us go to lunch, my friends—it is late."

PAGE 41

C'est leur. . . . "It's their damned facility."

APPENDIX OF TRANSLATIONS

PAGE 47

Tout comprendre. . . . To understand all is to forgive all.

PAGE 48

C'est la fin. "It is the end."

A mon élève. . . . To my pupil Malvina, sensitive sculptor, from her old master Auguste Rodin, the day that war was declared. *Paris, August 1914.*

Gardez ce livre. . . . "Keep this book in memory; you once said to me that the trees in the allee of my garden raise their branches toward the sky like hands in prayer; today, the whole world should lift their hands, for it is the end of our era of civilization."

Qui n'est, après tout. . . . "Which is, after all, only a coat of paint which washes off when the rain falls."

PAGE 53

Tu fus toujours. . . . "You were always thus, you always approached familiarly all terrible things."

PAGE 63 (ILLUSTRATION)

Voici des fruits. . . .

Here are fruits, flowers, leaves and branches,
And here too is my heart which beats
Only for you. . . .   (*Verlaine*)

PAGE 67

The quotation is from *Sonnets of Simonetta,* by Helen Gerry.

PAGE 76

Pour effrayer. . . . "To frighten some one at our pension."

Émilie, regardez. . . . "Emilie, look on the mantel, you will see a new boarder for Mlle. Guilhou . . .! Don't be frightened, he doesn't eat as much cake as we do."

PAGE 80

C'est la qualité. . . . "It is the quality of the soul which is lacking, Malvina. You know it as well in America as do we in Yugo-Slavia. They work with their hands and not with their souls."

PAGE 129

Vous n'avez rien. . . .

"You have nothing to declare? No? Well, will you give us the pleasure of breakfasting with us at the hotel in Zagreb tomorrow morning?"

"Yes, with pleasure, and thanks. . . . Is every one asleep? Where are we?"

"Shsh . . . yes, and soon we will be outside the war zone and you will be liberated. . . ."

PAGE 232

Il faut attraper. . . . "One must seize upon accidents and turn them into science."

PAGE 337

Je viendrai. . . . "I shall come early; I'm a sailor, even in Paris—next Thursday, then."

PAGE 345

A deux pas. . . . A few steps from the sea, which one hears thundering, I know a lost corner in the land of Brittany. . . . (*Paysage,* by André Theuriet)

PAGE 351

Il faut vouloir. . . . "One must want to live and know how to die."

PAGE 353

Nous écoutons. . . . "We are listening to the bells of the sunken cathedral."

PAGE 400

La main touche. . . .

Hand touches hand,
And we remember that we were walking together,
That the soul is eternal
And that yesterday is tomorrow.

INDEX

INDEX

Academy of Art (Hawaii), 189
Acropolis, the, 119
Adjim, 146
Adrenal gland, 238
Africa, 16, 78, 130 ff.
African types, 11, 149, 156
Ainus, the, 195, 205, 207 ff.
Aksu, 304
Alexander, John W., 32
Alexander, Prince, 122
Alpine type, the, 159, 165, 215
Amber, Palace of, 317
American Academy, Rome, 78
American Express Company, 182
American Yugo-Slav Relief Society, 117, 122
Anatomy, 42, 43; Institute of, 163, 164
Andaman Islander, the, 294, 297
"Annunciation," the, 81
Anthropological Institute Dahlem, Berlin, 163; Vienna, 164; Munich, 165
Apache, the, 374, 376
Apayaos, the, 250
Arabs, 134, 143, 144
Archæological Museum, 134
Arizona, 363
Armour, A. W., 3rd, 328
Art, instinctive, of primitive races, 114; of Indians, 361, 362, 391
Artist, 31, 264
Aryan, hair, 247; the Kashmir, 321
Asiatics, 13
Athens, 119
Athens Numismatic Museum, 120
Atlantis, 353
Audierne, 346
"Autumn Bacchanale," 57
Avalon, Arthur, 169; see Woodroffe
Awomori, 196
Aztec, the, 362

"Bacchanale," 57, 58
Bacon, Robert, 54, 58
Baguio, 250
Baillie, Robert, 75
Balfour, Lord, 75
Balkans, the, 16, 117 ff.
Bali, 249, 253 ff.
Balinese, the, 262, 263, 264
Barbizon, 86
Bardo Museum, the, 133
Barnum, P. T., 19
Bartlett, Paul, 51
Batavia, 272
Batchelder, Doctor, 205, 207, 215, 216
Batchelder, Yai, 205 ff.
Batchelder's Hotel, 23
Belgrade, 122
Belur, Ram Krishna Monastery, 306
Benares, 310
Bénédite, George, 51
Bénédite, Léonce, 51, 98
Benin Bronzes, 113, 114
Bernhardt, Sarah, 76
Bertelli, Riccardo, 56
Beuret, Rose, 44
"Bigouds," 347
Biron, Hotel, 47, 48
Bishop Museum (Honolulu), 184
Black, Doctor Davidson, 220, 221, 244
Blackfoot, the, 11, 12
Blondat, Max, 51
"Blue Boy," the, 47
Boar-hunting, 54
Bologna, Giovanni de, 98
Bombay, 319 ff., 327
Bontoks, the, 250
Borneo, 249
Borobodour Temple, the, 272
Bouchardon, Edmé, 110
Brahman, Kashmiri, 12

INDEX

Brahmanism, 262
Brahms, Johannes, 32
Brain Surgery Institute (Vienna), 165
Brancusi, 51, 86
Brearley School, 32
Bredon, Lady, 241
Bretons, 159, 345 ff.
"Bring 'em Back Alive," 282
Brinig, Myron, 386
British Museum, 217
Brittany, 15, 345 ff.
Bronze casting, 99 ff.
Brooklyn Museum, 79
Brooks, Romaine, 52
"Brothers Pribicevic," 127
Brown, Bellamy, 289
Buck, Frank, 282
Buck, Pearl, 247
Buddhist Shogun Temple, the, 194
Buddhists, 243; monks, 235, 236, 329
Burma, 290 ff.
Burmese, the, 290, 293
Bush House, 74
Bushmen, Kalahari, 155, 156; Australian, 215
Byrse, 134

Calcutta, 298, 303, 305 ff.
Calcutta Museum, 305
Calhoun, Mrs., 220
Calvé, Emma, 29
Cambodian settlement, Exposition Coloniale, 173
Camels, 146, 147
Carnac, 346
Carson, Kit, 372
Carthage, 134, 143, 353
Casting, "lost-wax," 85, 107, 108; plaster, 86, 95; bronze, 99 ff.; hollow, 107 ff.; Negocoll, 164, 165, 191, 307
Cathedral of Saint John the Divine, 67, 126
Cathedral of Saint Louis, 134
Cathédrales de France, Les, 48
Cellini, Benvenuto, 98, 107
"Century of Progress," the, 10
Ceylon, 321, 322, 327 ff.
Chanler, William Astor, 54
Chasens, F., 272

Chateaubriand, 347
Chicago, 3, 4, 10, 156, 189, 216, 333
Chien Lung Dynasty, 243
Chihli, Province of, 238
China, 218 ff.; bronze work of ancient, 98
Chop sticks, 238
Chopin, 70, 73
Churchill, Anthony, 284
Churchill, Winston, 284
Circus, 294
Citroën Expedition, 304
Cochiti, 362
Cockfighting, 270
Cocteau, Jean, 52
College of Physicians and Surgeons in New York, the, 42
Colombo, 330
Colony Club, 340
Columbia University, 43
"Column of Life," 44
Confucius, 222
Cook, Mrs. Montague, 189
Coolies, 233
Cooper, Major, 148
Criminal tribes, nomad, 315
Cushing, Doctor Harvey, 163

Dahlem, 163
Dakar, 354
Dalmatia, 126, 127
Dances, Russian, 56, 58; Temple, 173; Balinese, 173; Burmese, 290; devil, 330; Indian, 363, 364, 370, 382, 393, 394
Dandré, Victor, 58
D'Annunzio, 52, 129
da Vinci, Leonardo, 41, 75
Debussy, 53, 254
Delattre, Père, 134
de Monfreid, Henri, 334, 337, 338
Dempo, the, 332
Den Pasar, 263
d'Erlanger, Baron, 134, 144
Despiau, 97
Diaghileff's Ballet, 51
Dinars, 163
Dissection, 42, 43
Djibouti, 354
Dodge, Mabel, 51, 383 ff.
Doggon tribe, 382

Donatello, 98
Dorchester House, 46, 51
Draper, Muriel, 385
Draper, Paul, 30, 385
Draper, Ruth, 30, 232, 319
Draper, Dr. William Kinnicutt, 30
Draper, Mrs. William H., 30
Draper, Mrs. William K., 128, 191;
   see also Helen Hoffman
Druids, 346
Dutch Pavilion, The, 173
Dutch wife, 256
Dutchman, and native Papuan, 270
Duval, Georgie, 52, 53
Dyak, Borneo, 278, 279

Eames, Emma, 29, 177
Eickstedt, Baron Von, 164
Elephants, working, 329, 330
Emmet, Marie Louise, 118, 120, 125,
   127
Engert, Mr., 232, 244, 245
Eskimos, 215
Ethiopians, in Tokyo, 192
Evans, John, 386
Exposition Coloniale, 155, 172, 174

Fantasia of the Unconscious, 388
Field, Henry, 159, 160
Field, Stanley, 12, 216, 221, 247
Field, Mrs. William, 376
Field Museum, the, 3, 4, 10, 16, 70,
   150, 184, 189, 207, 216, 309, 327,
   330, 333, 340.
Finistère, 345 ff.
Fischer, Dr. Eugene, 163
Fiume, 127, 129
Flaubert, 134
"Flying Heart, The," 387
Fonderie Rudier, 113
Ford, John, 261, 262
Forest of Loches, 54
Forty-third Street, 19 ff., 30, 55
Fouesnant, 346
Four Horsemen, 77, 130
French, southern type, 159
Fugh, Doctor Philip, 232

Gabes, 144
Gainsborough, 47
Gamelon, 255

Gandhi, 319
Ganges, 15, 310
Garden, Mary, 52
Gaugin, 337
"Gavotte," 57
Geisha-girl, 193
George, Lloyd, 169
Germans, southern type, 159
Geronimo, 374
Ghiberti, Lorenzo, 98
Glazounoff, 57
Good Earth, The, 247
Goujon, Jean, 98
Grachanitza, the Temple of, 126
Grand Central Gallery, 68
Grand Hotel (Peiping), 219
Greeks, 159
Green, Gretchen, 181, 219, 222, 235,
   241, 247, 253, 289, 293, 298, 307
Greffuhle, Comtesse, 46
Griaule, Marcel, 354
Grimson, Samuel B., 30, 31, 44, 75,
   85, 133, 144, 163, 174, 177, 181,
   191, 192, 218, 222, 231, 241, 253,
   256, 269, 277, 281, 284, 287, 290,
   293, 298, 316, 317, 318, 322, 327,
   328, 330, 333, 334, 340, 348, 354
Guha, Dr. B. S., 305

Haardt, George Marie, 303, 304
Hakodate, 205 ff.
Haksar, Colonel, 166, 315
Hall of Man, the, 3–12, 16, 19, 73, 99,
   155, 165, 178, 184, 232, 309, 338–
   340, 360
Hamilcar, 353
Hamite, 156
Hara Kebira, 146
Hara Srira, 146
Harriman, Mrs. E. H., 109
Harrower, Dr. J. G., 272
Harvard University, 67
Harvey Hotel System, 364
Hava Supai Canyon, 363
Hawaii, 183 ff.
Hawaiian surf-board rider, 13, 184
Heaven, the Temple of, 242
Herodotus, 215
Hill, Doctor, 331
Hippodrome, 30
Hitler, 159

INDEX

Hoffman, Charles, 30
Hoffman, Elizabeth, 22
Hoffman, Fidelia Lamson, 24, 29, 52, 53, 56, 67
Hoffman, Helen (Mrs. William Kinnicutt Draper), 24, 30
Hoffman, Richard, 19, 23, 24, 29, 31, 32
Hoffman, Richard, Jr., 22
Hokkaido, 189, 195 ff.
Holland, 58
Hollow casting, 107 ff.
Holy City of Death, 310
Hong Kong, 246 ff.
Honolulu, 183 ff.
Hoover, Herbert, 117, 129
Hopis, 362, 373, 374, 382
Horsemen of the Apocalypse, 130
Horyogi, the Treasure Houses of, 216
Houdon, 68
Hsu Tse Mou, 219
Hubbell, Don Lorenzo, 372, 373
Huntington, Doctor George S., 42
Hu Shih, Doctor, 232, 241, 245
Hyashi, Count, of Hirotaro Imperial University, 189, 190, 194

Iacovleff, Alexander, 304
Iberians, 159
Ifugaos, the, 250
Igorotes, the, 250
Imperial Hotel (Tokyo), 190
Inao, 210
India, 298 ff.
Indians, American, 12, 13, 358 ff.; head of Ecuador Jivaro, 76; maharajas and princes, 166 ff.; Miska, 381
Indo-China, 238
Indo-Chinese subjects, 173
International University (Santiniketan), 309
International World's Fair, the, 10
Iroquois, the, 381
Isle of Impurity, 297
Italians, 159
Ituri pigmies, the, 148, 149, 156

Jaipur, 319; the Maharaja of, 317, 318
Jakuns, the, 272, 277, 278
Japan, 189 ff.
Java, 262 ff.

Javanese, the, 264, 269, 272
Jeffers, Robinson, 386
Jerba, 146, 147
Jews, of Jerba, 146
Jicarillas, the, 374
Jokjo, 269
Jokjokarta, 271

Kabuli, 309, 310
Kabunian, 250
Kachinas, 382
Kalingas, the, 250
Kamehameha the First, 187
Kam Yin, 246
Kanchow, 305
Kandy, 328, 329
Karlobac, 127, 128
Keams Canyon, 373
Keats, John, 77
Keith, Sir Arthur, 159, 160
Keller, 113
King's Library at Windsor, 75
Kintamani, 254
Kipling, 206, 235, 293
Kiowa, 362
Knoedlers' (Paris), 58
Kohonomoku, David, 183, 184
Kohonomoku, Sargent, 183, 184
Kossovo, 125, 126, 128
Kreisler record, 253
Kriss dance, 269
Kwannon, the, 216

Lack, Col. L. A. H., 293
"La Douleur est la Mère de la Beauté," 67
Lady Chatterley's Lover, 388
"La Peri," 57
Lamaists, 242, 243
Lamson, Fidelia, 19; *see also* Hoffman, Fidelia Lamson
Lattimore, Owen and Mrs., 237, 244
Laufer, Doctor Berthold, 189, 207, 216, 221, 232
Lauru, Mme., 238
Lawrence, D. H. (Lorenzo), 386, 387, 388, 391
Lawrence, Frieda, 386 ff.
"Le Bien Aimé," 110
Le Braz, 347
Le Goffic, 347
Leicester Gallery, 46

INDEX

Lemordant, Jean-Julien, 347, 357
Les Cathédrales de France, 48
"Les Orientals," 57
Lessing, Doctor, 222, 236, 242, 243
L'Île Joyeuse, 254
Lincoln, Abraham, 359
Lind, Jenny, 19
Lindberghs, the, 207
Little Boar's Head (New Hampshire), 23
Ljubliana, 122
London, 47, 74, 75, 159, 166, 169, 315
"Lost-wax" process, 85, 107, 108
Loti, Pierre, 347
Loudon, Mr., 173
Louis XV, 110–112
Loulou, 52
Louvre, the, 68
Luhan, Tony, 51, 385, 394
Luhan, Mrs. Tony, *see* Mabel Dodge
Lutten, Eric, 354
Luzon, 250
Lydig, Rita de Acosta, 68

Macassar, 249, 252
MacMonnies, Frederick, 51
Madagascar, 304
Made, 256
Maeterlinck, 52
Mahout, elephant trainer, 329
Maillol, 86
Malay Peninsula, 272 ff.
Malcolm, Doctor, 160
Malvina, the, 348, 351
Manchus, 13
"Mandala," the, 242
Mangbetu, the, 150, 156
Manila, 250 ff.
Man Who Died, The, 388
Maori, 188, 279, 381
Marble, 35, 36
Marco, Jean de, 108, 181, 222, 305, 308, 322
Marcus, George, 56
Mariados, 303, 310, 322
Marseilles, 331
Marshall Field & Company, 182
Masks, 381, 382
Matisse, 51
Medicine Man, 370
Medinin, 148

Mediterranean type, the, 159, 215
Mei Lan Fang, 241
Melba, 29
Memorial, war, 58, 67
Mescalero, the, 374
Mestrovic, Ivan, 45, 79 ff., 126, 133
Meudon, 43, 44, 51
Michelangelo, 41, 97, 98
Mignaty, Margherita Albana, 75
Minas, 256
"Modern Acropolis," 57
"Modern Crusader," 128
Modern Museum, the, 113
Modi, Doctor J. J., 321
Mongolians, 13, 218, 236, 369
Montandon, Doctor, 207, 215
Montrésor, Duc de, 54
Monvel, Boutet de, 51
Moon Year, The, 241
Morbihan, 346
Mordkin, 56, 57, 58
Mormons, of Hawaii, 187
Moros, the, 251
Mowbray, Colonel G. A. de C., 282]
Mu, 353, 354
Mud-carriers, 246
Mudras, 184, 222, 231, 269
Musée de l'Histoire Naturelle, 155
Musée Rodin, the, 51, 98, 117
Musées Nationaux, Les, 354
Museum, Archæological, 134
Museum, Athens Numismatic, 120
Museum, Bardo, 133
Museum, Bishop, 184
Museum, British, 217
Museum, Brooklyn, 79
Museum, Indian, 305
Museum, Modern, 113
Museum, Naples, 98
Museum, New Mexico, 359
Museum, Singapore, 277
Museum, South Kensington, 51
Museum, Taiping, 279
Museum, Vienna, 164
Museum, Wellcome Historical Medical, 160, 163
Music, 23, 24, 29, 31, 52

Naidu, Madame, 319
Nanking, 244, 245
Naples Museum, 98

INDEX

Nara, 216
Nats, 316
Nature, 53, 392
Navajo, 363, 369–373
"Negocoll," 164
Negritos, the aboriginal, 250
Nell, Doctor Andreas, 328, 330
New Delhi, 315
New Mexico, 51, 359 ff.; Museum of, 359
New Territory, 246
Nicobar Islands, 297
Nietzsche, 53
Nigeria, 113
Niiro, Doctor, 216
Nijinsky, 51
Ni Polog, 263
Nish, 120, 121
Noone, H., 279, 282, 289
Nordic type, the, 11, 159, 165, 215
Not I, but the Wind, 388
Novikoff, 58
Nuno, Christine, 191

Oahu, 183 ff.
Ochs, Adolph S., 57
Omon Gate of Tokyo, the, 192, 193
Oraibi, 372
Out of Life, 386

Pacific Islands, 360
Padaung tribe, 293
Paderewski, 70 ff.
Painting, 32
Palace at Peiping, the, 98
Palace of Amber, 317
Pantograph, 177
Papuan, 256
Paris, 10, 12, 24, 33–41, 43, 47, 52, 73, 75, 110, 155, 172 ff., 303, 304, 334, 338, 354
Parsees, the, 320, 321
Patiala, the Maharaja of, 169, 171; Yuvuraj, the, 171
Pavley, 57, 58
Pavlowa, Anna, 51, 56, 57 ff., 67, 330
Peace Monument, 57
Peiping, 217 ff., 234 ff.
Peking (Peiping) Union Medical College, 220
Pelléas et Melisande, 52

Penang, 289
Penmarch, 345
Peru, 76, 114
Peter, King, 122
Philippines, 249 ff.
Pigmies, Ituri, 148, 149, 156; Semang, 272, 284, 287; Andaman, 294, 297; Philippine, 250 ff.
Pilon, Germain, 98
Pisano, 98
Place de la Concorde, 52
Plançon, 29
Plaster-casting, 86–95
Plato, 353
Poland, 73
Poller, Madame, 164, 165
Polynesians, 187–189
Pont-l'Abbé, 348
Poona, 319
Port Blair, 297
Port Saïd, 332
Prambanan, the temple of, 271
Prague, 163
"Praying Kashmiri," 166
Precinct of Tanit, 134
Presentiment, poem by Emily Dickinson, 55
Pribicevic, Colonel Milan, 127, 128
Primitive art, 13, 14, 397; people, 15, 271; forces, 16; instinct, 114, 361, 362, 381, 398
Psychology, 15, 16
Pueblo Indians, 361, 362
Puppet actors, 236, 237
Pyrenees, 159

Races, study of, 12, 13, 16, 78, 117 ff., 150; Indian, 395, 396
Raffle's Hotel, 272
Rangoon, 290 ff.
Raphael, 41
Ravel, 53
Reading, Lady, 166
Reading, Lord, 315
Readymoney, Sir Kavasji Jehangir, 320
Repulse Bay, 247
Reszke, brothers de, the, 29
Returned Students' Club, 241
Revelation of Saint John, 77
Rich, Frances, 357

414

INDEX

Ringling, 150, 293
Riviere, George Henri, 354
Rivet, Doctor, 354
Robbins, Reverend Howard C., 126
Rockefeller Foundation, 122
Rockefeller Laboratory of Anthropology, 359
Rodin, 34 ff., 43, 46 ff., 86, 97, 232
Rodin, Rose Beuret, *see* Rose Beuret
Rome, 78, 133
Rosales, Emanuel, 45, 51
Royal College of Surgeons, 160
Rudier, Eugène, 110, 177
Ruskin, 134
Russell, Lillian, 20, 30
"Russki Tzar," 121

Sacré Cœur, 52
"Sacrifice, The," 67
St. Guénolé, 345–348, 351
St. Malo, 347
St. Mawr, 388
Sakais, the, 272, 279 ff.
Salammbo, 134
Salonika, 120
Samoans, the, 187
San Felípe, 363
San Ildefonso, 362, 383
Sanskrit, 309
Santa Fe, 359, 361, 364, 376, 383, 384
Santiniketan, 309
"Satrya, The," 256
Savage, Henry, 30
Savoy Hotel (London), 169
Savoyards, 159
Schelling, Ernest, 67, 70
Schuré, Edward, 75, 347
Scotti, Antonio, 29
Scudder, Janet, 385
Sculpture, 32, 33, 34, 45, 46, 69, 79; Negro, 113; school of, 264
Semang pigmies, the, 272, 284, 287
Semino, Charlie, 75
Senegalese types, 144, 145
Serbia, 119, 121 ff.
Shakti, 243
Shanghai, 219, 244, 245
Shellshear, Professor and Mrs., 246
Shilluk warrior, the, 156
Shirawoi, 207, 208
Shwe Dagon Pagoda, 293

Shogun temple, Buddhist, 194
Sicilian fisherman, 334
Sidi Bou Saïd, 143
Sikhs, 171, 172, 247
Sikkims, 309
Simard, Albert, 252
Simpson, James, 327, 328
Simpson, Mrs. John, 34
Singalese, the, 328, 329, 330
Singapore, 272 ff.
Singermann, 386
Slavs, 159
Solo, 269
Solomon Islander, 277
Samalis, 173
South Kensington Museum, 51
Spanish War, 30
Spittel, Doctor, 331
"Squeeze," 43
Stampar, Doctor, 122
Staples, B. I., 364, 369, 372, 376
Starri Grad, 80
Stein, Gertrude, 51
Stern, Maurice, 386
Stevenson, Doctor Paul H., 220, 221
Straits Settlements, 272
Strauss, Doctor, 165
Strauss, Richard, 32
Sumatra types, 272
Surf Rider, 184
Symbols, 210, 212, 231, 242, 243

Tagore, Abinandranath, 307, 308, 309
Tagore, Rabindranath, 307, 309
Tahitians, 189
Taiping, 279
Tamils, 321, 329
Taoist monks, 237
Taos, 383 ff., 394
Tapah Road, 279, 282
Tasmanians, the, 13
Temperament, artistic, 9
Temple of Grachanitza, 126
Temple of Heaven, 242
Temple of Prambanan, the, 271
Temple of the Cloud, the, 237
Temple of the Tooth, the, 329
Teusler, Doctor Rudolfe, 191
Thebaud, 293
Thin, Doctor Aung, 293
"Thinker, the," 44

INDEX

Thracians, the, 215
Tibetans, 305, 369
Tien Tsu Hui, 235
Tima Tittwar, 297
Todas, the, 215
Toddy wine collectors, 322
Tokyo, 190 ff.
Toltec, the, 362
Tomakomai, 205, 206
"Towers of Silence, The," 320
Trocadéro, the, 113, 334, 354
Tsugaro Strait, 205
Tunis, 133, 143
Tusla, 125
Tweed, John, 46
Tyroleans, Swiss, 159, 241

Ubangi, the, 149, 150, 156
United States Indian School, 361, 376
Urumchi, 304

Vaish, Hamman Pershad, 317
Valsuani, 102
Varennes, rue de, 43
Veddas, the, 331
"Venus de Milo," 97
"Venus Hottentot," 155
Vermont, 369
Vernay, Arthur, 282
Verrocchio, 98
Versailles, 113
Vienna, 164, 165
Villa Chauvelot, 172, 174
Vink, Doctor de, 271
Visva Bharati, 309
Vivekananda, Swami, 306

Wagons-Lits Company, 244

Waikiki Beach, 184
Walpi, 373, 374
War, 30, 48
Wayang players, the, 269
Weddell, Alexander, W., 119
Wellcome, Sir Henry, 163
Wellcome Historical Medical Museum, the, 160, 163
Wells, Kady, 386
Weninger, Dr. Josef, 164
Westminster, the Duke of, 46
White, Mrs. Stanford, 385
"White Horse Inn, The," 165
"Widows," 126
Wilders, the James, 183
"William and Mary," straits of, 303
Windsor, 75
Woman Who Rode Away, The, 388
Wong Wen Hau, Doctor, 232
Woodroffe, Sir John (Chief Justice of Bengal), 169
Wyle, Irene, 357

Yamakata, Mr., 205
Yarnall, Agnes, 77
Yokohama, 190, 193
Yoshiwara, 193
Yucatan, 363
Yugo-Slavia, 77, 78, 79, 117
Yuvuraj, the, 171

Zagreb, 79 ff., 128, 129, 133
Zarraga, Angel, 177
Zeus, 243
Zoroaster, 320
Zuloaga, Ignacio, 82, 85
Zuni, the, 382